SPARKING EUROPE'S NEW INDUSTRIAL REVOLUTION
A policy for net zero,
growth and resilience

Edited by Simone Tagliapietra
and Reinhilde Veugelers

BRUEGEL BLUEPRINT SERIES

SPARKING EUROPE'S NEW INDUSTRIAL REVOLUTION

A policy for net zero, growth and resilience

Simone Tagliapietra and Reinhilde Veugelers

Editor: Stephen Gardner

Layout and cover design: Hèctor Badenes Rodríguez

© Bruegel 2023. All rights reserved. Short sections of text, not to exceed two paragraphs, may be quoted in the original language without explicit permission provided that the source is acknowledged. Opinions expressed in this publications are those of the authors alone.

Bruegel

33, rue de la Charité, Box 4

1210 Brussels, Belgium

www.bruegel.org

ISBN: 978-9-07-891055-8

Contents

About the authors 5
Foreword 11

1 Industrial policy in Europe: past and future 13
   Simone Tagliapietra and Reinhilde Veugelers

2 An innovation-driven industrial policy for Europe 29
   Philippe Aghion

3 Productivism and new industrial policies: learning from the past, preparing for the future 42
   Dani Rodrik

4 Industrial policy and technological sovereignty 72
   Uwe Cantner

5 Cooperation or conflict? A transatlantic look at whether industrial policy will produce solutions or generate unmanageable conflicts .. 90
   Laura Tyson and John Zysman

6 Green industrial policy: the necessary evil to avoid a climate catastrophe 107
   Alessio Terzi

7 Industrial strategies for Europe's green transition 123
   Chiara Criscuolo, Antoine Dechezleprêtre and Guy Lalanne

8 A more globally-minded European green industrial policy.........153
Ricardo Hausmann and Ketan Ahuja

9 Europe's green industrial policy..166
Simone Tagliapietra, Cecilia Trasi and Reinhilde Veugelers

10 Smart green industrial policy..187
Ben McWilliams and Georg Zachmann

11 Industrial policy for electric vehicle supply chains and the US-EU fight over the Inflation Reduction Act..211
Chad Bown

12 A new pharma industrial policy for Europe? Lessons from COVID-19 257
Mathias Dewatripont

About the authors

Philippe Aghion is a Professor at the College de France and at the London School of Economics, and a Fellow of the Econometric Society and of the American Academy of Arts and Sciences. His research focuses on the economics of growth. With Peter Howitt, he pioneered the so-called Schumpeterian Growth paradigm, which has been used to analyse the design of growth policies and the role of the state in the growth process.

Ketan Ahuja leads a research programme on green growth at Harvard's Growth Lab and is a DPhil student in law at the University of Oxford. His research focuses on how to regulate market competition in ways that reduce inequality, share power more broadly and support innovation and economic growth.

Chad P. Bown is Reginald Jones Senior Fellow at the Peterson Institute for International Economics. His research examines international trade laws and institutions, trade negotiations and trade disputes. He was previously a senior economist for international trade and investment in the White House on the Council of Economic Advisers, and most recently was a lead economist at the World Bank. Previously, he was a tenured professor of economics at Brandeis University.

Uwe Cantner is Professor of Economics at Friedrich Schiller University Jena, where is also is Vice President for Young Researchers and Diversity Management. He is Professor of Economics at the University of Southern Denmark/Odense and Chairman of the Federal German Government Commission of Experts for Research and Innovation.

Chiara Criscuolo is Head of the Productivity and Business Dynamics Division in the Directorate for Science, Technology and Innovation of the Organisation for Economic Co-operation and Development. She is also one of eleven economists appointed to the French National Productivity Board and a Research Associate at the Centre for Economic Performance at the London School of Economics.

Antoine Dechezleprêtre is a Senior Economist in the Productivity, Innovation and Entrepreneurship Division, Directorate for Science, Technology and Innovation, OECD. He works on the role of innovation and technology diffusion for the green transition and the impact of environmental policies on innovation, technology adoption, carbon emissions, productivity and firm performance. Before joining the OECD, he was an Associate Professor at the Grantham Research Institute, London School of Economics, and then headed the Green Growth work stream at the OECD.

Mathias Dewatripont has been a Professor at Université Libre de Bruxelles since 1990. Between 1991 and 2001, he co-directed ECARES, which is now part of the Solvay Brussels School of Economics and Management of ULB. Between 1998 and 2011, he was Research Director of CEPR and Visiting Professor at MIT. He was also previously Executive Director of the National Bank of Belgium.

Ricardo Hausmann is the founder and Director of Harvard's Growth Lab, and is the Rafik Hariri Professor of the Practice of International Political Economy at Harvard Kennedy School. Previously, he was first Chief Economist of the Inter-American Development Bank. He was Minister of Planning of Venezuela and a member of the Board of the Central Bank of Venezuela. He also served as Chair of the International Monetary Fund-World Bank Development Committee.

Guy Lalanne is a Senior Economist at the Directorate for Science, Technology and Innovation Directorate of the Organisation for Economic Co-operation and Development. Previously, he held several positions in the French Treasury, notably as Secretary General of the macroprudential authority and Head of the Industrial Policy, R&D and Innovation Division, and in the French National Statistical Institute.

Ben McWilliams is an Affiliate Fellow at Bruegel. His work involves data-driven analysis to inform European public policy, specifically in relation to the energy sector and its decarbonisation. He has an MSc in Economic Policy from Utrecht University and a BSc Economics from the University of Warwick.

Dani Rodrik is the Ford Foundation Professor of International Political Economy at Harvard's John F. Kennedy School of Government. He is a co-director of the Economics for Inclusive Prosperity network and president of the International Economic Association. He is affiliated with the National Bureau of Economic Research and the Centre for Economic Policy Research (London), among other research organisations. His research focuses on globalisation, economic growth and development, and political economy.

Simone Tagliapietra is a Senior Fellow at Bruegel. He also is a professor of energy and climate policy at the Catholic University of Milan and at The Johns Hopkins University – School of Advanced International Studies (SAIS) Europe. He is the author of *Global Energy Fundamentals* (Cambridge University Press, 2020). He also is a Member of the Board of Directors of the Clean Air Task Force.

Alessio Terzi is the author of *Growth for Good* (Harvard University Press, 2022). He is an Economist in the European Commission's Directorate-General for Economic and Financial Affairs, and an Adjunct Professor at Sciences Po and HEC Paris. Previously, he was an Affiliate Fellow at Bruegel and a Fulbright Scholar at the Harvard Kennedy School.

Laura Tyson is a Distinguished Professor of the Graduate School at the Haas School of Business, University of California, Berkeley. She also chairs the Board of Trustees at UC Berkeley's Blum Center for Developing Economies, and is a Senior Fellow at the Berggruen Institute. She is an expert on trade and competitiveness and was the chair of the President's Council of Economic Advisers and chair of the National Economic Council during the Clinton Administration.

Cecilia Trasi is a Research Assistant at Bruegel. She completed a BSc in Economics at Università Cattolica in Milan, and then a Master's in Public Policy at the Hertie School in Berlin. Before joining Bruegel, Cecilia pursued a Blue Book traineeship at the European Commission focusing on renewable energy and green hydrogen and cooperation with countries in sub-Saharan Africa.

Reinhilde Veugelers is a Senior Fellow at Bruegel. She also is a professor at KULeuven in the Department of Management, Strategy and Innovation, and a non-resident senior fellow at the Peterson Institute for International Economics. She is a Centre for Economic Policy Research Research Fellow, and a member of the Royal Flemish Academy of Belgium for Sciences and of the Academia Europeana.

Georg Zachmann is a Senior Fellow at Bruegel. His work focuses on regional and distributional impacts of decarbonisation, the analysis and design of carbon, gas and electricity markets, and EU energy and climate policies. Previously, he worked at the German Ministry of Finance, the German Institute for Economic Research in Berlin, the energy think tank LARSEN in Paris, and the policy consultancy Berlin Economics.

John Zysman is Professor Emeritus at UC Berkeley and co-founder/co-director of the Berkeley Roundtable on the International Economy. He received his BA from Harvard and his PhD from MIT. His work covers the implications of platforms and intelligent tools for work, entrepreneurship and international competition, and the economic challenges and opportunities of climate change and the green economy.

Foreword

Economic policymaking in Europe has become a lot more complicated. It was hard enough when European Union policies focused on reconciling growth and efficiency with cohesion and social protection. But now – after a pandemic, a war, droughts and heatwaves, and soaring energy prices – there is a new focus: to forestall disaster. This requires fast decarbonisation not just in the EU but internationally. It also requires greater resilience in the face of shocks, particularly shocks related to trade and geopolitical conflict.

There is broad consensus that an economic model based solely on competition, open trade, emissions taxes and industrial polices benefiting all sectors – through skill formation and innovation, for example – is insufficient to meet this challenge. New problems and policy objectives require additional policy instruments, including new industrial policies.

There is no consensus, however, on the form that these policies should take. Many in the EU worry that state intervention in support of specific industries and projects could hurt the EU's main engines of prosperity: the single market and rules-based international trade. Furthermore, state intervention often involves public spending. But money is always a touchy subject in the EU. Who pays and who exercises control?

In this Bruegel Blueprint, we have asked some of the finest minds in economics how the new state intervention should be designed. Not surprisingly, there is no agreement – economists never agree fully. But the ideas, principles and trade-offs articulated in this volume do allow us to narrow down the set of policies that the EU should consider, while helping to avoid mistakes.

They also help answer some basic questions. Is it possible to deploy industrial policies that strengthen green growth and economic security without hurting competition, economic openness and cohesion in the EU? Is it possible to do so without stronger EU-level governance, backed by financial resources? To me, the answer to the first question is 'yes', and to the second, 'no'. But please read the Blueprint and draw your own conclusions.

My thanks goes to all authors for their contributions, to Simone Tagliapietra and Reinhilde Veugelers for pulling them together, and to Stephen Gardner and Hèctor Badenes for a formidable editorial and production job. I am also particularly grateful to the European Climate Foundation for generous financial support.

Jeromin Zettelmeyer, Director of Bruegel
Brussels, July 2023

1 Industrial policy in Europe: past and future

Simone Tagliapietra and Reinhilde Veugelers

1 Europe's industrial policy debate: a brief history

The debate about industrial policy has traditionally been about the role of the state in the economy, driven by difficult questions such as: why and to what extent should governments intervene in steering market mechanisms? When they intervene, how should they do it? Should governments pick 'winners' to be supported?

Over time, Europe's approach to industrial policy has evolved depending on different political and policy cycles.

After the Second World War, when the process of European reconstruction began, the focus was notably on the strategic industries of coal, steel, electricity and railways. Between the early 1950s and the mid 1970s, referred to as the heyday of industrial policy (Owen, 2012), most European countries were concerned with closing the income gap and reducing their dependence on the United States. During those years, some European governments, most notably France, ventured into interventionist, winners-picking sectoral policies, also defined as vertical industrial policies. These policies targeted sectors thought to be strategic and promising for the future, including steel, chemicals, machinery, communications and technology, aircraft and nuclear power. Europe went through a wave of nationalisation and strong intervention involving state-owned enterprises and other state-powered initiatives. It was during this period that France, for example, launched a programme to promote its national computer industry – the 'Plan Calcul' – and engaged in '*Grands Projets*'.

The European Coal and Steel Community (ECSC) was set up in 1952 with the goal of reducing overcapacity and modernising coal production. This first European-level industrial policy was considered a success, both in terms of outcome and coordination between participating states. The ECSC provided an interventionist framework within which national companies had to modernise.

The European Economic Community (EEC), established after the ECSC, progressively reduced tariffs in European markets. The first technology policy initiative at European Community level was PREST (*Politique de Recherche Scientifique et Technologique*), aimed at facilitating common European research projects. The motivation for this initiative was fear of European technology lagging behind the US. A notable milestone in this era was the Davignon Plan, adopted in 1977, under which European-wide solutions were sought for the so-called 'sunset' industries, while keeping national control of 'sunrise' industries, such as computers. It was in this context that the Airbus consortium was established, as a European industrial alliance for the production of aircraft.

The 1980s saw a new phase of liberalisation with market-oriented industrial policies, limited to setting the right framework within which economic processes could take place (horizontal industrial policy). Countries liberalised markets, trying to avoid the government failures of the typically vertical industrial policy and winner-picking initiatives of the past.

At European level, the inefficiencies of uncoordinated national industrial policies became clear, leading to the development of two important instruments at EU level: the internal market and competition policy, including state aid. The Single European Act (1986) laid the legal basis for affirmative action of the state in the area of research and development. During this period, different initiatives were undertaken at European Community level to promote cooperation on research and innovation. One example was ESPRIT (European Strategic Programme for Research and Information Technology), a five year-programme focused on collaborative research with the aim of *"bringing together companies, universities and research institutes across Europe"* with a specific focus on information technology (Owen, 2012). ESPRIT was born as an attempt to respond to the government-led initiatives that the Japanese Ministry for International Trade and Industry undertook, initiatives that successfully enabled Japan to catch-up quickly with the United States as a technological and economic leader, particularly in the field of semiconductors. ESPRIT is typically considered the precursor of the European Commission's framework programmes (starting in 1984), through which the Commission carries out science, technology and innovation policy and collaborative research initiatives. The current framework programme is Horizon Europe.

During the 1990s and early 2000s, liberalisation programmes continued in Europe. A consensus emerged at EU level on the preference for a more holistic, integrated and 'horizontal' approach to industrial policy. The role of the EU was to ensure the right framework conditions, focusing on the use of internal market and competition instruments, and stimulating R&D and innovation. This cumulated in the 2000 Lisbon Strategy: a programme *"to transform the EU into the most competitive and dynamic knowledge-based economy in the world capable of sustainable economic growth with more and better jobs and greater social cohesion"* (European Council, 2000). Its goal was to implement a comprehensive strategy of structural reforms by boosting innovation and investment in R&D and creating a more integrated and competitive internal market.

2 Europe's industrial policy revival

The Great Recession of 2008 marked the start of a new era, characterised by an industrial policy revival across Europe.

In 2012, the European Commission published a new industrial policy communication, 'A Stronger European Industry for Growth and Economic Recovery' (European Commission, 2012), which started from the premise that *"Europe needs industry"* and sets out a roadmap for reindustrialising Europe, with the aim of *"raising the share of industry in GDP from the current level of around 16 percent to as much as 20 percent in 2020"*. Although the Commission stressed the need for a comprehensive vision *"mobilising all the levers available at EU level, notably the single market, trade policy, SME policy, competition policy, environmental and research policy in favour of European companies' competitiveness"*, the communication returned to a more targeted approach, identifying six priority action lines, including key enabling technologies, clean vehicles and smart grids. The communication was followed by action plans for specific sectors, such as steel (European Commission, 2013)[1].

The increasing pressure to put Europe on a trajectory towards climate neutrality and the need to respond to growing international tensions added to the significance of this policy development. This has been particularly the case since the adoption in 2019 of the European Green Deal as Europe's flagship programme or, as the European Commission defines it, as its *"new growth strategy"*[2]. In March 2020, the Commission presented a 'New Industrial Strategy for Europe', built on the twin objectives of managing the green and digital transitions while avoiding external dependencies in a new geopolitical context, especially with China considered a *"systemic rival"* (European Commission, 2019). Among the key policy goals in the strategy were securing the supply of clean technologies and critical raw materials, stepping up investment in green research, innovation, deployment and up-to-date infrastructure, and creating lead markets in clean technologies by making more strategic use of single-market regulations, public procurement rules and competition policy.

On the day after the publication of the new strategy, the World Health Organisation declared the COVID-19 outbreak a pandemic.

---

1   See also Veugelers (2013).
2   See European Commission press release of 11 December 2019: https://ec.europa.eu/commission/presscorner/detail/en/ip_19_6691.

That shock, with all the issues related to the emergency procurement of personal protective equipment and vaccines, triggered a substantial revision of the new industrial strategy, which came in May 2021. The updated strategy centered on the strengthening of the resilience of the single market. It did so by putting a strong focus on the need to improve Europe's *"open strategic autonomy"* in key areas including health and green and digital technologies by diversifying international partnerships, developing Europe's strategic industrial capacities and monitoring strategic dependencies (European Commission, 2021).

Since then, the issue of 'open strategic autonomy' has became more and more central to Europe's industrial policy debate, also as a result of the war in Ukraine, the subsequent energy crisis and the overall increase in international tension linked to the geopolitical decoupling of the United States and China. At the core of this issue stand the risk of supply disruption for critical items (including vaccines during a pandemic, natural gas during a major energy crisis, and critical raw materials and clean technologies during the green transition) and the consequent quest for 'de-risking'.

This paradigm change first became evident with the European Chips Act proposed by the European Commission in February 2022 to address the shortage of chips during the COVID-19 crisis. The Act has the double objective of improving the resilience of the semiconductor ecosystem in the EU to minimise future supply chain disruptions and increasing Europe's domestic capacity for chip production. It rests on three pillars: research and innovation policies, subsidies for cutting-edge chip manufacturing plants, and measures to monitor and intervene in chip-supply crises. The Act seeks to attract foreign investment and coordinate with global partners (European Commission, 2022). Yet, it has also raised concerns about its emphasis on protectionism and its potential to create competition distortions (Poitiers and Weil, 2022).

When it comes to resilience in the face of supply risks associated with the green transition, the European Commission published in

March 2023 two legislative proposals reflecting its new policy framework in this area: the Critical Raw Materials Act (CRMA) and the Net-Zero Industry Act (NZIA).

The CRMA is an attempt to respond to the supply disruption risk in critical raw materials, mainly by boosting their domestic production, refining and recycling. The proposed Act identifies a list of strategic raw materials that are considered crucial for the manufacturing of green, digital and defence technologies, and then sets precise domestic targets to be achieved by 2030. The CRMA aims to make the issuing of permits to relevant industrial projects subject to a common EU deadline. The proposed act also includes provisions on supply chain monitoring, stockpiling and improving the recyclability of CRMs. The CRMA acknowledges that, while important, domestic actions will never make the EU self-sufficient in critical raw materials. The Act thus also puts forward an international strategy to diversify the EU's imports of critical raw materials and strengthen its global partnerships with emerging markets and developing economies, and to consider a 'critical raw materials club' for like-minded countries.

The proposed NZIA meanwhile aims to tackle the supply disruption risk in clean technologies by:

1. Listing the net-zero technologies that are considered to be strategic: solar photovoltaic and solar thermal technologies; onshore wind and offshore renewable technologies; battery/storage technologies; heat pumps and geothermal energy technologies; electrolysers and fuel cells; sustainable biogas/biomethane technologies; carbon capture and storage (CCS) technologies; grid technologies.

2. Adopting an overall headline target of reaching a manufacturing capacity for these technologies of at least 40 percent of the EU's annual deployment needs by 2030. It also proposes a target for an annual injection capacity in CO2 storage of 50 million tonnes of carbon dioxide by 2030, to spur the development of CCS.

3. To achieve these targets, EU countries can identify Net-Zero Strategic Projects (NZSPs) that will be granted priority status at national level and fast-tracked in permitting procedures.

3 Europe's industrial policy trilemma

The final shape of the NZIA and CRMA will ultimately emerge from the EU legislative process, ongoing at the time of writing (Tagliapietra et al, 2023). However, both proposals are clearly underpinned by a de-risking approach, that has recently become an integral part of policy for both the EU (Von der Leyen, 2023) and G7[3].

The historical discussion in section 1 shows how such concerns are not new to Europe or the world. Discussions about the economic and security challenges posed by China's emergence as a global economic power mirror the unease felt by European governments in the 1970 and 1980s about the technological leadership of the United States and Japan.

Old industrial policy questions are emerging again, yet with a new level of complexity because of the urgent need to move forward with the green transition. In a globalised world grappling with the impacts of climate change, industrial policy needs to address multiple objectives, including global decarbonisation, world competitive economic value and job creation, and strategic autonomy. When these objectives conflict, they present policymakers with a challenging trilemma: how to combine decarbonisation with economic growth and jobs and world competitiveness, while also reinforcing resilience and sovereignty/autonomy/security of supply? What is the best way socio-economically to achieve decarbonisation and resilience? How and how far to go in moving towards sovereignity/autonomy/resilience, and

---

3   See Council of the European Union press release of 20 May 2023: https://www.consilium.europa.eu/fr/press/press-releases/2023/05/20/g7-hiroshima-leaders-communique/.

what does this means in terms of moving away from the traditional economic efficiency paradigm? How far to move away from a horizontal policy approach to shaping of framework conditions, such as through strong competition policy and open trade? To what extent can technologies and projects deemed to be strategic be selected, requiring resilience/autonomy to secure supplies? How can these trade-offs be minimised, for example by fostering technological innovation to substitute critical inputs, rather than investing in expensive import substituting local projects? How can resilience be turned into an opportunity to create quality jobs and accelerate, rather than impede, the decarbonisation process?

This book tries to tackle some of these difficult questions. In the volume, a consensus emerges on the legitimacy and significance of revitalising industrial policy. Authors agree that governments have a pivotal role to play in managing the transition from fossil fuels to low-carbon energy systems, while addressing social challenges. Leaving the challenges to market forces is not an option in view of the externalities and path dependencies that can slow down or interrupt the course of private actions. The focus lies on the necessity of a future-proof industrial policy infused with strong 'green' elements. The question is what such an industrial policy should look like.

Although the details of such an industrial policy are not yet clearly laid out, there is a consensus in this volume's chapters that a mix of policy instruments is needed. Effective industrial policies should recognise the complementary nature of both supply- and demand-side instruments, combining public support with regulatory frameworks, target setting and carbon pricing. In the contributions, there is a strong consensus that priority should be given to support for innovation capacity building. Authors concur that governments can and should shape technological progress in line with societal needs and should enhance the skills of the workforce. The objective is to ensure that industrial policies coexist with competition, facilitating structural change and business dynamics. Safeguarding competition and enabling the entry of new firms to challenge less efficient incumbents is crucial.

There is also agreement on the need for more directionality in industrial policymaking. *Ex-ante* choices will have to be made about technologies and projects that contribute most to the multidimensional objectives, but which are impeded by market, system and transition failures, even if the risk of selection failures is high. Managing this risk of government failure calls for a good mix of vertical and horizontal instruments, bottom-up and top-down selection, limiting support in time and the importance of ensuring competition as a level playing field. Recommendations range from establishing agencies modelled after the United States Defense Advanced Research Projects Agency (DARPA) to conducting complexity analysis of value chains, all with the goal of developing flexible policies that can be evaluated regularly and adjusted accordingly.

The success of industrial policy will be defined ultimately by whether it succeeds in unleashing private-sector investment to meet society's targets in a globally competitive and resilient manner, putting public-private partnerships at the core of industrial policymaking. The authors in this volume call for explicit policies and continuous collaboration between firms and governments to establish objectives that promote the creation of 'good jobs'.

Building coalitions at domestic and international levels, even among countries that may be rivals in other areas, is of paramount importance to navigate the green transition and other transformative processes effectively. The regional dimension is particularly crucial for a 'smart industrial policy', whether focused on green initiatives or not. While some argue that efficiency and a region's inherent comparative advantage should guide industrial policy, others caution against straying too far from industry economics. Caution is also advised when pursuing national interests through industrial policy, as this may trigger an international race for subsidies, adversely affecting developing countries and potentially accelerating deglobalisation. Overall, this

Blueprint offers recognition of the benefits of an industrial policy that supports international coordination and even cooperation, rather than adopting a short-sighted Europe-first approach. These reflections are addressed in different ways by the contributing authors, as follows:

Chapter 2, *An innovation-driven industrial policy for Europe* (Philippe Aghion), asserts that industrial policy is essential for the competitiveness of EU industry and to catch up with the technology frontier. The core question is how to redesign the governance of industrial policy to make it more compatible with competition and innovation-led growth. Governments should focus support on skill-intensive sectors or sectors subject to high competition, to stimulate productivity growth more efficiently. However, by subsidising incumbent firms, governments should not deter new, higher-performing firms from entering the market. The author also calls for updated interpretations of the Stability Pact, competition policy and the single market, and EU borrowing to enhance Europe's investment capacity, make it more competitive at the global level and avoid irreversible decline. The author also advocates a European DARPA to ensure the competitiveness of EU industry, with projects funded from participating nations' budgets and by joint-EU borrowing.

Chapter 3, *Productivism and new industrial policies: learning from the past, preparing for the future* (Dani Rodrik), turns to the labour aspect of industrial policymaking. The author proposes a new paradigm of 'productivism' to enhance the productivity of all parts of society through a collaborative effort involving government agencies and private firms. Productivism focuses on incentivising worker-friendly technologies and improving the quantity and quality of jobs available for less-educated and less-skilled members of the workforce. Industrial policies should encourage improvements on both the demand and supply sides of the labour market. This requires customised and targeted business incentives, and dialogue between government agencies and companies to identify constraints and opportunities and design interventions accordingly. To help create 'good jobs', regional business bureaux should be set up – or strengthened – to work alongside public employment services to provide customised services to local firms and investors.

Chapter 4, *Industrial policy and technological sovereignty* (Uwe Cantner), focuses on the main driver of industrial policy at EU level: innovation and how to assure that innovation works as driver for industrial policy while assuring strategic autonomy or sovereignity in technology. The chapter discusses what obtaining technological sovereignty entails, what policies could be needed to achieve this, and when it is better to leave it to the market. The chapter sets this discussion in the context of relevant key technologies and of radical change and innovation.

Chapter 5, *Cooperation or conflict? A transatlantic look at whether industrial policy will produce solutions or generate unmanageable conflicts* (Laura Tyson and John Zysman), outlines how international collaboration among allies is essential for the success of industrial policies. The authors discuss the implications for the global economy and the international political economic order of US industrial policies, including the CHIPS and Science Act and green industrial policies. The argue that the success of these policies will depend on US cooperation with its allies, but the policies are likely to raise tensions precisely with those allies, even though industrial policies need not disadvantage foreign firms relative to domestic firms, and success will require allies to adopt complementary policies. Meanwhile, building domestic coalitions for industrial policies and rewarding local constituencies may generate conflicts between nations, whether allies or not. Competing national industrial policies, while well motivated, can quickly lead to counterproductive and wasteful bidding wars.

Chapter 6, *Green industrial policy: the necessary evil to avoid a climate catastrophe* (Alessio Terzi), offers an economic-development perspective on green industrial policy. The author considers industrial policy an essential but imperfect tool to tackle climate change. Market imperfections and distributional concerns imply that instruments such as carbon pricing will be insufficient to ensure speedy decarbonisation. The use of industrial policy in the service of national interest may lead to an international subsidy race, to the detriment of developing countries. Moreover, policymakers need to be aware of the negative effects of industrial policy on innovation, particularly at the technological frontier. Protectionist approaches might slow technological innovation in a time when speed is of the essence.

Chapter 7, *Industrial strategies for Europe's green transition* (Chiara Criscuolo, Antoine Dechezleprêtre and Guy Lalanne), postulates that green industrial policy should go beyond carbon pricing and should leverage the complementarities of supply- and demand-side instruments. The current pace of innovation is too slow to face the challenge of climate change; a range of barriers and market failures remain at the root of the problem. To resolve these, a mission-oriented industrial strategy for the green transition is needed. The authors suggest a taxonomy of industrial policy instruments to deploy in concert. Effective green industrial policy should make strategic use of different policy instruments supporting innovation and technology adoption, carbon pricing and framework instruments (such as standards and regulations and policies to encourage skills). Industrial policies are not necessarily incompatible with competition and should be designed so that they do not slow down structural change and business dynamics.

Chapter 8, *A more globally minded European green industrial policy* (Ricardo Hausmann and Ketan Ahuja), further enlarges the scope of the discussion by providing a Global South perspective on Europe's green industrial policy, illustrating how a more global European industrial policy would be better suited to deal with the trade-offs the continent faces. The authors argue that Europe should not pursue a 'Europe first' approach, but should only engage in strategic competition over the parts of the value chain in which Europe holds a comparative advantage. Bottom-up techno-economic cost modelling and economic-complexity analysis of emerging clean supply chains can help identify these parts. EU green industrial policy should also recognise the economic reality of energy distribution, and relocate accordingly the production steps that can be more efficiently decarbonised. This means helping third countries build clean-tech value chains and developing economic constituencies and political forces behind green industries in Europe's trading partners, to counterbalance fossil-fuel interests that resist change in those countries. Finally, Europe should focus on growing the overall global green economy and increasing overall demand for the green products and services in which Europe has a comparative advantage. A global green industrial policy would benefit European workers, shareholders and consumers, as well as the rest of the world.

Chapter 9, *Europe's green industrial policy* (Simone Tagliapietra, Cecilia Trasi and Reinhilde Veugelers), gives an overview of the green industrial policy measures being implemented in Europe. The authors argue that the current fragmentation of policy measures calls for a new approach to green industrial policymaking at EU level. A new and effective EU green industrial policy should aim at an overall improvement in the attractiveness of the EU single market as a location for green investment, via both horizontal measures to enhance market functioning and specific measures in support of clean technologies. Examples of these measures include better regulation, better green procurement rules and EU-level financing to promote new or earlystage clean tech, in which EU firms can achieve sustainable competitive positions. An EU-scale green industrial policy will require a stronger governance model to ensure better coordination and longer-term commitment.

Chapter 10, *Smart green industrial policy* (Ben McWilliams and Georg Zachmann), takes a regional development perspective to illustrate how regions should develop a smart green industrial policy. Drawing upon empirical and theoretical literature, the authors argue that regions have unique technological, knowledge and institutional capacities, and that these are a crucial indicator of the ability of a region to absorb new knowledge. It is possible to identify these comparative advantages at a regional level. Policymakers can map desirable green technological capacities against existing regional capabilities, and thus increase the likelihood that a region will respond successfully to green industrial policy.

Chapter 11, *Industrial policy for electric vehicle supply chains and the US-EU fight over the Inflation Reduction Act* (Chad Bown), examines how the Inflation Reduction Act (IRA) of 2022, its implementing regulations, policy decisions on leasing and potential critical minerals agreements all have the potential to affect the electric vehicle supply chain. This case study showcases the political-economic complications involved in US and EU attempts to cooperate over clean energy transition policy to address the global externality of carbon dioxide emissions. Electric vehicles are one example of the challenge facing partners with integrated supply chains and similar levels of economic development that share concerns about climate change, rising inequality, workers, other social issues and democracy itself. The author argues that the electric vehicles conflict laid bare the differing US and EU prioritisation of these issues relative to economic efficiency, World Trade Organisation rules, the approach to non-market economies and national security vulnerabilities

Chapter 12, *Developing a European industrial policy: lessons from COVID-19* (Mathias Dewatripont), focuses on the innovation part of industrial policy by bringing into the analysis Europe's experience with COVID-19 vaccines. While Europe has a solid foundation in the health sector, it suffers from suboptimal coordination between parties, especially between providers of funding. The author argues that the EU should put in place a renewed support strategy for the development and commercialisation of innovative technologies modelled on DARPA. This approach would enhance competition, mix top-down and bottom-up approaches, and support innovation while prioritising affordability. Industrial policy should also aim at improving bargaining positions through EU-wide coordination of negotiations with pharma companies, to limit their ability to play countries off against one another. This would be valuable particularly for rare diseases, for which pan-EU purchasing could offer higher sale volumes to companies and make lower prices more sustainable for the industry.

References

European Commission (2012) 'A Stronger European Industry for Growth and Economic Recovery Industrial Policy Communication Update', COM/2012/0582 final, available at https://eur-lex.europa.eu/legal-content/EN/TXT/?uri=celex%3A52012DC0582

European Commission (2019) *Strategic Outlook*, JOINT/2019/5 final, available at: https://eur-lex.europa.eu/legal-content/EN/ALL/?uri=CELEX%3A52019JC0005

European Commission (2020) 'A New Industrial Strategy for Europe', COM/2020/102 final, available at https://eur-lex.europa.eu/legal-content/EN/TXT/HTML/?uri=CELEX:52020DC0102

European Commission (2021) 'Updating the 2020 New Industrial Strategy: Building a Stronger Single Market for Europe's Recovery', COM/2021/350 final, available at https://eur-lex.europa.eu/legal-content/EN/TXT/?uri=COM:2021:350:FIN

European Commission (2022) 'A Chips Act for Europe', COM/2022/45 final, available at https://eur-lex.europa.eu/legal-content/EN/TXT/?uri=CELEX:52022DC0045

European Council (2000) 'Presidency conclusions, Lisbon European Council, 23 and 24 March 2000', available at https://www.consilium.europa.eu/uedocs/cms_data/docs/pressdata/en/ec/00100-r1.en0.htm

Owen, G. (2012) 'Industrial Policy in Europe since the Second World War: What Has Been Learnt?' *ECIPE Occasional Paper* 1/2012, European Centre for International Political Economy, available at https://www.econstor.eu/handle/10419/174716

Poitiers, N. and P. Weil (2022) 'Is the EU Chips Act the right approach?' *Bruegel Blog*, 2 June, available at https://www.bruegel.org/blog-post/eu-chips-act-right-approach

Tagliapietra, S., R. Veugelers and J. Zettelmeyer (2023) 'Rebooting the European Union's Net Zero Industry Act', *Policy Brief* 14/2023, Bruegel, available at https://www.bruegel.org/policy-brief/rebooting-european-unions-net-zero-industry-act

Veugelers, R. (ed) (2013) *Manufacturing Europe's future*, Blueprint Series Volume XXI, Bruegel, available at https://www.bruegel.org/book/manufacturing-europes-future

Von der Leyen, U. (2023) 'Speech on EU-China relations to the Mercator Institute for China Studies and the European Policy Centre', 30 March, available at https://ec.europa.eu/commission/presscorner/detail/en/speech_23_2063

2 An innovation-driven industrial policy for Europe

Philippe Aghion

1 Introduction
With the stated objective of both curbing inflation and fighting global warming, the American administration has enacted the so-called Inflation Reduction Act (IRA). This law gives the green light to a considerable increase in public spending of $737 billion over ten years, including $369 billion in tax credits and subsidies.

The protectionist consequences of the IRA are fairly obvious. In particular, it provides for a subsidy of up to $7500 for any American consumer who purchases an electric car assembled in the United States, and that has batteries relying on at least 40 percent US input components. It also offers generous tax exemptions to any producer of solar panels that chooses to operate on American soil, and it heavily subsidises green research and development activities that are being carried out in the United States. Consequently, some companies have decided to freeze projects elsewhere and relocate to the US.

The IRA penalises not only European producers of electric cars, such as BMW or Fiat, but also European firms that operate already in the US but which rely on production chains partly located in other countries.

How can Europe react to the IRA and preserve its competitiveness worldwide? How can it stop and hopefully reverse the declining trend in its industrial production and exports? How can it avoid being leapfrogged by China and becoming an innovation laggard? European industrial policy is part of the answer, provided it is adequately designed and financed.

2 The case for industrial policy

In the years following the Second World War, national industrial champions were at the forefront of industrial policy in many developed countries. In France, this pro-champion policy was a pillar of the reconstruction of the economy and of the thirty years of post-war growth. In the United States, it played a decisive role in particular for the defence, aeronautics and aerospace industries in pursuit of supremacy over the Soviet Union. At the same time, the World Bank, under the direction of Robert McNamara, supported trade protection and import substitution in developing countries, to allow them to nurture their infant industries.

The infant industry doctrine can be summarised as follows (List, 1841). Consider a developing country with two sectors of activity: a large agricultural sector and a nascent domestic manufacturing sector. This country wishes to develop its manufacturing sector because of the resulting positive technological externalities on the economy as a whole. Manufacturing, however, entails high initial fixed costs that will decrease over time thanks to experience and learning-by-doing. Total and immediate liberalisation of international trade would lead this country to import manufactured products from developed countries, where they are initially cheaper to produce. This in turn would lead to less local manufacturing activity, less learning-by-doing, and thus less technological progress and domestic growth. To avoid these repercussions, proponents of the infant industry argument endorse temporary protectionist policies, such as provisional tariff barriers, so that infant industries can grow and catch up to the technological frontier.

Over time, industrial policy fell out of favour. Little by little, economists became aware of the problems it creates in practice. First, it favours existing large domestic firms – the national champions – thus limiting or distorting competition. But we know that product market competition is key for innovation and productivity growth: more competition induces firms to innovate more intensely in order to surpass their rivals (Aghion *et al*, 2005). Second, governments are not great at picking winners, that is, choosing which firms they should support with subsidies or tariffs, as they do not have access to all of the relevant information. Furthermore, they may be receptive to lobbying by large incumbent firms. The larger the resources of these firms, the more they are in a position to influence public policy. Anne Krueger (1993, 1995) was among the most forceful and vocal opponent of industrial policy.

This challenge led to a preference for what are known as 'horizontal' policies for stimulating innovation and growth, meaning policies that apply to all sectors of the economy (Acemoglu et al, 2006; Aghion and Howitt, 2006). Among the main vectors of horizontal policy are: 1) investing in the knowledge economy (especially higher education and research); 2) reforming labour and product markets to make them more dynamic, through appropriate policies for competition, unemployment insurance and professional training; and 3) developing venture capital and private equity to provide funding for innovation.

Are these horizontal measures enough? Or does the state still have a role to play in industry, and if so, what is that role? Objections to industrial policy from the 1950s through the 1980s are difficult to counter, especially because later work, such as that of Laffont and Tirole (1993), pointed to several sources of inefficiency in state intervention, because of asymmetric information or the potential for collusion between some private actors and the state. Still, this alone does not disqualify state intervention, which remains legitimate for several reasons. One reason is the existence of positive knowledge externalities, such as patents, that individuals do not take into account. An individual deciding whether to invest in education or in R&D does not take into account the positive externalities on his or her co-workers, or on the economy as a whole. As a consequence, individuals tend to underinvest in education and in R&D. Credit constraints exacerbate this tendency. Still, this does not justify state intervention that is not purely horizontal.

A first argument in support of a non-horizontal industrial policy is the phenomenon known as path dependence. A quintessential example is green innovation. For example, car manufacturers that innovated in combustion engine technology in the past will tend to innovate in combustion engine technology in the future because of path dependency (Aghion *et al*, 2016). Imposing a carbon tax or subsidising green innovation makes it less costly to adopt a new technology and redirects the innovation activities of car manufacturers to electric engines. This example shows that governments have a role to play, not only in stimulating innovation in general, but also by directing innovation through targeted interventions.

Another argument has to do with problems of coordination. Bolton and Farrell (1990), and Rob (1991), suggested that government action can help resolve coordination problems, thereby enabling or accelerating entry into strategic sectors where the initial fixed costs of entry are high. Consider a new potential market for which entry is costly and where future profits are uncertain and depend on information (such as the level of consumer demand) that cannot be known until the market is active. No single firm wants to be the first to pay the fixed costs of entry. Every firm prefers to let other firms bear the fixed costs first, and then to benefit from the information they generate, without bearing the risk and cost of acquiring this information. In other words, the absence of state intervention leads to the free-rider phenomenon, which results in delay or even an impasse in creating the market. To solve this problem, the state can subsidise the first entrant, which encourages other firms to follow its example.

This coordination argument explains the success of state intervention in the aeronautics industry (Boeing, Airbus), where fixed costs are high and demand is uncertain. It also explains the success of the US Defense Advanced Research Projects Agency (DARPA), established in 1958 to facilitate the transition from basic research to applied research and marketing for breakthrough innovations ('tough technologies'), where this transition entails substantial fixed costs and requires coordinated efforts by various economic actors (Azoulay *et al*, 2019). We discuss DARPA in more detail below.

3 Governing industrial policy

Once we recognise that industrial policy can be useful, how can we determine in which sectors the state should intervene? Policymakers should first address economic and social priorities including fighting climate change and developing renewable energies, health, and defence. After that, they should focus on sectors that use highly skilled labour or have a high degree of competition. Thus, a study analysing international microeconomic data showed that public investments targeting skill-intensive sectors are more effective in stimulating productivity growth (Nunn and Trefler, 2010). Similarly, a study based on Chinese data showed that targeting more competitive sectors helps stimulate productivity growth (Aghion *et al*, 2015).

The question then arises of the governance of industrial policy and sectoral state aid. A priority is for industrial policy to be competition-friendly. Thus, Aghion *et al* (2015) showed that sectoral aid stimulates productivity growth more when it is not concentrated on a single firm or a small number of firms – in other words if the aid operates to maintain or increase competition in the sector.

Equally important is to minimise the extent to which subsidising incumbent firms discourages the entry of new, higher-performing firms (Acemoglu *et al*, 2018). Subsidising established firms can hinder the entrance of new, more innovative firms as a result of a reallocation effect: incumbent firms increase the demand for skilled labour and other factors of production, thereby increasing their cost. This extra cost in turn reduces the profits that potential new entrants can expect, discouraging them from entering the market.

Aghion *et al* (2019) illustrated this reallocation effect in an analysis of how the Eurosystem's Additional Credit Claims (ACC) programme, implemented in February 2012 by the European Central Bank, affected firm dynamics in France. Mario Draghi, ECB president at the time, created this programme to prevent a recession in the euro area following the 2008-2009 financial crisis. The idea was as follows: in the euro area, banks could pledge high-quality corporate loans as collateral for refinancing from the ECB. These loans thus enabled banks to obtain additional liquidity. Firms that are most likely to repay their debt have a rating of 1. They are followed by the firms rated 2, then 3, then 4, then 5, with decreasing probabilities of repaying their debt. A rating of P means the firm is close to bankruptcy. Before February 2012, commercial banks could use only loans to firms rated better than 4 as collateral for refinancing from the ECB. The ACC programme extended eligibility to firms rated 4.

What happened after implementation of the ACC programme? The first consequence was that loans to firms rated 4 increased relative to loans to firms with a rating worse than 4, in particular those one step below, at 5+. The second consequence was that the productivity growth of firms rated 4 increased. In other words, relaxing credit constraints on these firms allowed them to invest, in particular in innovation. But this positive effect was offset by a reallocation effect: the implementation of the ACC programme reduced the fraction of firms rated 4 that exited the market, and the biggest impact was on the lowest-performing firms in terms of initial productivity. In other words, the ACC programme impeded the replacement of the lowest-performing firms rated 4 by new, potentially higher-performing firms.

The existence of a reallocation effect pointed out by the above-mentioned studies suggests that any public policy to subsidise firms should take into account the impact of the policy not only on existing firms, but also on potential new entrants to the sector.

Next, sectoral state aid should be regularly reassessed to avoid the perpetuation of programmes that prove ineffective. Co-financing by state and private investors, such as development banks, can facilitate the establishment of adequate exit mechanisms.

Overall, industrial policy is not a 'yes or no' issue; the question is rather to redesign the governance of industrial policy to make it more compatible with competition and, more generally, with innovation-led growth.

4 The DARPA model

The so-called DARPA model is a successful attempt at reconciling industrial policy with competition and entry. DARPA is a research agency within the US Department of Defense, responsible for innovations with military applications. The history of DARPA's success demonstrates that a well-managed industrial policy can successfully foster rather than inhibit innovation. DARPA was created after the United States lost a battle in the space race against the Soviet Union: in October 1957, the Soviet satellite Sputnik became the first artificial satellite to orbit the earth. This event had a huge international impact. It substantiated the advance of the Soviet space programme and stunned the American public. Lyndon B. Johnson, then a senator, wrote of *"the profound shock of realising that it might be possible for another nation to achieve technological superiority over this great country of ours"* (Johnson, 1971). Within five months, in February 1958, even before the creation of NASA, President Eisenhower established DARPA as America's primary tool in the military race and the space race against the Soviet Union.

DARPA still exists, and its novel model has been studied in detail (Azoulay *et al*, 2019). In areas such as defence and space exploration, it is difficult to make the transition from basic research to implementation and marketing. This can be represented by an S curve. The beginning of the curve represents the origin of a concept to which not much development effort has been devoted because the returns on such efforts are low. The median part of the curve corresponds to the take-off phase: returns on development efforts are higher, enabling the technology to advance more quickly. Lastly, the phase of maturity implies diminishing returns to development efforts and slower improvements to the technology. Because the initial phase requires substantial efforts, the anticipated social gains from future exploitation must be considerable in order for the project to generate interest and be eligible for DARPA funding. Accordingly, DARPA projects have three characteristics: they are midway between basic and applied research; it is possible to organise research toward a precise objective; and the existence of coordination problems makes large-scale funding and testing of the technology difficult without public intervention.

This model of scientific development enabled the United States to catch up steadily with the Soviet Union in the space race. Even though in the initial years after DARPA was created the USSR had a series of successes, thanks to an equally ambitious space programme (for example, the first animal in space in 1957, the first man and first woman in space in 1961 and 1963, respectively, and first unmanned lunar landing in 1966), the United States ultimately won the race in 1969, when it first landed humans on the moon. Today, DARPA's annual budget is over $3 billion, and it funds over one hundred programmes. DARPA has played a decisive role in the development of high-risk projects with high social value, such as the internet, originally called Arpanet (at the time DARPA had been renamed ARPA), and GPS.

The DARPA model is particularly interesting because it combines a top-down approach with a bottom-up approach[4]. On the top-down side, the Department of Defense funds the programmes, selects the programme heads and hires them for a three- to five-year period. On the bottom-up side, the programme heads, who come from academia or the private sector, or who are investors, have full latitude to define and manage their programmes. They can freely organise partnerships between start-ups, university labs and large industrial firms, and they enjoy great flexibility in recruiting collaborators.

And most importantly, programme heads elicit new competing projects. A good example is BARDA (the Biomedical Advanced Research and Development Authority), which is the equivalent of DARPA for the US biotech sector. During the COVID-19 crisis, BARDA financed

---

4 The top-down approach refers to a hierarchical process in which the state is the decision maker and imposes its decision on decentralised actors. Conversely, in a bottom-up approach, the state sets out the broad lines of a policy, but allows local actors flexibility to determine how to implement it.

several competing vaccine projects, including BioNTech and Oxford-AstraZeneca, which were initiated outside the US.

5 The case for European DARPAs

Having to compete with the US and China, both of which are promoting very assertive industrial and innovation policies, why not create European DARPAs? A first reason for creating European DARPAs is to enable Europe to assume greater responsibility for its own defence. A more fundamental motive is that Europe faces major technological challenges, in particular in the energy and environment, digital and healthcare sectors. The projects of these European DARPAs would be funded directly from participating nations' governmental budgets, and also from borrowing by the European Union as a whole.

Most importantly, as it is already the case for the funding of basic research by the European Research Council (ERC), the selection of projects by these European DARPAs should escape the *juste retour* principle, according to which each member state expects to receive, in monetary returns, at least as much as it contributes. Project selection by European DARPAs should also avoid member states' obsession with veto rights. Some EU countries have expressed the fear that European DARPAs would systematically favour larger EU members at the expense of the smaller. Here again, governance is the adequate response and there are at least two models one can build upon. First, BARDA during the COVID-19 crisis: it included labs located outside the US when selecting which vaccines to push for mass production; in particular it took BioNTech and Oxford-AstraZeneca. Second, the European Research Council and its international jury panels: excellence, not nationality, is the primary criterion for selecting those research projects that receive ERC funding.

Who should take part in these European DARPAs? Our preference would be for an open 'coalition of the willing', with the possibility for the United Kingdom to also join, given their academic and industrial expertise in defence, health and energy.

6 Moving beyond Hayek

Our call for establishing EU-funded European DARPAs is somewhat at odds with what mainstream European policy advisers would advocate. Thus, Kleimann *et al* (2023), on responding to the US IRA, wrote: *"the EU should not just seek to protect its competitiveness relative to the US but to pursue broader aims, including competitiveness in general ... these aims imply that the EU should not impose local-content requirements of its own, should not loosen state-aid rules and should not mimic the IRA's approach to manufacturing subsidies. Rather, it should focus on boosting its structural competitiveness".*

In other words, in response to the IRA and the climate challenge, Europe should not change its doctrine, in particular it should not contemplate the possibility of new sectoral state aid – those are seen as being anti-competitive *a priori* – but should instead deepen its reliance on structural reforms and adequate carbon taxes and regulations.

A contrasting view is that, in the face of fiercer competition from China and the United States, both of which implement forceful industrial policies, the EU should rethink its economic doctrine: not to throw it away, but rather to adapt it to the new circumstances. The EU doctrine took shape in the late 1980s. Centred around the idea of a large single market and a broad set of regulations, but with a very small EU budget, this paradigm is directly inspired by Hayek. The basic idea, well explained in *The Road of Serfdom* (Hayek, 1944), was that Europe and its institutions should be thought of primarily as a federation, with the main objective of preventing member states from yielding to local political and social pressures. Hence the three pillars of European economic governance: 1) the single market and the European Commission's primacy with regard to competition policy – in particular it is up to the Commission to detect and punish sectoral state aid in member states; 2) the Maastricht Stability and Growth Pact, which limits the budgetary power of individual member states – the Commission ensures the compliance with the 3 percent deficit rule; and 3) an EU budget of only 1 percent of European GDP.

Interestingly, following the enactment of the IRA, some new ideas have been put forward by the European Commission, which depart from a literal interpretation of the Hayekian doctrine. A first suggestion is to soften the rules governing sectoral state aid. This has raised strong criticisms from some countries, including the Netherlands and Sweden, which see it as a threat to the single market, and something that would favour large countries at the expense of smaller member states[5]. This objection should not be disregarded, yet in the previous section we argued that suitable governance of European DARPAs would help avoid such an undesirable outcome. A second idea is to use the €750 billion of the post-COVID-19 Resilience and Recovery Fund and to even increase Europe's investment capacity by creating a European Sovereign Fund for Industry, which, like the Recovery Fund, would be financed by a loan directly contracted by the European Union. This second idea met strong reluctance from countries such as the Netherlands[6], for which this is just a trick to circumvent the budgetary rules of the Union.

We are not calling here for a phase-out of the existing rules. In particular, in Aghion *et al* (2005), we provided strong empirical evidence of the importance of competition and the single-market as the main drivers of innovation-led growth. We also strongly support the Growth and Stability Pact, which underlies the credibility of the euro and guarantees macroeconomic stability in the euro area, both of which can only favour innovation-led growth. Yet, the current circumstances call for an updated interpretation of the rules.

- *Stability Pact*: countries that successfully engage in structural reforms and show seriousness in the use of public funds, should

---

5   See for example *Euractiv.com with Reuters*, 'Eleven EU countries urge 'great caution' in loosening state aid rules', 15 February 2023, https://www.euractiv.com/section/economy-jobs/news/eleven-eu-countries-urge-great-caution-in-loosening-state-aid-rules/.

6   Sam Fleming, 'Netherlands opposes new EU money to counter US green subsidies', *Financial Times*, 24 January 2023, https://www.ft.com/content/f1cfc042-2620-453d-b0c0-585c79571d9a.

be granted an entry ticket to invest more and better in education, innovation and energy transition.
- *Competition policy and the single market*: rather than *a priori* forbidding any kind of sectoral state aid *ex ante*, an *ex-post* approach should be adopted and sectoral aid should be tolerated as long as it does not result in a decline in product market competition or in obstacles preventing the entry of new innovative firms.
- *EU borrowing*: Europe's investment capacity should be enhanced using EU borrowing, to fund new – and properly governed – European DARPAs aimed at making Europe more competitive in the world economy.

Without any accommodation of the rules and any evolution in the underlying doctrine, Europe runs the risk of an irreversible decline.

References

Acemoglu, D., P. Aghion and F. Zilibotti (2006) 'Distance to Frontier, Selection, and Economic Growth', *Journal of the European Economic Association* 4(1)

Acemoglu, D., U. Akcigit, H. Alp, N. Bloom and W. Kerr (2018) 'Innovation, Reallocation, and Growth', *American Economic Review* 108(11): 3450-3491

Aghion, P., N. Bloom, R. Blundell, R. Griffith and P. Howitt (2005) 'Competition and Innovation: An Inverted-U Relationship', Quarterly Journal of Economics 120: 701-728

Aghion, P. and P. Howitt (2006) 'Appropriate Growth Policy: A Unifying Framework', Joseph Schumpeter Lecture, *Journal of the European Economic Association* 4(2-3): 269-314

Aghion, P., J. Cai, M. Dewatripont, L. Du, A. Harrison and P. Legros (2015) 'Industrial Policy and Competition', *American Economic Journal: Macroeconomics* 7(4): 1-32

Aghion, P., A. Dechezleprêtre, D. Hemous, R. Martin and J. Van Reenen (2016) 'Carbon Taxes, Path Dependency, and Directed Technical Change: Evidence from the Auto Industry', *Journal of Political Economy* 124(1): 1-51

Aghion, P., A. Bergeaud, G. Cette, R. Lecat and H. Maghin (2019) 'The Inverted-U Relationship between Credit Access and Productivity Growth', *Economica* 86: 1-31

Azoulay, P., E. Fuchs, A.P. Goldstein and M. Kearney (2019) 'Funding Breakthrough Research: Promises and Challenges of the "ARPA Model"', *Innovation Policy and the Economy* 19: 69-96

Bolton, P. and J. Farrell (1990) 'Decentralization, Duplication, and Delay', *Journal of Political Economy* 98(4): 803-826

Hayek, F. (1944) *The Road to Serfdom*, University of Chicago Press

Johnson, L.B. (1971) *The Vantage Point: Perspectives of the Presidency, 1963-1969*, New York: Holt, Rinehart and Winston

Kleimann, D., N. Poitiers, A. Sapir, S. Tagliapietra, N. Véron, R. Veugelers and J. Zettelmeyer (2023) 'How Europe should answer the US Inflation Reduction Act', *Policy Contribution* 04/2023, Bruegel

Krueger, A.O. (1993) *Political Economy of Policy Reform in Developing Countries*, Cambridge, MA: MIT Press

Krueger, A.O. (1995) 'Policy Lessons from Development Experience since the Second World War', in J. Behrman and T.N. Srinivasan (eds) *Handbook of Development Economics*, vol. 3B: 2497-2550, Amsterdam: Elsevier

Laffont, J.-J. and J. Tirole (1993) *A Theory of Incentives in Procurement and Regulation*, Cambridge, MA: MIT Press

List, F. (1841) *Das nationale System der politischen Ökonomie*, Stuttgart: J.G. Cotta

Nunn, N. and D. Trefler (2010) 'The Structure of Tariffs and Long-Term Growth', *American Economic Journal: Macroeconomics* 2(4): 158-194

Rob, R. (1991) 'Learning and Capacity Expansion under Demand Uncertainty', *Review of Economic Studies* 58(4): 655-675

3 Productivism and new industrial policies: learning from the past, preparing for the future

Dani Rodrik

1 Introduction[7]

Throughout history, economic ideology has swung from one end of the pendulum to the other, from the reification of markets to reliance on states and then back again. Superficially, we appear to be in the midst of one of these periodic realignments. It was perhaps inevitable that the excesses of neoliberalism – the increase in inequality, concentration of corporate power, neglect of the threats to the physical and social environment – would cause a backlash.

But new paradigms get established by developing novel approaches and not by just emulating the old. When after the 1930s, the New Deal and the welfare state replaced the freewheeling capitalism that preceded them, they did not simply revert to the mercantilist practices of old. They established new modes of regulations, new institutions of social insurance and explicit macroeconomic management in the form of Keynesianism.

Similarly, if the new turn to 'productivism'[8] is to be successful, it

---

7 This chapter is based on, and draws heavily from, Rodrik and Stantcheva (2021) (a report for French President Emmanuel Macron), and from Dani Rodrik, 'Getting Productivism Right', *Project Syndicate*, 8 August 2022, https://www.project-syndicate.org/commentary/will-productivism-supersede-neoliberalism-by-dani-rodrik-2022-08.

8 Dani Rodrik, 'The New Productivism Paradigm?' *Project Syndicate*, 5 July 2022,

will have to move beyond conventional social protection, industrial policies and macroeconomic management. It will have to internalise lessons learned from the failures of some of those policies in the past, and adapt to fundamentally new challenges.

State intervention aimed at reshaping the structure of an economy – so-called industrial policy – has traditionally been faulted for being ineffective and getting captured by special interests. 'Governments cannot pick winners', as the old adage goes. In reality, much of this criticism is overdone. While there have been notable failures, systematic recent studies find that industrial policies incentivising investment and job creation in disadvantaged regions have often done surprisingly well (Criscuolo *et al*, 2019).

Public initiatives have been behind some of the most startling high-tech successes of our time, including the internet and GPS. For every Solyndra – a solar cell manufacturer that failed spectacularly after half a billion dollars in government loan guarantees – there is often a Tesla, the phenomenally successful electric battery and vehicle manufacturer that also received government support at a critical phase of its development.

Nevertheless, there is much room for improvement. The most effective industrial policies are those that entail close, collaborative interaction between government agencies and private firms, through which firms receive critical public inputs – financial support, skilled workers or technological assistance – in return for meeting soft and evolving targets on investment and employment. This kind of industrial policy is likely to work much better – whether in promoting local economic development or in directing major national technological efforts – than open-ended subsidies or tax incentives.

As the name suggests, productivism focuses on enhancing the productive capabilities of all segments and regions of a society. While

https://www.project-syndicate.org/commentary/new-productivism-economic-policy-paradigm-by-dani-rodrik-2022-07.

traditional forms of social assistance, especially better access to education and healthcare, can help in this regard, connecting people with productive employment opportunities requires interventions that go beyond these. It requires improvements on the demand side of the labour market as well as the supply side. Policies must directly encourage an increase in the quantity and quality of jobs that are available for the less-educated and less-skilled members of the workforce, where they choose (or can afford to) live.

In the future, most of these jobs will come not from manufacturing, but from services such as health and long-term care and retail. Even if policy succeeds in reshoring manufacturing and supply chains, the impact on employment is likely to remain limited. The experience of East Asian manufacturing superstars such as South Korea and Taiwan provides a sobering example. These two countries have managed to rapidly increase the share of manufacturing value added in GDP (at constant prices), yet they have experienced steady declines in manufacturing employment ratios.

This is important since so much of the policy effort in the United States and Europe is focused on promoting high-tech manufacturing and digital industries. For example, the US CHIPS and Science Act provides $52 billion in funding for semiconductors and related manufacturing. The initiative is aimed at both enhancing national security *vis-à-vis* China and creating good jobs. Unfortunately, even if the first objective is met, the second objective is likely to remain elusive. A similar point can be made about the subsidies to green technologies that are a core component of President Biden's Inflation Reduction Act. Without question, the green transition is an urgent priority that the new paradigm needs to tackle. But here too, governments cannot kill two birds with one stone. Policies that target climate change are not a substitute for good-job policies, and vice versa.

Shoring up the middle class and disseminating the benefits of technology broadly through society requires an explicit good-jobs strategy. Such a strategy would not be so fixated on competition with China; it would target services instead of manufacturing, and it would focus on incentivising worker-friendly technologies.

2 Business incentives with a good-jobs focus

Economists tend to be cautious, if not downright hostile, towards industrial policies. This attitude derives less from economic theory than from practical considerations. The externalities and market failures that industrial policy aims to fix – learning spillovers, coordination failures, agglomeration effects and, increasingly, the social benefits of good jobs – are widely understood to be widespread in contemporary economies. The concern is that governments lack the knowledge to identify accurately where these market failures are ('governments cannot pick winners'), or that they will be subject to political lobbying and capture once they put themselves in a position to select industries to support.

In recent years, policymakers have articulated the need for industrial policy more explicitly and forcefully. The challenges of transition to a green economy, geographic divides, digitalisation and, increasingly, the perceived threat of Chinese competition in high-tech industries, have highlighted the urgency of public action to stimulate investment and innovation in particular industries and regions. The European Union acknowledged the importance of industrial strategy explicitly in the Juncker Plan of 2014. The European Commission's Horizon 2020 Report targeted an increase in the manufacturing share of GDP in the EU from 16 percent to 20 percent (a target that was missed). The EU is already a massive provider of business incentives through a variety of funds. While the bulk of the EU's structural and cohesion funds are invested in infrastructure, about 10 percent takes the form of direct grants to firms, which makes the programme *"one of the largest enterprise subsidy schemes in the world"* (Murakosy et al, 2020).

In France, business incentives centre on three schemes. First, there are tax credits for R&D spending (*Crédit d'Impôt Recherche*), the stated objective of which is to increase the competitiveness of the country through innovation. Second, there is investment support for SMEs (through the *Banque Publique d'Investissement*, BPI), which channels government and EU funds to support investment and innovation through various financial instruments (credits, credit guarantees or buying shares). The BPI works closely with client firms through the life cycle of projects, providing counselling and management training. Third, there are publicly funded 'competitiveness poles' (*Pôles de compétitivité*). These are designed to promote clusters in specific regions or industries – bringing together small and large firms, training organisations and research labs – through financial support and tax incentives.

It is fair to say that while employment is almost always a subsidiary goal of these programmes, they are rarely designed with employment as the key objective[9]. In the main, they target increased productivity and global competitiveness and try to foster new digital and green industries. In the EU Industrial Strategy Package (2020), for example, high-quality jobs and employment are occasionally referred to, but the emphasis is clearly on digital innovation and green tech. Employment is generally viewed as part of the social agenda, distinct from the productivity and economic growth agendas.

A second consideration is that business incentives work best when they are customised and targeted to specific needs of firms, and when they are part of an iterative dialogue between firms and government agencies. The traditional conception of industrial policy is represented by the East Asian caricature: bureaucrats independently choose a set of economic activities to be promoted, select pre-determined incentives (tax rebates or subsidised credit), and then impose hard conditionality on the receiving firms (they either perform or else). This type of policy hardly works well, and in fact was never quite how industrial

---

9   This is a general feature of business promotion schemes. In a global review of such programmes, Robalino *et al* (2020) wrote: *"In practice, projects are seldom selected for public support based on the jobs impacts the investments are likely to generate ... Often, the beneficiaries of demand-side programs are selected, subject to the size of the firm, on a first-come-first-serve basis."*

policy was actually implemented in Japan, Taiwan, South Korea or China. Successful programmes tend to revolve around a process of strategic collaboration in which firms' needs, market opportunities, and appropriate remedies are discovered over time, with policies revised as learning takes place.

Tim Bartik of the Upjohn Institute has been a long-term observer of business incentives in the US, and his synthesis of the evidence provides a valuable perspective that applies equally well to Europe (Bartik, 2019, 2020). In summary: public policy focusing on job growth in distressed areas can be effective and generate persistent gains in employment-to-population ratios, but current systems are not very effective. They are based on significant tax breaks that often go to large corporations and are not properly targeted or designed. He makes several recommendations. First, business incentives should focus on areas that are distressed – that is, areas that truly need them. Second, the incentives should focus on sectors or firms that are likely to have high job-creation multipliers. Third, public assistance should focus less on tax incentives (and encouraging physical investment) and more on specific public services needed by firms, such as customised business services, zoning or infrastructure policies, local amenities and skills training. Fourth, business assistance should be viewed as a portfolio of services rather than a particular incentive, with the actual mix attuned to local conditions. The second, third and fourth of these recommendations are especially relevant to France (and Europe more broadly).

Bartik's recommendations echo ideas that have developed over the last couple of decades into a new conception of industrial policy (Evans, 1995; Hausmann *et al*, 2008; Rodrik, 2007, 2008; Sabel, 2007; Fernández-Arias *et al*, 2016; Ghezzi, 2017). Under this conception, the government is not presumed to know where the market failures are beforehand and, therefore, does not determine *ex ante* what the specific policy instruments are. Industrial strategy consists of a collaborative process of 'discovery' involving business and agencies of the state, where the objective is to identify the constraints and opportunities over time, and to design interventions appropriately. As learning takes place, policies are revised, refined and sometimes reversed.

Rodrik and Stantcheva (2021), in relation to France, proposed the setting up of regional business promotion agencies that operate alongside existing public employment services (PES, *pôle emploi*) and cover the same territories. These could be called *"regional business bureaux"* (RBB). The main thrust is to create a structure for job-enhancing productivity assistance to firms that runs in parallel (and in cooperation) with the worker-oriented pôle emploi.

The objective of RBBs (or their equivalent) would be to provide a portfolio of services to local firms or prospective investors with the overarching goal of assisting them to increase productivity while creating good jobs[10]. Many of these services would normally be administered by other agencies, in which case the role of the RBBs would be mainly to coordinate those agencies and help firms navigate through them. For example, RBBs may cooperate with the PBI to help SMEs get access to financing or business advice. They may coordinate with the local PES to identify suitable workers and help recruit them. They may organise training providers to ensure the requisite skills are built up. They may help with infrastructure needs of SMEs, for example with respect to internet and cloud services where pooling of fixed costs could be an advantage. They may also act as a go-between with the local bureaucracy as regards local regulations such as zoning. And they could be provided with additional resources to provide other services as well, as the needs reveal themselves. In general, RBBs would be in a position to assist with the financing (through their own or other agencies' resources) of any productivity and employment-increasing

---

10 One question is whether EU state aid rules are sufficiently flexible to permit the kind of scheme we describe. We note that those rules allow a substantial number of exceptions, particularly with respect to smaller enterprises, funding of innovation and disadvantaged regions. 'Disadvantaged' regions presently cover about a quarter of the French population (European Commission, 2013).

spending or reorganisation on the part of firms. Investment subsidies would not be prioritised over other incentives.

The RBBs would take a customised, individualised approach to their relationship with firms, on the understanding that different firms/sectors have different needs. They would maintain an open-ended relationship with them, trying to understand their problems and opportunities.

Firms would make proposals to the RBB for use of one or more particular services, say a training programme or purchase of a particular advanced technology system. In return, they would make commitments on specific quantities of jobs they will create at different qualification levels (ie low-salaried employees, medium-salaried employees, etc). Firms would be encouraged to pool proposals when they make use of common inputs, as would be the case for workers with particular skills or infrastructure.

It is particularly important that the process of soliciting proposals be open to new or young firms. In particular, new firms may be deterred by regulations or sectoral agreements that act as entry barriers. In addition to encouraging proposals from such firms, RBBs might also be empowered to grant young firms certain temporary exemptions from sectoral regulations or agreements, in order to ease business formation. This would obviously have to be done in exchange for good-job conditionalities and in agreement with social partners. Failing agreement with social partners, new firms might be provided with financial incentives that compensate for the cost of the relevant regulations.

RBBs would then screen proposals for suitability. They would evaluate the overall desirability of the proposed project, paying attention to the quality of the project, its feasibility and plausibility, the additionality of the jobs that are to be created and the likelihood that the RBB can deliver the services needed on the timescale required. Larger, more expensive proposals might be evaluated by outside consultants. At this stage, the RBB might also negotiate additional requirements with the firm. For example, the firm might be asked to work with its local suppliers to improve their management or technological capabilities. Or a firm that is considering outsourcing part of its production to a foreign county might be asked to delay doing so for a number of years, in case productivity improvements at home render those plans unnecessary. The firm could be required to arrange for additional training for some of its employees. The project would then be given an overall score, to compare with others on a single scale.

Once projects are approved and launched, there would be periodic audits designed to check whether firms are making sufficient progress towards their commitments, especially on employment. It would be understood that there is a certain provisionality – inevitable in light of uncertainty and unforeseen circumstances – to both the targets and the package of assistance being deployed. The audits would reveal that some projects are clearly not working out. Those would be terminated. Some other projects may underperform because of unanticipated changes but may still be salvageable with existing (or revised) support. Those would continue to receive support. In other words, the audits would be as much an opportunity to revise policies and targets as they would be an occasion to make binary, up-or-down decisions.

To the greatest extent possible, the proceedings of the RBB would be open and transparent. Packages of support and targets agreed to by firms would be public information. Any revision of supports or targets would also be carried out in a transparent fashion, with firms' justifications for revising targets open to public scrutiny. Transparency over these matters would be essential both to limit public corruption and to ensure firms have limited ability to game the bureaux.

Finally, at the end of the first five years (and each subsequent five years) a certain number of RBBs would be subject to rigorous evaluation. The objective would be to see whether the bureaux are achieving their central objective: creation of productive job opportunities. If the bureaux were being phased-in gradually, such evaluations could be carried out initially using randomisation or synthetic-control (comparing each *région* with a synthetic control group) methods. Subsequently, evaluations could be carried out within *régions* using regression discontinuities (comparing firms just below and above the cutoffs on the overall score).

We note that much of the resources which the bureaux would help coordinate and direct are already allocated via other programmes, such as the BPI, *pôle emploi* or municipal budgets. Additional resources may well be needed for new initiatives along the lines we have suggested.

3 Governance considerations for RBBs

It is worth saying a bit more about the regulatory model that underlies this approach, since it differs from the standard, arm's length regulation model of economists[11]. In the conventional regulatory approach to the mitigation of externalities, firms have to meet clear guidelines, and consultation between the regulator and firms is limited typically to resolving differences. The costs of mitigation are known to firms but not to the regulator. Firms use this informational edge to minimise their adjustment costs while regulators devise ways of eliciting the cost information without being captured by the firms. There are fixed limits on permissible behaviour and a schedule of fines for violating them.

This model does not apply well to the present context because the objective itself ('good jobs') is imprecise and multi-dimensional; it needs to be operationalised in a way that is both evolving and context-dependent. Furthermore, creating good jobs depends on a wide array of decisions on investment, technological choice and business organisation, the consequences of which are unknowable *ex ante*. Technological and operational possibilities are highly uncertain, and neither firms nor government agencies have the information needed to devise concrete behavioural schedules from the outset. Hence the interaction between RBBs and firms must take as its starting point the

---

11 The discussion here follows closely Rodrik and Sabel (2019).

provisionality of ends and means and the need for disciplined review and revision. Targets and instruments for good-job creation must remain provisional, to be revised as new information comes in. The task of governance is to establish an information exchange regime that induces firms to cooperate with RBBs and adjust their strategies in the desired direction in a context of extreme uncertainty.

Instead of defining each party's obligations precisely, our proposed governance system would establish broad goals and a regime for evaluating their achievement. Such practices have become established in industries as diverse as biotechnology, IT and advanced manufacturing, and in policy regimes such as food safety, water quality, civil aviation and the promotion of advanced technologies (Gilson *et al*, 2009; Rodrik and Sabel, 2019). They entail:

"regular, joint reviews of progress towards interim targets or milestones, procedures for deciding whether and with what exact aim to proceed or not, and mechanisms for resolving disagreements. The information exchanged under such a regime allows the parties to develop a more and more precise idea of the shared goal while allowing each to assess with increasingly reliability the capacities and good faith of the other: to observe if the capable stranger can become a reliable partner and the long-trusted partner is capable of innovative tasks. As collaboration progresses, each party comes to rely increasingly on the capacities of the other, deterring opportunistic defection and generating or activating norms of reciprocity. Joint regular review and deliberate consideration of the interim results thus create the conditions in which informal norms and self-interested calculations bind the parties to continue promising collaboration in good faith. Trust and mutual reliance are the result of agreement to collaborate, not its precondition, just as the precise aims of cooperation are the outcome, not the starting point of joint efforts" (Rodrik and Sabel, 2019).

In our specific context, the RBBs would consult local firms extensively and then establish an ambitious, open-ended outcome: 'good jobs,' as measured by a number of metrics that reflect community preferences and national standards. Firms would be encouraged to enter into partnerships with the RBB to gain access to RBB services (of the type discussed previously) customised to their needs. In return, they would be required to make plans to achieve 'good job' targets and to report their results regularly. RBB benefits would continue as long as firms report their progress (or lack thereof) accurately, and they make certifiable good-faith efforts to meet their targets. Targets would remain soft, and failure to meet them would not necessarily call for withdrawal of support during the early stages, as long as there is demonstrable progress and good-faith efforts. The objective of the regime would be to incentivise cooperation, information sharing and ongoing revision of instruments and targets. In the words of Rodrik and Sabel (2019), *"fostering good jobs is likely to depend on solving highly idiosyncratic, place-specific problems: failures of coordination between local firms and training institutions; between firms and their (potential) supply-chain partners; and the managerial breakdowns or skill gaps within individual firms and institutions to which the coordination problems point."* With enough success on some of these aspects, more firms could be drawn into such schemes, generating a virtuous cycle of new production practices and learning spillovers.

Beyond these broad governance principles, there is no how-to manual that can guide government officials in this work. Discretion on the part of government bureaucrats remains an integral part of such incentive regimes. But it is disciplined, on one side, by requirements of transparency and professional norms and, on the other, by the demands and needs of firms. Since experimentation by RBBs can add value, local autonomy is useful and can trigger learning across regions. Ultimately, success depends on the development of organisational cultures that internalise the behavioural norms of this type of governance.

Like all public policies, the proposed scheme may fail or turn out to be ineffective. However, it is important to be clear that key elements of what we have sketched out exist already in the public-policy arsenal. For example, the BPI already has considerable experience of working closely with SMEs, using a wide range of instruments (loans, guarantees, equity participation, export credits, training, management counselling, access to technology and networks). The BPI has the capacity to screen firms, monitor their progress and intervene at various stages of their lifecycle. Effectively, the BPI acts as a public equivalent of venture capital. The proposed RBBs could leverage this capacity with additional instruments and resources, and in a more employment-friendly manner.

The RBB proposal does not entail a significant increase in capacity compared to institutional arrangements that have already proved feasible in other, similar contexts. The novelty, to the extent there is any, lies in the focus and orientation of the business-promotion programme: a closer coordination of business incentives with labour market/training policies, more customised business services instead of *ex-ante* tax incentives, explicit targets for employment and job upgrading ('good jobs'), greater room for revision in light of changing circumstances and more intensive evaluation.

4 Labour-friendly innovation policies

In 2016, Elon Musk announced that Tesla's Model 3 would be built in a new, fully automated car factory. Codenamed 'Alien Dreadnought,' with obvious connotations of science fiction and hyper-advanced technology far beyond current practice, the project would enable essentially workerless production. Complete automation would allow the factory to operate beyond human speed: *"raw materials would go in one end and finished cars would roll out the other. In between, robots would do everything, at very high speed – speeds too dangerous to risk around frail human bodies"*[12]. Only a few human experts would be

---

12 Matthew DeBord, 'Tesla's Future Is Completely Inhuman — and We Shouldn't Be

needed to ensure everything was running smoothly.

The factory was supposed to become fully operational by the end of 2018. But the plans proved hard to implement, and by mid-2018 it was clear that production bottlenecks would not be solved easily. The operation was experiencing "*production hell*" and was "*within single-digit weeks of death*," in Musk's words. The dire situation forced the company to launch a new assembly line inside a sprung structure (what Musk described as a "*tent*") on the grounds of the factory. Built in three weeks, the new assembly line increased production by 50 percent and returned the company to financial health.

When CBS News correspondent Leslie Stahl visited the "*tent*" sometime later, accompanied by Musk, she observed that the new Model 3 factory was in fact full of human workers. Musk laughed, responding "*people are way better at dealing with unexpected circumstances than robots*"[13]. On Twitter, he conceded that "*excessive automation at Tesla was a mistake ... Humans are under-rated*"[14].

Tesla's automation mistake is revealing for several reasons. First, it highlights how production techniques relying on human labour can still dominate automation when it is impossible to fully account for uncertainty and routinise all tasks. Second, it is indicative of the excessive faith many business leaders often place on new technologies. Third, it reminds us that technology adoption is a choice: businesses face a range of options about what kind of innovations to use and deploy – choices that have significant implications for the workforce but are not typically internalised in the decision-making process.

In his magisterial book *Inequality*, the late Anthony Atkinson stressed that there are three reasons why the direction of technological

---

Surprised', *Business Insider*, 20 May 2017, https://www.businessinsider.com/tesla-completely-inhuman-automated-factory-2017-5?r=UK.

13   Simon Alvarez, 'Inside Tesla's 'Tent'-Based Model 3 Line That Set a Path to Profitability'. *Teslarati*, 10 December 2018, https://www.teslarati.com/inside-tesla-tent-based-model-3-production-assembly-line-profitability/.

14   See https://twitter.com/elonmusk/status/984882630947753984.

change cannot be left to firms and innovators alone (Atkinson, 2015, pp. 115-118). First, technology choices have distributional implications – the share of capital in value added and the level of wages – to which society may not be indifferent. Second, the replacement of labour with robots and other modes of automation typically entails the substitution for a joint product – a human service alongside manual labour – and there is no guarantee that laissez-faire is efficient in the presence of joint supply. Third, today's innovations have long-range implications for the future and may foreclose technological paths that are more friendly to human workers. The social benefits of good jobs we have already discussed can be considered a fourth broad reason.

Technological change is probably the single most important force that has been driving the polarisation of labour markets. As automation, AI and other new technologies alter the type and composition of skills demanded in labour markets, workers with skills that are in less demand face significant challenges.

The usual discussion around the labour-market implications of new technologies is curiously one-sided. The direction of technological change – whether it augments or replaces labour – is taken to be essentially exogenous and out of our control. All the adjustment, therefore, falls on the labour force. Typical statements exhort workers to acquire better education and training to ensure they have the skills required by new technologies. Here is, for example, how a McKinsey report (2020) on the future of work in Europe puts it:

> *"Automation will require all workers to acquire new skills. About 94 million workers may not need to change occupations but will especially need retraining, as technology handles 20 percent of their current activities. While some workers in declining occupations may be able to find similar types of work, 21 million may need to change occupations by 2030. Most of them lack tertiary education. Newly created jobs will require more sophisticated skills that are already scarce today"* (McKinsey, 2020, p. iv).

What is striking in such statements is the degree of technological determinism. It is as if technological innovations and their likely impacts on future jobs are completely exogenous, shaped by forces outside the economy, institutional arrangements and government policy.

In reality, the kind of innovations that are fostered depend on several conditions that may be amenable to control.

First and most directly, government-funded and directed innovation programmes make decisions about what kind of innovations to promote. Those priorities are often shaped by considerations about which activities are the industries of the future (eg *Programme d'investissements d'avenir in France*), or what specific societal goals need to be fulfilled (eg green technologies in the context of the European Green Deal, or defence-related technologies at the national level). These priorities in turn determine what kind of research projects are funded and developed. Employment-friendly technologies – those that augment rather than replace labour – could be part of those priorities, though they are not at present.

Second, private-sector innovation incentives can be skewed because of prevailing financing methods or policies. Venture capital, for example, plays a relatively important role in financing innovation in the US. VC naturally seeks areas where the returns can be capitalised relatively quickly by investors. As Lerner and Nanda (2020) pointed out, this may exclude innovations where the gains are longer term or reaped by society at large. There are also many policies that indirectly shape private-sector technological investments because of the market incentives they generate. For example, most advanced economies subsidise capital formation (through depreciation allowances and various incentives of the type we discussed previously) and tax labour (through personal income taxes and labour charges). An unintended consequence of the tax system is to induce firms to economise on labour by investing in machinery, to an extent that may be socially suboptimal. Acemoglu *et al* (2020) found that a shift to an "*optimal*" system of factor taxation would increase US employment by nearly 6 percent. There is no reason why such indirect and unintended consequences on the direction of technical change could not be taken into account if tax (and other) policies were subject to a fuller evaluation.

Third, beyond the economic incentives they face, there is an informal set of norms that guide innovators' decisions. The high-tech community often operates under a shared set of values and expectations with respect to what is a desirable direction for technological change. In the US, groupthink is aggravated by the very high concentration of VC funding in a small number of firms and cities (such as San Francisco, Boston and New York City). "*Venture firms based in other cities might have chosen very different firms to invest in given their perspectives on their local economies,*" wrote Lerner and Nanda (2020)[15]. Automation and replacing human labour or ingenuity can be prized beyond the true economic value. Elon Musk's misplaced confidence in the benefits of full automation was perhaps a reflection of such values. Such norms might be amenable to change as society begins to attach specific value to employment-friendly technologies. An analogy might be drawn here with the growing ecological consciousness households and firms have exhibited in recent decades, as the climate change challenge has become part of the everyday consciousness.

Finally, the direction of technological change also depends on the balance of power between employers and employees. When workers have a say in the workplace, management has to get buy-in from them before major technologies are deployed and work is restructured. This can reflect itself in a modern version of Luddism – aversion to any kind

---

15 Those who finance innovation are very unrepresentative of the societies in which they live. Lerner and Nanda (2020) reported about top venture firms: "*Eighty percent of partners are male; among the set of partners with at least one board seat, 91 percent are male. Three-quarters of partners with at least one board seat attended either an Ivy League school, or one of Caltech, MIT, or Stanford; moreover, nearly 30 percent of these individuals are graduates of just Harvard Business School or the Stanford Graduate School of Business. In terms of location, 69 percent are based in the Bay Area alone and over 90 percent are based in either the Bay Area, Greater Boston, or New York.*"

of innovation that appears to threaten jobs. But it can also be a useful counterweight to adverse incentives in the system encouraging too much automation or the adoption of what Acemoglu and Restrepo (2019) called *so-so technologies*. For example, businesses that take stakeholders' interests into account are more likely to deploy new technologies in a manner that empowers workers, rather than replace them or reduce them to mechanical, routine work. Sophisticated technologies can allow managers to monitor their workers' every movement and measure their efficiency, enabling companies to set ever-more demanding standards of productivity, at some cost to workers' physical and mental health. Alternatively, new technologies can empower workers to increase their autonomy and control their work environment.

In short, there are reasons to believe that the direction of technological change, in addition to its rate, depends on a wide range of factors, many of which could be influenced by societal and governmental decision-making. And if so, it may be possible to direct technology to better serve the existing workforce's needs, in addition to preparing the workforce to match the requirements of technology.

5 Margins of technological choice

Firms faced with the challenge of upgrading productivity face all kinds of decisions. Their options may range from installing robots (which kind?) to modernising existing capital equipment, to using advanced analytics to optimise performance. The technology that will work best is unclear *ex ante*, and rarely comes in ready-made, off-the-shelf form. These choices create the margins around which better or worse decisions can be made.

Technology choices that firms make are closely linked to the organisation of production and the degree to which employees benefit from autonomy and a learning environment. Under Taylorist production, workers perform repetitive tasks on the assembly line: jobs may be plenty, but they are hardly satisfying. Under lean production, machines replace routine human labour, but work remains under hierarchical control and offers little autonomy.

In 'learning organisations,' by contrast, workers take part in decision-making, have considerable autonomy, and are engaged in problem-solving and continuous learning. The learning mode of production not only increases worker satisfaction, it is also more conducive to increased productivity and dissemination of innovations over time[16]. In particular, the introduction of new technologies along with organisational changes can allow less-skilled workers, such as shop floor operators, to identify productivity improvements and engage in appropriate actions. There are plenty of examples of firms that have made a conscious choice to move towards this learning form of organisation[17].

---

16 Based on data from European Conditions of Work Surveys (ECWS), France Stratégie (2020) reported highest levels of job satisfaction in 'learning organisations.' Also, rates of innovation seem to be correlated with proportion of learning firms at the national level.

17 A joint programme between the World Economic Forum and McKinsey focused on *"lighthouses,"* firms that are introducing new technologies that have the potential to revolutionise production in a human-centred way, empowering workers and giving them greater agency in the process of introducing innovations (WEF/McKinsey, 2019b). Studying these lighthouses provides many valuable insights. For example, the French company Schneider Electric *"is implementing, testing and rolling out ideas for innovation in an organized approach in a 'Smart Factory Program' A strong focus on workforce engagement ensures that the changes and new technologies are supported by employees and therefore adopted quickly. For instance, at the company's Le Vaudreuil site in France, it has created a 3D virtual reality model of the entire factory to use in testing and validating innovative ideas. This is then used to engage operators so they can see how their day-to-day work will change..."*. In another example, *"a large manufacturer had deployed autonomous mobile robots (AMRs) for a point-to-point material transfer workflow moving parts from kitting stations to an assembly cell. Workers in another cell noted that their colleagues experienced fewer delays waiting for parts, and they also noticed that the robots would wait in an idle queue between tasks. They approached the floor supervisor and requested that the robots also be assigned to support their cell.... As a result of their independent and collaborative action, the workers and local staff were able to increase their productivity and also increase the utilization of the robot, making it a win for all involved".* In the words of a machine operator at Foxconn, *"my role has changed from loading and other manual tasks to monitoring, diagnostics and problem-solving"* (WEF/McKinsey, 2019b).

Firms will have diverse motives in choosing among these modes: management capacity, organisational culture, relations with workers and not least imagination. Technological features themselves are rarely the sole determinant. A France Stratégie (2020) study noted that learning organisations have become common in Nordic countries but are still scarce in France[18]. The study highlighted the need for public policies that pay attention to how firms make choices over production modes, instead of treating firm organisation as a black box.

Moreover, different technologies can survive side-by-side. In a study of small and medium-sized manufacturers in Ohio, Waldman-Brown (2020) found her respondents took two different approaches to the competitive challenges they faced. One approach was to build new greenfield plants that were fully automated, typically in a different country, with the intention of phasing out existing operations. In her sample, one company was building a plant in Mexico and another in Romania. This strategy naturally resulted in job losses in Ohio (and did not create many new jobs in the outsourced countries in view of the extent of automation). But a second group of firms were engaged with *"ongoing tinkering with existing plants,"* and this did not seem to result in much job loss. The retrofitting and modernisation of existing plants seemed to be a profitable strategy for those firms that took this path. The majority of the SMEs Waldman-Brown (2020) interviewed *"claimed to have found robust competitive niches"* and *"very few of these legacy firms seemed to be laggards."* Firms pursuing the tinkering strategy *"were constantly*

---

18 The report cites a rare French example, Favi, an automotive subcontractor: *"As early as the mid-1980s, [Favi] chose to focus its strategy on product quality and the use of innovative technologies, with a focus on the health and safety of its employees. It also focused on the autonomy of its employees - especially the workers - by creating 'self-organized units,' i.e., mini-plants of 5 to 25 employees, each taking charge of a production line in a customer/supplier approach. As at Volvo, employees developed their own methodological tools for monitoring and improving production processes. The operators themselves made contact with customers instead of the sales staff, thus acquiring greater control over their work and a cross-functional view of the production line"* (France Strategie, 2020).

on the lookout for new technologies that could meet their demands for affordability and versatility, and most were not concerned about being out-competed by automation at home or cheaper labor abroad." Such studies suggest the possibility of different technological paths to firm success, with sharply varying consequences for labour.

An important series of papers by Acemoglu and Restrepo (2018, 2019) argued that it is possible to resist present technological trends and push innovation in a direction that creates new, labour-absorbing tasks. They cited three areas. First, they suggested AI could be used in education to create more specialised tasks for teachers, personalise instruction for students, and increase effectiveness of schooling in the process. They noted that individual students have different learning styles, which requires teaching to be adapted to their specific needs. By generating real-time information on learning and making recommendations, AI tools can enable customised, smaller-group teaching. They can also allow instruction to respond more rapidly to evolving technologies and labour-market needs. Such tools are unlikely to replace teachers; they might in fact increase the demand for teachers (as well as redefine their roles) by enhancing the return to individual or small group instruction.

Second, Acemoglu and Restrepo (2019) noted a similar potential in healthcare, which is perhaps closer to realisation. AI tools can significantly enhance the diagnostic and treatment capabilities of nurses, physicians' aides and other medical technicians. They can, in effect, allow *"less skilled"* practitioners to perform tasks that only physicians with many more years of professional education have traditionally undertaken. The same logic also applies to other areas to boost job opportunities for those without the most advanced skills. For example, AI systems already enable the drawing up of simple contracts (such as wills) and the provision of many other services without the actual involvement of lawyers. To date, such systems have replaced primarily paralegals rather than lawyers themselves, but more advanced systems could enable paralegals to perform more advanced tasks, such as document review, due diligence and document drafting (Remus and Levy, 2016). Machine learning and neural networks can enable mid-level finance professionals to do financial risk assessment, loan underwriting and fraud detection tasks that would otherwise be undertaken by more senior professionals (McKinsey, 2018).

Third, Acemoglu and Restrepo (2019) mentioned the use of augmented and virtual reality technologies in manufacturing, enabling humans and robots to work together in performing precision tasks (rather than the latter replacing the former). Such technologies are based on smaller, more nimble robots that also enable greater customisation of production in response to specific customer needs. *"This will not just help workers keep some of the tasks that might have otherwise been automated; it could also create new tasks in which humans, augmented by digital technology and sensors, can be employed and contribute to productivity"* (Acemoglu and Restrepo, 2019). More broadly, shop floor apps augment relatively unskilled labour by allowing workers to carry out operations that more-skilled employees typically perform. A WEF/McKinsey white paper (2019a) noted that such apps *"enable manufacturers to bridge the skill gap."* Real-time performance feedback and guidance through manufacturing analytics allow *"experienced and new operators* [to] *work side by side with manufacturing apps"* (WEF/McKinsey, 2019a).

Product customisation is one of the imperatives that have pushed some car companies to moderate their ambitions with respect to automation. Beyond Tesla, companies including BMW and Mercedes are building their automation plans around human work, which they have found allows both greater reliability and more customisation in production. McKinsey (2018) reported:

"after years of building robotic factories, BMW in South Carolina is ramping up hiring of human workers. [BMW] *says that combining people with machines on its automotive assembly lines increases the flexibility to build multiple models in smaller*

batches and thus respond to shifting customer demands more quickly."

In new BMW factories, lightweight robots ('cobots'), which do not have to be physically separated from workers, allow humans and machines to perform complementary tasks. For example, to install the insulation inside a door, a worker may first put in place the foil with the adhesive bead, and then the robot applies the heavy pressure needed to seal it[19]. Similarly Mercedes-Benz has replaced some of its older generation robots with AI-enabled cobots, redesigning its processes around human-machine collaboration. This allows the company to build more customised S-class sedans, something that older systems could not do as well. In the plant, human workers customise cars on the fly using hand-held tablets, with the automated work being performed by the light-weight robots (Wilson and Dougherty, 2018). In general, lightweight robots have opened up new potential for human tasks that cannot be routinised.

In sum, there are many margins of technological choice. First, the kind of automation that amounts to replacement of labour, pure and simple, is far from destiny. Second, investing in 'learning organizations' can pay off in terms of both worker satisfaction and productivity. Third, many AI systems have the potential to complement low and middle-skilled labour instead of high skills. Fourth, appropriately steered innovation can lead to an increase in labour-requiring tasks through greater customisation in manufacturing and individualisation of services. Some of the examples we have provided suggest that firms can make innovation decisions that are simultaneously labour-friendly and profitable. But the mix of incentives they face is distorted by existing policies as well as by their lack of internalisation of the social benefits of good jobs.

---

19 BMW Group Press Release, 'Innovative Human-Robot Cooperation in BMW Group Production,' 9 October 2013, https://www.press.bmwgroup.com/global/article/detail/T0209722EN/innovative-human-robot-cooperation-in-bmw-group-production?language=en.

6 Is there a role for policy?

"The direction of technological change should be an explicit concern of policy-makers, encouraging innovation in a form that increases the employability of workers and emphasizes the human dimension of service provision," wrote Atkinson (2015). The question is what this implies for specific policies.

First, it would be useful to review the prevailing fiscal regime with a view to ascertaining whether there are excessive incentives for investment in automation (as appears to be the case in the US; Acemoglu *et al*, 2020). If the answer is yes, corrective instruments may need to be put in place. Possibilities would include an increase in the taxation of capital that directly substitutes for labour (eg robots), providing tax preferences for cobots over traditional robots and, of course, reducing labour charges.

Second, it may be possible to incorporate employment considerations directly into the existing regime of tax incentives for R&D. In the presence of a good-job objective, traditional R&D externalities have to be modified to take into account the likely employment effects of innovation. The selection criteria could revolve around the margins of choice we discussed previously: innovations such as automation that directly replace labour would be favoured the least, and innovations that augment labour of low and medium skills and create new, labour-absorbing tasks would be favoured the most.

While it may be difficult to ascertain those employment consequences, especially of different types of work, research does provide some rough guidelines. For example, Webb (2020) provided a mapping from different kinds of research in AI (measured through patents) to the employment structure. This kind of work could guide policymakers in providing a more differentiated structure of R&D incentives, favouring the kind of R&D that is more labour-friendly. Acemoglu (2021) suggested policymakers should look at the labour share of value added. None of the existing methods are likely to be particularly reliable at the outset. The expectation is that paying attention to employment in this context might lead eventually to the development of better measurement frameworks regarding labour-market implications.

Third, and in a similar vein, governments could apply a 'prospective employment test' when determining their public-spending priorities for innovation. At the EU level, for example, employment considerations appear to play virtually no direct role in the construction of the innovation portfolio. Horizon Europe has identified five specific research and innovation missions for the 2021-2027 period: adaptation to climate change; cancer; climate-neutral and smart cities; healthy oceans, seas, coastal and inland waters; soil health and food[20]. No doubt each of these areas is important. But encouraging labour-friendly innovation is no less important. Its absence from the list reflects an unwarranted determinism about the direction of technological change[21].

The European Fund for Strategic Investments (EFSI) partners with the European Investment Bank (EIB) to finance investment in innovation. The areas it lists as priorities are *"infrastructure, energy efficiency and renewable energy, research and innovation, environment, agriculture, digital technology, education, health and social projects."* It also provides risk finance to small businesses to help them innovate. One possibility would be to devote a portion of EFSI funds experimentally to developing labour-friendly technologies – just as in the case of green technologies.

The European Green Deal (EGD) provides a more specific opportunity for making employment a focus of innovation. The social component of the EGD consists almost entirely of 'compensation,' the idea being that those regions and groups of workers that are adversely affected by investments in decarbonisation should be made whole

---

20 See European Commission, 'Horizon Europe (HORIZON),' https://ec.europa.eu/info/funding-tenders/opportunities/portal/screen/programmes/horizon.

21 Atkinson (2015) provided another example: "*Did the European-based Euroka consortium* [in autonomous vehicles] *consider the distributional issues when launching PROMETHEUS (Programme for a European Traffic System with Highest Efficiency and Unprecedented Safety)? The fact that 'efficiency' is picked out in its title suggests that 'equity' was not at the forefront.*"

in some way[22]. An equally important strategy might be to take good-job considerations explicitly into account in selecting investment priorities within the EGD. In particular, different decarbonisation strategies may have different implications for labour markets. Some programmes, such as retrofitting building and transport systems, waste management, and public transportation, tend to be much more labour-friendly than others, such as carbon capture and storage (CCS) or nuclear energy. Employment considerations may yield a different portfolio of innovations and investments within the EGD than would be selected in their absence.

Fourth, the government can directly encourage the introduction and dissemination in the private sector of learning organisations that empower workers. The goal would be for such organisational forms – based on teamwork, development of cognitive, social, and soft skills, workers' autonomy and continuous learning – to replace Taylorist or lean organisational models where feasible. Along these lines, France Stratégie (2020) recommended the creation of a French national programme for managerial and organisational innovation to raise awareness of firms and to assist in the implementation of the requisite organisational changes. Since the requisite investments may require both public assistance and skills training, it would be natural for such a programme to work together with the public employment services and the regional business bureaux we discussed previously.

Finally, public policy can play a role in shaping public consciousness about the social and employment consequences of innovation. A public that is more aware of the choices we have is likely to expect more from innovators. Acemoglu (2021) drew an analogy with environmental consciousness and concerns about nuclear weapons: "*in*

---

22 The EGD includes a Just Transition Mechanism to raise and transfer funds to regions dependent on coal, lignite, oil shale and peat, and greenhouse gas-intensive industries. Region-specific 'territorial just transition plans' are contemplated for reskilling, development and regional rehabilitation needs, though plans remain vague at time of writing.

the same way that millions of employees demand that their companies reduce their carbon footprint and in the same way that many nuclear physicists would not be willing to work on developing nuclear weapons, AI researchers should become more aware and more sensitive to the social consequences of their actions." One might also add to these examples the increasing concerns about privacy that digital innovations have created. The requisite change in public norms will have to come from within society at large. But the government can play an important role as well in articulating the appropriate narrative on the need for labour-friendly innovation.

The public narrative we might need is one that qualifies the single-minded focus on the imperative of adjustment by workers and their skills to new technologies. This is an oddly one-sided remedy. As a matter of logic, the gap between skills and technology can be closed in one of two ways: either by increasing education to match the demands of new technologies, or by redirecting innovation to match the skills of the current (and prospective) labour force. The second strategy, which gets practically no attention in policy discussions, might be worth a shot too.

References

Acemoglu, D. And P. Restrepo (2019) 'The Wrong Kind of AI? Artificial Intelligence and the Future of Labor Demand', *Cambridge Journal of Regions*, Economy and Society, available at https://doi.org/10.1093/cjres/rsz022

Acemoglu, D. And P. Restrepo (2018) 'Artificial Intelligence, Automation and Work', *Working Paper* 24196, National Bureau of Economic Research, available at https://doi.org/10.3386/w24196.

Acemoglu, D., A. Manera and P. Restrepo (2020) 'Does the U.S. Tax Code Favor Automation?' BPEA Conference Drafts, *Brookings Papers on Economic Activity*, Spring

Acemoglu, D. (2021) 'AI's Future Doesn't Have to Be Dystopian', *Boston Review*, 20 May, available at https://www.bostonreview.net/forum/ais-future-doesnt-have-to-be-dystopian/

Atkinson, A.B. (2015) *Inequality: What Can Be Done?* Harvard University Press, Cambridge, MA

Bartik, T.J. (2020) 'Using Place-Based Jobs Policies to Help Distressed Communities', *Journal of Economic Perspectives* 34(3): 99–127

Bartik, T.J. (2019) 'Should Place-Based Jobs Policies Be Used to Help Distressed Communities?' W.E. Upjohn Institute for Employment Research, 1 August

Criscuolo, C., R. Martin, H.G. Overman and J. Van Reenen (2019) 'Some Causal Effects of an Industrial Policy', *American Economic Review* 109(1): 48-85

European Commission (2013) 'Guidelines on Regional State Aid for 2014-2020', 2013/C 209/01, *Official Journal of European Union*, 23 July

Evans, P.B. (1995) *Embedded Autonomy: States and Industrial Transformation*, Princeton University Press

Fernández-Arias, E., C. Sabel, E.H. Stein and A. Trejos (2016)*Two to Tango: Public-Private Collaboration for Productive Development Policies*, Inter-American Development Bank, Washington DC

France Stratégie (2020) *Promoting Learning Work Organizations: Issues and Challenges for France*, available at https://www.strategie.gouv.fr/sites/strategie.gouv.fr/files/atoms/files/note_de_synthese_-learning_organisation.pdf.

Ghezzi, P. (2017) 'Mesas Ejecutivas in Peru: Lessons for Productive Development Policies', *Global Policy* 8(3): 369–80, available at https://doi.org/10.1111/1758-5899.12457

Gilson, R.J., C.F. Sabel and R.E. Scott (2009) 'Contracting for Innovation: Vertical Disintegration and Interfirm Collaboration', *Columbia Law Review*, 2009: 431–502, available at https://doi.org/10.2139/ssrn.1289428.

Hausmann, R., D. Rodrik and C. Sabel (2008) 'Reconfiguring Industrial Policy: A Framework with an Application to South Africa', *Working Paper* No. RWP08-031, Harvard Kennedy School, available at https://papers.ssrn.com/sol3/papers.cfm?abstract_id=1245702

Lerner, J. And R. Nanda (2020) 'Venture Capital's Role in Financing Innovation: What We Know and How Much We Still Need to Learn', *Journal of Economic Perspectives* 34(3): 237–61

McKinsey (2020) *The Future of Work in Europe: Automation, Workforce Transitions, and the Shifting Geography of Employment*, McKinsey Global Institute

McKinsey (2018) *Skill Shift: Automation and the Future of the Workforce*, McKinsey Global Institute

Remus, D. And F. Levy (2016) 'Can Robots Be Lawyers? Computers, Lawyers, and the Practice of Law', mimeo, available at https://papers.ssrn.com/sol3/papers.cfm?abstract_id=2701092

Robalino, D., J.M. Romero and I. Walker (2020) 'Allocating Subsidies for Private Investments to Maximize Jobs Impacts', *Jobs Working Paper* No. 45, World Bank

Rodrik, D. And S. Stantcheva (2021) *Economic Inequality and Insecurity: Policies for an Inclusive Economy*, Report Prepared for Commission Chaired by Olivier Blanchard and Jean Tirole on Major Future Economic Challenges, Republic of France

Rodrik, D. (2022) *An Industrial Policy for Good Jobs*, Policy Proposal, The Hamilton Project

Rodrik, D. And C. Sabel (2019) 'Building a Good Jobs Economy', *Faculty Research Working Paper* No. RWP20-001, Harvard Kennedy School

Rodrik, D. (2007) 'Industrial Policies for the Twenty-First Century', in D. Rodrik, *One Economics, Many Recipes: Globalization, Institutions, and Economic Growth*, Princeton University Press

Rodrik, D. (2008) 'Normalizing Industrial Policy', *Working Paper* No. 3, Commission on Growth and Development, available at https://drodrik.scholar.harvard.edu/files/dani-rodrik/files/normalizing-industrial-policy.pdf

Sabel, C. (2007) 'Bootstrapping Development: Rethinking the Role of Public Intervention in Promoting Growth', in V. Lee and R. Swedberg (eds) *On Capitalism*, Stanford University Press

Waldman-Brown, A. (2020) 'Redeployment or Robocalypse? Workers and Automation in Ohio Manufacturing SMEs', *MIT Work of the Future Working Paper* 03-2020, MIT

Webb, M. (2020) 'The Impact of Artificial Intelligence on the Labor Market', mimeo, available at https://papers.ssrn.com/sol3/papers.cfm?abstract_id=3482150

Wilson, H.J. and P.R. Daugherty (2018) 'Collaborative Intelligence: Humans and AI Are Joining Forces', *Harvard Business Review*, 1 July, available at https://hbr.org/2018/07/collaborative-intelligence-humans-and-ai-are-joining-forces

WEF/McKinsey (2019a) *Fourth Industrial Revolution: Beacons of Technology and Innovation in Manufacturing*, White Paper, World Economic Forum (in collaboration with McKinsey), available at https://www3.weforum.org/docs/WEF_4IR_Beacons_of_Technology_and_Innovation_in_Manufacturing_report_2019.pdf

WEF/McKinsey (2019b) *Global Lighthouse Network: Insights from the Forefront of the Fourth Industrial Revolution*, White Paper, World Economic Forum (in collaboration with McKinsey), available at https://www3.weforum.org/docs/WEF_Global_Lighthouse_Network.pdf

4 Industrial policy and technological sovereignty

Uwe Cantner

1 Introduction

In times when the prosperity and welfare of an economy depend on mastering and using the latest technologies and, if necessary, also generating them, the question of the extent to which an economy has the skills and knowledge to succeed in doing so becomes important. If an economy has and maintains such capabilities and knowledge, then it can make sovereign decisions about the use of the latest technologies.

This sovereignty and its preservation have gained attention in politics, media and in the broad public. It started with so-called digital sovereignty which has been closely related to the topic of cybersecurity – mainly driven by the significant increase in cyberattacks worldwide. Meanwhile it is not only the digital sphere that is concerned with the issue of sovereignty. Sovereignty is also important in the spheres of raw materials and energy, electronic devices, international value chains and key technologies. The sources of constraints on technological sovereignty are various, ranging from new geopolitics and economic wars, to intense technology competition and vicious-virtuous cycles of development. Trajectories of technological and economic divergence, patterns of severe economic inequality and noticeable structural changes arising from radical changes that broadly affect – positively and negatively – all sectors and industries, give rise to political considerations and concepts that seek to preserve and regain technological and, in particular, digital sovereignty.

Policymakers have been quick to identify intervention points and to arm themselves with industrial and foreign trade policy tools. The belief that the markets can solve these problems is fading, and forces are gaining ground that see active government intervention via industrial policy measures as the silver bullet. The Inflation Reduction Act in the United States, the European Green Deal and China's Belt and Road Initiative are examples. Industrial policy flourishes.

Against this background, the question remains of whether these policies are conceptually appropriate to cope with the issue of technological sovereignty. This issue takes on particular importance in phases of far-reaching structural change and fundamental transformation processes. Radically new technologies come into play, new key technologies emerge and the question is which economies can best contribute to these processes and occupy prominent positions (economically, technologically and in terms of driving the Sustainable Development Goals). Particularly in relation to key technologies, new constellations of international technological leadership will emerge, which may lead to dependencies and restrictions on technological sovereignty.

This chapter introduces the concept of technological sovereignty as a microeconomic issue. It then discusses this sovereignty and restrictions on it, in the context of a technology-gap trade model with endogenous processes of generating new knowledge and hence innovation. The chapter ends with a brief dive into industrial policy and measures to cope with and prevent technological sovereignty.

2 Technological sovereignty: the concept

The concept of technological sovereignty is described and defined in varying ways. The common denominator is that technological sovereignty is about the degree to which one can master a certain technology in its application and use, and also about the degree to which that technology is available or the degree to which one has access to it. Mastery is measured on a spectrum of the existing know-how and competencies that must be built up and kept ready for the production of a technology or its use. Availability results from a positioning on a spectrum from pure self-production to complete procurement.

For the purpose of this chapter, the following definition of technological sovereignty is used (EFI, 2022):

"A national economy has technological sovereignty if it can itself provide and further develop a technology it deems critical for its welfare, competitiveness and ability to act, and if it can participate in its standardisation and is able to apply and to source this technology from other economic areas without one-sided structural dependency" (translated from German).

2.1 Technological sovereignty as a microeconomic problem

The use of technologies in the production and use of goods and services is subject to the decisions of companies, whether private or public, public institutions and infrastructures, and users, especially in the household sector. Sovereignty in the use of technologies thus first and foremost concerns microeconomic actors.

At the micro-level, operators or users are sovereign in a technology (i) when they master it, and (ii) when it is available to them. As to mastery, a sovereign approach to technologies means that they are well understood by their operators and users in accordance with the respective objectives. For that understanding, proper technological knowledge, comprising know-how and competencies, is required. One is not sovereign in these technologies if one does not have the knowledge to master them (lack of mastery). As far as availability is concerned, one is sovereign in dealing with a technology if one has it at hand and can use it. The availability of a technology is limited if one cannot afford it or does not have access to it for other reasons (lack of availability).

Lack of mastery and lack of availability – alone or together – mean that one is dependent on others to use a certain technology and, hence, is no longer sovereign in this respect. Such dependence is associated with high usage costs, which can be so high that one does not use a certain technology at all, although it is useful in its own right.

2.2 Technological sovereignty: between autarky and division of labour

How do operators and users of certain technologies achieve technological sovereignty? Well, the greatest degree of sovereignty in a technology is achieved when one generates this technology oneself and makes it available to oneself. In such cases, one is autarkic in this technology with full technological sovereignty.

This argument, however, neglects the positive effects of the division of labour – or the underlying managerial decision to 'make or buy'. Individual economic autarky does not guarantee that the best technology is available, but only the quality of technology that one is able to provide oneself. And this quality may well not be at the top of the range. In such a case, it may make sense to acquire better technology in the marketplace. If there are suppliers of a corresponding technology, then a calculation of the advantages according to the 'make-or-buy' principle must be made, in the sense of comparative performance-price ratios. In doing so, the price of procuring the technology needs to include the costs of building up and maintaining the corresponding competences and skills needed to operate and use the purchased technology, so-called absorptive abilities (Cohen and Levinthal, 1989). Comparing the performance-price ratios of buying and of making comprises the make-and-buy decision.

If this comparison leads to the decision to buy, then the degree of technological sovereignty of the buyer results from the quality of the absorptive capabilities (mastery) on the one hand, and the possibility of acquiring the technology on national or international markets (availability) on the other. Risks and resulting costs that may limit technological sovereignty must be contrasted with the costs and disadvantages that would arise if opportunities from the division of labour were not exploited and autarky were pursued.

2.3 Restrictions on individual economic sovereignty

Restrictions on individual technological sovereignty are not likely to occur in the case of in-house production of technologies. If technologies are acquired from others, then restrictions on individual technological sovereignty can be caused by two factors: restrictions on the ability to acquire the technology (lack of availability) and lack of technological knowledge (lack of mastery).

When companies acquire technologies on markets, there may be constraints on the procurement side. For example, it is possible that the supplier of a technology encounters problems that lead to supply-chain disruptions, delays, quality degradation or even a complete supply stoppage. If the acquiring company has not diversified its procurement and instead relies entirely on one or a few suppliers, its sovereignty is compromised by a lack of availability. In the international context, trade embargoes and other trade restrictions, however justified, can limit the technological sovereignty of companies. Even though the problem of availability is primarily caused by the supply side, it is really triggered by the lack of a corporate diversification strategy on the part of the procuring company. Obviously, such a strategy is not costless as the firm has to manage numerous procurement relationships, with different prices and qualities of the technology concerned.

As an alternative to diversifying procurement, a firm's willingness to reshore a technology when sovereignty constraints arise can also help maintain or restore its sovereignty. Costs are involved in this decision too. Significant factors influencing these costs are the know-how and the competences to generate and develop the technology for which reshoring is considered. To the extent that the necessary know-how and competences are lacking, they must first be invested in.

In case the reshoring firm's level of know-how and competence is close to that of a supplier of the 'critical' technology, costs of reshoring are comparatively low – an expression of technological sovereignty. However, if the supplier's know-how and competence in the critical technology are far ahead, then the reshoring firm's own provision of the technology is associated with potentially high costs. These include the time costs of building up the know-how and competences related to the technology, or losses in the quality and performance of the technology – cost related to a lack of mastery. Hence, retaining sovereignty in the mastery of a technology via reshoring is costly, and these costs express the degree of dependency on the supplier.

2.4 Technological sovereignty and its policy relevance
Technological sovereignty at the individual economic level is one of the problems that the management of every firm has to cope with. Being able to successfully counter restrictions on technological sovereignty in a preventive manner and anticipating associated problems at an early stage depends on the quality of management. It is part of the normal business reality that in this context management is also subject to misjudgements and, viewed ex post, can make wrong decisions that sometimes lead to considerable losses, and even to company bankruptcy. When markets are efficient, they ensure that these errors are detected and evaluated. This problem of firm management is of political relevance, if at all, only if the markets do not fulfil their tasks accordingly. Seen in this light, technological sovereignty must be regarded as a problem of individual economic actors. It is not relevant to the economy as a whole, and thus possibly not relevant to economic policy.

At the aggregate level, however, the assessment may be different if many companies and users in an economy, entire industries and sectors, are restricted in their technological sovereignty. This can occur with systemically relevant technologies that are of great importance to a broad spectrum of industries, companies and users. These include digital technologies in particular, along with other so-called key technologies from new manufacturing, bio- and life sciences, or the field of new materials. These represent important input factors in a number of industries and are the key to further developments. Furthermore, they are not easily substitutable by alternative technologies in the short and medium terms. A restriction of sovereignty in a key technology thus has negative consequences not only for the supplier and/or buyers of this technology, but also for many other players who depend on this technology. Digitalisation technologies, especially memory chips and semiconductors, show these characteristics.

Key technologies are of outstanding importance for the development of an economy and the international competitiveness of its industries. For this reason, the problem of technological sovereignty in key technologies is of particular importance. If the companies in an economy do not master a certain key technology, or have only limited access to it, dependencies arise because of a lack of technological sovereignty. Because of the systemic nature of such technologies, a problem arises for the economy as a whole, and not just a problem of individual economic actors. And accordingly, technological sovereignty becomes an issue relevant to economic policy.

3 Conceptual foundations of technological sovereignty in an international context

Policy interventions to establish and secure technological sovereignty can be justified in the context of industrial policy and trade policy considerations. The relevant theoretical basis is provided by technology-gap growth models (eg Fagerberg, 1987; Verspagen, 1992; Stiglitz, 2015) and models of technology-gap foreign trade (eg Krugman, 1985, Cantner, 1989; Dosi *et al*, 1990). Both model types have in common the concept of the so-called technology gap.

The comparison of actors on the basis of their respective technological knowledge, comprising know-how and competences, can be expressed as a technology gap. Technology gaps depend on two characteristics of the knowledge generating activities: (1) new (technological) knowledge is, instead of being treated as pure public good accessible to everyone, considered as a latent public good that offers innovators considerable protection against immediate imitation; (2)

new (technological) knowledge is endogenously generated and used, hence differs between actors, and is not distributed evenly among all actors.

The characterisation of new knowledge as a latent public good (Nelson, 1991) implies that its widespread use after invention occurs only after a certain period, during which users and imitators need to build up appropriate absorptive capacities (Cohen and Levinthal, 1989). Accordingly, such new knowledge is not immediately available to all actors to the same extent. This gives rise to technology gaps between actors. These gaps can change over time, depending on the relative rate of knowledge accumulation between economies, and technological spillovers between them.

Endogenous modelling of the generation of new knowledge is associated with external learning effects (positive dynamic scale effects): the stock of technological knowledge built up – or what has been learned so far – has a positive influence on its further development, ie on its improvement through new technological knowledge. Because of such learning, knowledge differences between actors, however small they may be, increase continuously.

3.1 Technology-gap growth models

Technology gap growth models are based on the endogenous formulation of the growth of economies. The core driving factor is technological knowledge, which grows endogenously over time. This gives rise to innovation and productivity growth. Models of this kind are suitable to explain non-converging comparative growth of economies. Based on the aforementioned learning dynamics, an economy with a higher volume of production (Stiglitz, 2015) or a higher accumulated knowledge level (Verspagen, 1992) than another, exhibits comparatively stronger growth of productivity or knowledge stock, and thus of GDP. Accordingly, the leading economy grows faster than the following economy – a diverging dynamic.

An economy lagging in terms of this growth dynamic may learn from or imitate the leading economy by tapping into its superior or more advanced stock of knowledge. This use of external knowledge, so-called spillover effects, creates the potential for catching-up via additional growth of knowledge and hence innovation and productivity growth. This counteracts the tendency for the lagging economy to fall further behind in growth. The magnitude of the addressed learning effect depends on the level of the technological gap between economies in two ways. First, the larger the gap, the more can be learned. Second, the larger the gap the more difficult it is for the lagging economy to understand (absorptive capacities) the latest knowledge of the leading economy. The combination of both relationships results in an inverted U-shaped pattern of exploitable spillovers. Accordingly, up to a certain threshold value of the technological gap, a lagging economy can increasingly take advantage of spillovers and catch up through external learning. Above this threshold value, however, spillover effects diminish in potency, leading to reduced catching up or even falling further behind.

3.2 Technology-gap trade models

Comparative advantages in the production of tradeable goods (including services and technologies) determine – in combination with factor prices – the foreign trade structure of an economy. In technology-gap trade models, these comparative advantages arise from internationally differing technological knowledge entering production and application of these goods, and are therefore directly related to the technology gaps between trading economies.

In a multi-goods context, the comparative advantages of one economy over another in these goods can be ranked in ascending order. This so-called comparative advantage function is a measure of how much the two countries differ in the level of technological knowledge that goes into their production of goods: it thus stands for the technological gap. The function takes the value 0 if there is no gap. As the deviation from 0 increases, there is an increasing gap. With negative values, one country leads, with positive values the other leads. The slope of this function indicates how much the technological gap changes as one moves from one good to the next.

Some goods, such as raw materials or rare earths, cannot be delivered by all trading countries, and substitutes for them do not exist. With these goods, the supplying economy has an absolute advantage. In terms of the comparative advantage function in these goods, the slope is infinite, implying an infinite technology gap. In cases in which both economies could provide a certain good, the comparative advantage can be so great that it comes close to an absolute advantage on the part of the technology-leading economy.

The conversion of the comparative advantages of an economy into competitive advantages takes place via the relative factor prices compared to another economy. These competitive advantages in turn determine the trade structure of an economy. The higher the relative factor prices of an economy, the greater the technological lead in producing a given good has to be, in order to be competitive in that good. This means that economies with relatively high factor prices tend to export goods in which they have a larger technological lead. Economies with low relative factor prices are able to export goods for which the other economy's technological lead is much less pronounced (or even reversed).

Technological change and changes in relative factor prices between economies affect the patterns of foreign trade. By applying the above model of endogenous new knowledge generation based on learning effects, the comparative advantages in the production of goods in which an economy has a technological lead will improve continuously. Relative factor prices are affected via the trade balance adjustment. In case of an export surplus of the technologically leading economy over another economy – due to, for example, new knowledge leading to goods of improved quality-price ratio – relative factor prices of the technology leader need to increase. This changes the trade structure by shifting the production of some goods to the lagging economy, thus restoring the trade balance.

The strength and the direction of the combined effect of new knowledge generation and changes in relative factor prices depend on the demand structure in the trading economies and on the pattern of technology gaps between them (function of comparative advantages). Assuming stable demand structures, in case the increase in the technological lead is stronger than the increase in relative factor prices, the range of goods the technology leader produces and exports will increase. In case of a reverse relationship between changes in the technology gap and relative factor prices, the range of goods the lagging country is able to take over in terms of production and export will increase.

3.3 Dynamic positioning and sovereignty of a country in a technology-gap context
On the basis of the endogenous learning-driven process of generating new knowledge, a country that gained through its technological lead a comparative advantage in some goods will not lose, but rather reinforce that advantage over time. Four trade-technology constellations are interesting in this respect:

North-North: In the North-North trade context, the trading countries will each have a technological lead on some goods but a lag on others. As more new knowledge is generated in all of these economies, and goods are improved accordingly, the basic structure of comparative advantage will change little, but will become more pronounced for each good. The changes in relative factor prices required to restore trade balances in such a constellation are rather modest, so the terms of trade of the economies do not change much. In terms of technological sovereignty, the specialisation of each economy in certain goods where its respective technological advantage is increasing means a weakening of the other economy's ability to master those technologically advanced goods. Dependencies can arise for both economies, so they are mutual in nature. In the event of availability problems due to strategic trade policies, the 'attacked' economy has a bargaining chip at its disposal: the goods in which it has a technological lead allow to it to counteract the strategy.

North-South: In a North-South context however, countries in the

North have technological leads in all high tech-based goods, whereas the South has advantages in no- or low-tech goods. As high-tech will increasingly be important in the North's economies, the North will be at an advantage, while the South will be at a disadvantage. With the generation of new knowledge in the North and in the South, high-tech goods will be more improved in the North than in the South, and high-tech goods will be improved more than low-tech goods. Hence, the structure of comparative advantages will change in favour of the North and deteriorate for the South, leading to trade imbalances. To restore this balance, factor prices in the North need to increase relative to the South. This increase is usually not large enough to compensate for the increasing technological lead of the North, inducing a continuous improvement of North's terms of trade and worsening of South's. The increase in the North economy's technological lead in a rather broad range of goods weakens the South economy's ability to master them. In case of availability problems induced by strategic trade policy, the South has few tools to counteract. Bargaining chips via goods the South in which has a technological lead are rare and presumably not powerful enough. However, retaliatory trade policy could be implemented.

Old technologies-new technologies: While generating new knowledge to upgrade and further develop existing technologies might limit opportunities to existing incumbents that have long mastered these technologies, in new technologies for new goods there are still major opportunities. In a trade structure in which one economy is rather specialised in old goods and another in new goods, comparative advantages in old goods do not change much in response to newly generated knowledge. For new goods, however, comparative advantages change quite intensely and may reach a level close to absolute advantage. In such cases, changes in relative factor prices leave the specialisation structure more or less unaffected. The terms of trade of the economy producing new goods improve, whereas those of the other economy worsen. Over time, technological sovereignty becomes an issue: for the economy specialised in old goods, the ability to master new goods and the technology behind them tends to weaken, as does the power of old goods to serve as bargaining chips in case of availability issues.

Key technologies: Key technologies are a crucial input into innovative development of a large number of technologies. The importance of mastery and availability of key technologies thus goes way beyond their own industries. In an international trade context with an endogenous process of generating new knowledge, further development of key technologies has impacts in three ways. First, if an economy does not specialise in a key technology, its technological gap in that technology increases and so does its lack of mastery of it. Second, the comparative advantage of the economy producing and exporting the key technology increases because of its growing technological lead. Changes in international relative factor prices required to restore trade equilibrium lead to a higher international price for the key technology. As the terms of trade of the lagging economies deteriorate, it becomes increasingly expensive for them to acquire the key technology. This reduces the ability of these economies to acquire a key technology – availability becomes increasingly limited and technological sovereignty declines. Third, in the lagging economies, the reduced availability of the key technology and its higher price will constrain the process of improving goods in all industries that use the key technology as an input. Consequently, the process of generating new knowledge in these industries slows, leading to a further deterioration of the terms of trade.

The interrelationships described above and the associated loss of technological sovereignty of an economy in a key technology apply in particular if lagging economies do not themselves specialise in a key technology, and thus do not seek related comparative advantages. However, key technologies are quite broad and often represent a bundle of different individual technologies. In this case, there may be an international division of labour and thus a specialisation structure within a key technology. In such a context, the question of technological sovereignty may arise less.

3.4 Dynamic comparative advantages

In an environment of endogenous, learning-driven processes of generating new (technological) knowledge, the main outcome is a pattern of divergent development. Applied to international trade, this results in an uneven distribution across economies of the welfare-enhancing effects of new knowledge. The concept of comparative advantage – or, in conjunction with factor prices, competitive advantage – determines this outcome because it establishes a particular pattern of international trade that is difficult to escape under endogenous learning.

Hence, for an economy attempting to position itself in international trade more favourably, following this principle of comparative advantages will not be helpful. These comparative advantages determine the structure at a given point in time and are thus static. To overcome that problem, an economy could look at dynamic or created comparative advantages. They are relevant for the goods for which an economy can change the comparative advantages in its favour over time through its own research and innovation activities – and thus also its positioning.

In a dynamic context, what matters for a country is not simply to specialise, but in which goods it specialises. In order to prevent the technology gap in an economy from becoming too large over time, the aim should be to specialise in goods with high potential for improvement through new knowledge, science and innovation.

In these, the economy may not yet have comparative advantages at a given point in time. In such a situation, moving via static comparative advantage into a trade structure in which the economy specialises in established but less-dynamic goods would be statically efficient but dynamically inefficient (eg Stiglitz, 2015; Cypher and Dietz, 1998). In order to comply with dynamic efficiency, static inefficiencies must be accepted, ie specialisation must take place in goods that do not (yet) have comparative advantages, but for which there is high technological innovation potential. In this way, the technology gap of an economy can at least be kept small. This has positive effects on income and prosperity, and on the level of knowledge required to be able to use high-tech goods manufactured abroad.

The focus on dynamic comparative advantages is especially significant in situations of major structural upheaval and transformation, driven by radical new technologies, and in which new technological leadership is emerging. Concepts of free trade based on certain assumptions, including the non-existence of external learning effects (knowledge accumulation), are less helpful here (for example, Greenwald and Stiglitz, 2014).

4 Industrial policy to establish and safeguard technological sovereignty of an economy

Decreasing technological sovereignty, as illustrated by the endogenous processes of generating new knowledge described above, and thus increasing the technological dependence of an economy on other economies, is a problem of political relevance. For an economy to avoid such vicious circles, a way out is to choose a trade structure consisting of goods with high potential for further innovative development. Such an ambition might go against its static comparative or competitive advantages, but can be justified by dynamic comparative advantages. To maintain such a specialisation requires industrial and foreign trade policy interventions to protect the chosen patterns of trade until they become self-sustaining.

Lack of mastery: Key to technological sovereignty is the knowledge to master technologies. Decreasing innovation capacity and technological know-how should be an alarm bell for firms. And it should also be so for policymakers, as this can in aggregate be seen as a systemic failure at national level. In terms of the mastery of goods and technologies, measures are needed to build up knowledge and hence know-how and as competencies. For key technologies, this needs to apply to the area of the key technology itself, but also, and especially, to the areas of user industries. The promotion of science and research, of training, further education and academic education, of transfer activities to the economy and society, and of innovation activities in these fields are primarily to be thought of here. Hence the large toolbox of research and innovation policies is applicable, with two reservations. First, the effects of these measures will be seen only after some years. Second, the knowledge required to create, develop and use the goods and technologies concerned will probably not be built up to the required quality entirely without in-house production. In order to counter this, it is then necessary to think about measures to keep or even build up the production and further development of these goods and technologies in the domestic market – even against static comparative advantages.

Mastery through availability: Industrial and foreign trade policy measures are suitable for keeping the process of generating new knowledge and the production of goods in a national economy. These could include subsidies for selected goods and (key) technologies or other means of export promotion, protectionist measures against imports of superior goods and technologies, and support for reshoring and even for building up facilities of production and of entirely new development in the domestic economy. Such measures ensure that these goods and technologies are produced and further developed domestically (availability) and that learning effects can be generated and used (mastery).

This has two consequences for policy implementation. First, these measures should be implemented for a limited period – at most until international competitiveness in the good or technology is achieved. Second, as far as can be identified, the measure should be implemented when a good or (key) technology is still young, the rate of exploitation of its technological and economic potential is still high, and the technology gap compared to the technology leader not too large. Particularly in the young phase of a new (key) technology, the risk is still quite high of being left behind internationally right from the start. Arguments in favour of young-industry protection or young-technology protection are relevant here.

However, the more mature and established a good or a technology is at the international level, the less one should think of bringing their production home. In such circumstances, other concepts for maintaining technological sovereignty need to be considered. Industrial policy support can also be thought of as supporting goods and technologies only in selected areas. This addresses the structure of an intra-industry and intra-technological specialisation. Several economies are technology leaders in an industry or a (key) technology, but each in a different subsector or niche. This contributes to mastery and availability, albeit in specialised areas. In principle this calls for a portfolio view, implying the technological sovereignty of an economy depending on its mastery of a balanced portfolio of (key) technologies – in some a comparative advantage is achieved, in others not.

Special availability concerns: Availability concerns are an issue when it comes to rigid strategic trade policy and trade wars. The factor of mastery is rather a side aspect here. In such cases, the solution depends on the balance of power. If each of the involved economies has a bargaining chip at hand, any 'attack' on sovereignty can be reciprocated. If such an interdependency does not exist, and on the contrary a situation of overdependency exists, then a country might be tempted to opt for an industrial policy directed towards self-sufficiency and import substitution to cut its over-dependency. However, this is not as straightforward as is looks. In case the availability issue is credible and expected to last, the price of the blocked good or technology goes to infinity, creating domestic business opportunities. Domestic but also international investors may jump in. Public support is not necessary here, or could involve only complementing certain research infrastructure (research organisations, universities, etc). This has the advantage that in case the original private investment pulls out the research infrastructure can be continued in the same or a different direction.

In view of these various measures, industrial policy appears to offer a toolbox that can effectively cope with lack of technological sovereignty and can preserving technological sovereignty. Governments around the world are increasingly resorting to this type of measure. It is to be hoped that this does not open the door to the widespread use of industrial policy, under the guise of preserving technological sovereignty.

References

Cantner, U. and H. Hanusch (1993) 'Process and Product Innovations in an International Trade Context', *Economics of Innovation and New Technology* 2: 217-36

Cantner, U. (1990) *Technischer Fortschritt, neue Güter und internationaler Handel*, Physica-Verlag HD

Cohen, W.M. and D.A. Levinthal (1989) 'Innovation and learning: the two faces of R&D', *The Economic Journal* 99(397): 569-596

Cypher, J.M. and J.L. Dietz (1998) 'Static and Dynamic Comparative Advantage: A Multi-Period Analysis with Declining Terms of Trade', *Journal of Economic Issues* 32(2): 305-314

Dosi, G., K. Pavitt and L. Soete (1990) *The Economics of Technical Change and International Trade*, Harvester Wheatsheaf

EFI (2022) *Gutachten zu Forschung, Innovation und technologischer Leistungsfähigkeit Deutschlands 2022*, Expertenkommission Forschung und Innovation

Fagerberg, J. (1987) 'A technology gap approach to why growth rates differ', *Research Policy* 16: 87-99

Greenwald, B. and J.E. Stiglitz (2013) 'Industrial policies, the creation of a learning society, and economic development', in J.E. Stiglitz and J.Y. Lin (eds) *The Industrial Policy Revolution I*, Palgrave Macmillan, London

Krugman, P. (1985) 'A 'technology gap' model of international trade', in D. Hague and K. Jungenfeldt (eds) *Structural adjustment in developed open economies*, Palgrave Macmillan, London

Nelson, R.R. (1991) 'Why do firms differ, and how does it matter?' *Strategic Management Journal* 12(S2): 61-74

Stiglitz, J.E. (2015) 'Leaders and followers: Perspectives on the Nordic model and the economics of innovation', *Journal of Public Economics* 127: 3-16

Verspagen, D. (1992) *Uneven Growth between Interdependent Economies*, UPM

5 Cooperation or conflict? Will industrial policy produce solutions or generate unmanageable conflicts?

Laura Tyson and John Zysman

1 The core of the matter

Industrial policy is back on the political agenda in the United States. The CHIPS and Science Act (Chips Act), the Inflation Reduction Act (IRA) and the Bipartisan Infrastructure Bill pursue significant national policy goals, in particular national security and climate goals, by nurturing particular sectors. The tools used – subsidies and tax credits to promote business activity, investment and demand – are standard industrial policy tools, designed to foster research, production and employment by the private sector in the United States in the targeted sectors. In this chapter, we examine the implications for the global economy and for the international political economic order of the move to overt industrial policy by the US.

We argue that the return of American industrial policy – which we classify into the two categories of 'chips' and 'green' – raises several potential tensions with US allies and trading partners. The Chips Act is at once both a geoeconomic and a geostrategic initiative. It is a response to substantive state actions abroad that have made the US reliant on semiconductor fabrication by a few major suppliers headquartered in Asia. It focuses on China's industrial policies and on the inherent national security risks for the US. But industrial policies in Taiwan have also played a significant role in the emergence of TSMC (Taiwan Semiconductor Manufacturing Company) as the major global supplier of advanced semiconductors for both defence and non-defence purposes (Breznitz, 2011). Competitive advantage in the semiconductor industry has been shaped by industrial policies around the world, and the Chips Act signals that the US will join the competition, using industrial policy levers to make the US a desirable location for the industry.

The goal of 'chips' is to ensure continuation of national, or at least allied, industrial and security leadership in this critical 'dual-use' technology sector. In semiconductors, as in other key technologies including quantum computing, AI and clean energy, the goal of US industrial policy is to maintain as large a technological lead as possible, while impeding technological advances in China, Russia and other countries that pose national security risks. Export controls and restrictions on inflows and outflows of investment to keep advanced technologies out of the hands of geopolitical rivals are complementary tools to achieve this goal.

The green bills in the US, in contrast, are designed to foster the production of green technologies and products in the US to speed and scale the transition to a low-carbon economy, a move from one energy and economic equilibrium to another. This requires a global, not just national transition, one that forces open the questions of who gains from the transition and who bears the costs domestically and internationally.

The success of both the chips and green industrial policies depends on cooperation with US allies. Cooperation, however, is complicated by the fact that US policies will affect the gain/cost calculus of allies and their own industrial policy goals. Moreover, the alliances required for chips and green goals are different. The pursuit of the different alliances required for the chips and green goals raises the question of how the choices of one state (or in the case of the EU, an association of states) influence the gain/cost calculus of others. Achieving the goals of the Chips Act requires cooperation between friends and allies. The climate goals of the 'green' bills require cooperation around the world.

Taken together the American initiatives raise broader questions[23]. In this chapter, we set aside the normative question of the role of the 'state' in domestic economic policy: whether it should extend beyond making the rules to shaping markets to actual intervention to overt support for particular firms and sectors. Industrial policies involve picking winners: with chips, the semiconductor industry, and with the green bills, the energy and climate mitigation and adaptation sectors. For the United States, overt industrial policies would seem to be a shift in the terms of debate and discussion. The US has certainly had extensive policies of sector-focused intervention, arguably very successful, for example, in the health sector and, of course, in defence-related technologies and sectors. Government policies to foster R&D and technological breakthroughs, and to provide demand, have been critical in the development of the commercial aircraft industry, the biotechnology industry and the internet. The rapid development of COVID-19 vaccines is the most recent dramatic example of industrial policy intervention and success in the US.

Generating domestic political support for overt intervention tilts policy choices towards favouring of national firms over foreign firms, or at least towards production on national soil. That distinction matters. It is reasonable for nations to use their own resources to encourage research, production and employment at home to benefit directly their own communities, and this inevitably raises issues with trading partners, and has done so even when embedded in defence policy. These activities, however, can be done by both domestic and foreign firms; industrial policies need not disadvantage foreign firms relative to domestic firms. The goal need not be to create national champions or to prefer national firms, but to promote economic activities in preferred sectors at home.

The success of the green and chips policies will require allies. For allies to adopt complementary policies, their governments will likewise

---

23 We wrote about many of these same issues in 1983. It was a radically different political and economic time, but many of the issues continue to be relevant. See Tyson and Zysman (1983).

need to create advantages and benefits for their local communities. This raises another issue. Overt national favouritism forces the issue of how to reconcile in international commerce and rule-making the diverse, competing, national objectives and varied national policy strategies to promote national firms or local production.

International economic negotiations always involve balancing benefits, but those negotiations are likely to be more difficult, and more public, when favouritism of national players or locations is direct, as in industrial policy[24]. The initial disagreement between the US and France over the Chips Act and Inflation Reduction Act is a clear signal of the frictions likely to arise among allies and trading partners[25]. The old international political economic order anchored by the United States was 'rule bound.' Although the rules themselves were built from debates about who would capture advantage, the new fragmentation and disorder are centred on national competitive advantage and self-sufficiency through onshoring, nearshoring and friend shoring. And the new economic nationalism is reflected in growing impediments to trade and global capital flows.

Negotiations about the several national industrial policies are likely to be even more difficult because enduring commercial and national advantage will be created in both green industries and in semiconductors. These considerations are not far from policymakers' minds. That comparative advantage can be created is evident in the Taiwanese success with TSMC and advanced foundries, and in China's success in solar panels. Another more mundane example is how Danish policies supporting early deployment of digital hearing aids helped Danish firms

---

24 Certainly differences in national policies, even policies without direct trade or development intent, can spill over into international trade conflicts. The case of the European steel cartel is a perfect example; see European Commission press release of 4 April 2011, 'Antitrust: Commission fines prestressing steel producers € 269 million for two-decades long price-fixing and market-sharing cartel', https://ec.europa.eu/commission/presscorner/detail/en/IP_11_403.

25 Dave Lawler, 'Biden's "Made in America" push alienates allies', *Axios*, 1 December 2022, https://www.axios.com/2022/12/02/biden-inflation-reduction-electric-cars-macron.

in global markets. Familiar mantras like 'we're all in this together' justify compromises to achieve the needed alliances, yet national interests in national champions and local production are real and will cause tensions. The new twin US industrial policies, green and chips, are likely to exacerbate such tensions.

Now as the US pursues broad security and climate goals, albeit goals shared by different sets of economic and political allies, it also overtly seeks competitive advantage and industrial leadership in chips and green technologies. There was a time when the US would rail against the 'state actions' of France, Japan and other market economies to create competitive advantage for their firms. Now the US is turning to the lessons from China's successful industrial policies to justify its own actions. There is a clear shift in US policies from trade policies to stem imports from China and other developing economies, based on their labour-cost advantages and state policies of industrial promotion, to industrial policies to bolster innovation, investment, production and employment in the US. Is the new US industrial policy irreconcilable with existing trade and foreign direct investment rules that the US has helped write and enforce? The competition among nations for both green industries and semiconductors will make establishing a new rule-bound order much more difficult. Will it make it impossible? Does the green/chips duality of US industrial policy show that the existing order is dead and gone? If so, what takes its place?

This new iteration of American industrial policy forces us to consider two seemingly competing logics. First, the green transition requires the needed technologies to be produced as fast and at as large a scale as possible. Second, fear of great-power conflict or other supply chain disruptions requires friend shoring, nearshoring or onshoring of production of critical technologies (semiconductors being the most complex and systemically important), including climate technologies. Impeding technological development by geopolitical rivals is a key goal, certainly of the US semiconductor policies and arguably of green policies as well. But autarky is both impossible and undesirable and working with allies is essential. Complicating matters is that China is a rival in the chip world and must be in some sense an ally in pursuing global climate objectives. Before delving more deeply into the two cases, let us consider industrial policy itself.

2 Situating industrial policy

Industrial policy justifications are traditionally associated with national competitiveness, jobs and technological advancement. Those goals are to be achieved by nurturing a particular sector/industry in a place, country, region or sphere. Importantly, it is not just about nurturing a sector/industry and, often, specific firms, but about nurturing them in a specific place, a particular nation[26]. State action is intended to alter the market results of firms and sectors, to achieve outcomes that are unlikely otherwise in the market. The objective is changing, or maintaining the economy's production profile, for example, by moving from agriculture to industry, or in the case of China moving from labour-intensive sectors to technology-driven sectors. Sometimes industrial policy is a story of broad transformations and sometimes it is a story that focuses on particular problems or sectors[27]. Industrial policy instruments are as diverse as the actual policy goals. Many policy instruments are available to achieve these goals: subsidies, tax incentives, R&D support, trade and foreign direct investment restrictions that discriminate in favour of local production, whether by domestic or foreign firms, and against foreign competitors. The goals and purposes, not the tools in particular, define industrial policy.

We should situate industrial policy in an historical context. Industrial

---

26 Of course, nurturing particular firms makes the policy open to corruption, that is for those with access to government, and the capability to influence its decisions, to direct the benefits of the policy to themselves. Arguably all economic policy, from tax and savings through regulation, has the same ability to benefit some firms and sectors differentially. However, industrial policy, which rewards as a goal particular sectors and firms, makes the link to political influence direct.

27 In a sense it is a shift from one equilibrium to another, and the incentives in an initial equilibrium may not induce the better outcome. Hence the question then becomes how to get from a less-attractive equilibrium to a better one.

policy has long been associated with a drive toward national power, whether in seventeenth century France with Colbert, nineteenth century Germany with List, or indeed – less well known – sixteenth century Britain when the need for wood for ships began a policy push to shift from wood to coal (Gerschenkron, 1962). More recently, French strategies after the Second World War to move from a predominantly agricultural to a modern industrial economy were about structuring market incentives to favour the modernisation of firms and activities (Zysman, 1983). The Japanese modernisation in the nineteenth century and its restructuring after the Second World War similarly were rooted in the objective of establishing, and re-establishing in Japan's case, a global economic position. After the Second World War, the United States was the dominant economy, and the dominant Western political force. It led the construction of a neo-liberal system of global trade/finance rules, which it is now regularly violating, and it reconciled both its geopolitical, strategic objectives and its domestic economic and political goals with these rules. Consistent with these rules, the US responded to import pressures in a wide variety of sectors from shoes to televisions, and from a wide variety of trading partners, through trade protections, often in the form of anti-dumping measures and voluntary export restraint agreements. These measures allowed the US to espouse free trade while restricting market access in sharply impacted sectors[28]. But, importantly, direct market intervention to support domestic firms was limited and even trade-adjustment assistance, announced firmly, was limited and used ineffectively. Companies, workers and communities were left to bear the costs of lost production and lost markets from low-cost imports and export competition. The local costs were concentrated and devastating, gradually undermining political support for free trade and stirring the rise of populist 'nationalist' movements on both the left and the right (Autor *et al*, 2016).

---

28 Arguably hypocritical, these restraints were triggered at a much high level of imports than would have been tolerated in other polities.

The track record of industrial policy is mixed. Certainly, the cases of Germany, France, Japan and now China contain successful stories of economic transformations steered by the state. They make clear that policies of purposeful development and creating competitive and comparative advantage can succeed. At the sectoral level there are European successes such as Airbus, to set alongside the questionable Concorde project. The failure of Minitel, or the French Machine Bull efforts, need to be set alongside France's success in high speed railways. In the case of the US, the defence-driven creation of the internet and the emergence of the biotechnology industry are two outstanding success stories. But most of the other specific industrial policies to protect employment in sectors or firms from import competition have been expensive failures (Hufbauer and Jung, 2021). What might be expected, then, from green industrial policy with its goal of fundamental economic transformation aimed at containing global warming? Can the chips industrial policy succeed in its geostrategic move to maintain for the US, or the US and its allies, leadership in a critical dual-use technology as a foundation for success in the rest of their chip-dependent digital sectors? What will be the consequences of these industrial policies for international trade and investment? Are the twin goals in inherent conflict: green requires everyone; chips is intended to contain China, Russia and other strategic rivals?

3 A green transformation

Green industrial policy in the United States is aimed at generating and accelerating an economic transformation, a transition from a carbon-based energy system to a green/alternative energy system. In a simple real sense, this involves electrifying everything and decarbonising electricity. History is replete with other energy system transitions, from wood to coal to steam to oil to electricity. Each has involved both markets and governments, prices and policies. The current transition, however, is particularly urgent: there isn't time to rely on markets to drive the transition from fossil fuels to renewables and more efficient uses of energy resources to achieve the net-zero commitments made by the US and the majority of UN countries. Green policy in the US and abroad is driven by the assumption that markets alone will not get to the goal of decarbonisation at sufficient speed and scale to realise these commitments and avoid climate disaster.

The US has defined its green goal in the IRA as a 40 percent reduction in carbon emissions compared to 2005 levels by 2030. The strategy is to use a variety of specific policies to achieve this goal: generous incentives on both the supply side, for firms, state and local governments, for R&D and for talent development, and on the demand side for consumers. Certainly, some of the subsidies for green tech, development and deployment can be viewed as offsetting ongoing policy support for the fossil-fuel energy system. Tit-for-tat green subsidies are likely around the world. The EU is already considering a European version of the IRA to allow its member states to counter the competitive challenges posed by US policies, and many other nations are making investments to speed the transition to green energy. Many of the poorest countries facing the greatest threats from climate change, however, do not have the financing to make such investments[29].

Securing a stable global climate – combating climate change – is a shared goal to provide a global public good of a sustainable climate[30]. Coordinated policies of nations around the world are required to achieve this goal. That said, 'green policy' in each country, as is evident in the IRA in the US, also pursues nationally specific objectives of local production and jobs. US policy is aimed overtly at assuring that green technologies, products, production and employment are developed in the United

---

29 Grantham Research Institute on Climate Change and the Environment press release of 8 November 2022, 'COP27 report calls for international investments of $1 trillion annually by 2030 in climate action in developing countries', https://www.lse.ac.uk/granthaminstitute/news/cop27-report-calls-for-international-investments-of-1-trillion-annually-by-2030-in-climate-action-in-developing-countries/.

30 There are significant historical parallels in which massive state involvement and investment was part of transformations altering the underlying infrastructure of the economy, including the interstate highway system driven in part by defence justifications, the railroad system and the electricity grid.

States, whether by US or foreign firms. US policy is also driven by making certain that China does not dominate green technologies and products. But US green industrial policies to make the US the competitive location for green technologies and products can conflict with the objectives and goals of US allies, whose own energy transformations are essential, and who likewise want to pursue national advantage in green sectors and technologies.

A purely national or autarkic success, even if possible in industrial terms, will not address the global climate challenge: success requires all nations to participate. There will however be rivalries over who wins and loses in the process of building the new energy systems. Consequently, a significant challenge for green industrial policies will be building coalitions both at home and abroad to share the economic adjustment costs and benefits of the transition. Global coalitions will require the engagement of China, India and Russia, posing very different coalitions that reconcile ambitions amongst like-minded allies.

A core challenge will be building domestic coalitions for the energy transformation that also permit, if not facilitate, global alliances[31]. Certainly policy must support and reward the emerging green technologies. But there are losers as well as winners. Who will pay the costs of transition? Will the losers be compensated? The fossil-fuel sector will continue to fight to maintain its position, arguing in some settings that the climate challenge is exaggerated or unreal. The French *gilets jaunes* movement is about resistance against higher prices that reflect the carbon costs of those who use fossil-fuel products. Since time is of the essence, delay is a profound challenge. The losers will not easily be displaced. Can they be bought off at a price and within a timeframe that allows nations to honour their commitments to net zero? The necessity of building domestic coalitions for green industrial policies means that each nation will seek to shape such policies to reward their local

---

31 On domestic coalitions, see Meckling *et al* (2015). On international coalitions, see Meckling (2021).

constituencies. Indeed, building domestic coalitions for the green transition seems likely to generate conflicts among nations about industries and competitiveness, conflicts that make building global coalitions on a shared public good more difficult. The challenge of harmonising national competitiveness and economic goals in green sectors with global climate goals should not be underestimated.

At stake in the transition is who will control the industries of the future. In theory, the development of green technologies and products in one country can benefit all countries, speeding and scaling the global energy transition. In practice, however, the rise of one nation's green industries can undermine the same industries in another nation. Consider China and solar panels. Chinese producers, supported by generous state industrial policies, drove down costs, making solar energy much less expensive. But the subsidised rise of China's solar panel industry also damaged actual and potential producers in the US and elsewhere. That is not just a market issue of lost domestic producers and production, but the loss of potential allies in domestic green industries in a domestic coalition to offset the political weight of domestic fossil-fuel producers.

There are many distinct yet crucial sectors in the energy transition. Supplying electrical energy involves wind and solar equipment, batteries and critical minerals required for those systems. Adapting energy use to electricity involves, as examples, transportation goods, from cars and trucks today to perhaps aircraft tomorrow, and heating systems for offices and homes. Diverse and complex, widely dispersed, global supply networks in the materials and components are involved. One consequence is that a policy drive toward predominance in one sector – say electric-vehicle design and assembly – risks retaliation in others. There are choke points throughout whether, as examples, those are the materials that go into products, the components of full systems, or mastery of battery manufacturing[32]. Targeting domestic firms alone or

---

32 Choke points in a supply network occur when one firm or one country has an effec-

local production exclusively assures international conflicts, higher costs and slower transition. Green policy must find political solutions and coalitions at two levels: domestic and international[33].

In the effort to find solutions that will ensure domestic support and avoid damaging trade conflicts that undermine the collective good of a green transition, existing products and technologies must be distinguished from the development of new next-generation technologies. Existing technologies are about who produces for today's markets. Existing products and technology – electrical generation, batteries, wind, solar power and the like – as well as the conversion of products to electrical operation, entail direct market competition. Next generation breakthrough technologies, in contrast, might be a basis for joint pre-commercial development.

Reconciling the several national green policies is essential to accelerate the transition. There are no panaceas. As a starting point, creating and maintaining a green roadmap that identifies potential choke points, and seeking cooperative solutions to them or identifying lines of potential collaborative pre-competitive research, might be useful first steps. But those who control current or future choke points are not likely to give them up willingly, and as technological breakthroughs come closer to market implementation, collaboration will not necessarily be comfortable. Since carbon-related border taxes are on the table, certainly seeking a tax deal, global or between friends, should be considered. Another option worth considering is the development of a sectoral trade agreement that covers trade in green products and services. Some would consider the IT sectoral trade agreement that began in 1996 and today has 82 participants and covers 97 percent of global trade in IT products to be an example of a successful sectoral trade agreement that has fostered trade and reduced barriers. Another option worth consideration

---

tive monopoly or dominates the market, creating leverage. Examples can be found in materials, components and final products, such as solar systems.

33 The classic statement of this is in Putnam (1988).

is joint pre-competitive research and funding by the US and its allies on green breakthrough technologies, such as nuclear fusion and carbon sequestration.

4 Chips with everything

The chips story poses very different problems to the green story. The Chips Act is focused both on maintaining US and allied leadership and on impeding China's advances in one sector – micro-electronic components. Semiconductors are essential dual-use technologies, inputs throughout much of the economy and critical to security concerns. Advanced countries have national economic and security interests in nurturing a resilient, secure supply of both mature and cutting-edge chips to meet growing non-defence and defence demand. Remaining at the frontier of technological change in chips requires semiconductor production: technological change and production go hand in hand. A nation needs a strong production base to remain at the technological frontier of chips: "*you can't control what you can't produce*" (Cohen and Zysman, 1987).

But, technological and market autarky will not be possible in this sector. In the words of Morris Chang, founder of TSMC: "*If you want to re-establish a complete semiconductor supply chain in the US, you will not find it as a possible task*"[34]. Consequently, market and policy alliances will be needed. In foundries, where leading-edge chips are produced, Taiwan's TSMC is dominant with Korea's Samsung and perhaps the US's Intel as enduring scale players. Production equipment, apart from the materials that go into production, is widely dispersed across Europe, the US and Asia with the Dutch company ASML dominating the essential domain of advanced lithography. ASML has announced that it will limit exports of its most advanced equipment to China, consistent with the goals of US policy to slow the growth of China's semiconductor industry.

---

34 Cheng Ting-Fang and Lauly Li, 'The resilience myth: fatal flaws in the push to secure chip supply chains', *Financial Times*, 4 August 2022, https://www.ft.com/content/f76534bf-b501-4cbf-9a46-80be9feb670c.

Japan has also announced that it will limit exports of such equipment to China. In design, the US has very strong positions with companies like Qualcomm. Europe's ARM, still owned by Japanese holding company SoftBank, is a major player.

We have previously defined the economic and geostrategic goals of US industrial policy in the semiconductor industry in the following way:

"For the sake of both national and economic security, the United States needs a multifaceted strategy for providing a competitive, resilient, secure, and sustainable (CRSS) supply of semiconductors. Such a strategy must address all parts of the industry, from design, fabrication, assembly, and packaging to materials and manufacturing equipment.

"Each of these elements of the supply chain is critical. Competitive market conditions must prevail throughout the industry, because excessive market power in any one segment can jeopardize supply. The system must also be resilient to shocks like fires, droughts, earthquakes, and geopolitical tensions and upheavals. And it must be secure in two senses: the US must maintain reliable access to cutting-edge chips and the means of producing them, and chip supplies need to be protected from threats like counterfeiting, theft, cyberattacks, and espionage. Finally, the supply must be sustainable, accounting for the significant environmental and energy costs of chip production.

"CRSS does not mean national autonomy in the semiconductor industry. That goal would be neither feasible nor economically rational, given the complex global supply system and the dispersion of industry knowledge, talent, and production. What CRSS does mean is that the US should cooperate closely with the European Union, Japan, Singapore, Israel, and others who form core parts of its secure supply base" (Tyson and Zysman, 2021).

The American calculus is driven principally by the national security concerns of maintaining substantial leadership over China – indeed, of rapidly moving the US and allies forward while slowing the Chinese. Not all countries share the US view of China, or at least they calculate their national interests differently. Many US allies and other nations are as concerned about the dominance of US tech companies as they are about the China challenge. Our concern is that competing national industrial policies, however well motivated, can quickly lead to counterproductive and wasteful tit-for-tat bidding wars of the sort we have seen before, both among US states and among European countries. The recent downturn in semiconductor demand will make this more acute. Governments will both be called on to support sagging companies while political pressure from the chip customer base will ease. The cyclical character of the industry makes sustained support both tricky and important. In contrast, collaborative policy could include pre-competitive public-private R&D partnerships to share equipment and other costs among participants. Perhaps a similar 'commons' approach could be extended to chip production as well. Further along the collaboration development chain, there may be possibilities in defining together the needs of sectors such as the automotive sector for semiconductor chips that differ from those that have been driven by the needs of the leading US tech companies. Finally, there is a need for allied coordination of export controls and controls over foreign direct investment in semiconductors and other strategic sectors and technologies.

5 Conflict or collaboration?

With 'industrial policy' resurgent, several questions arise. First, are the goals and policies of green and chips industrial policy in inherent conflict with each other? Green has the objective of a universal energy transformation. That requires a broad alliance, including China, even with competitive conflicts in green production and employment. Chips requires a more restricted alliance of allies and friends that confront

China, in which the underlying purposes of the allies are not all the same. China's ambition to establish leadership, indeed dominance, in crucial digital technologies is both a security and an economic challenge. For the United States, the security challenge is primary. The choices are not straightforward for other countries, which are trying to ensure in the name of 'sovereignty' their capacities for sustained autonomous technology development, to keep pace with US technology firms, while maintaining access to the Chinese market for their exports. An overarching question is whether the US-driven policy of containing China in the semiconductor industry will undermine China's willingness to participate in global solutions and trading rules in green technologies and products. If China is identified as an enemy in the semiconductor industry, will it be an ally in green industries?

Second, a more general problem is how to manage the conflicts generated by competing national industrial policies, and more specifically by the policies adopted by the United States. The existing trade and foreign direct investment rules do not provide comfort. The dispute settlement mechanism of the World Trade Organisation is moribund, killed off by the United States. The American ability to use access to its domestic market as leverage in international negotiations has dwindled in its effectiveness. The US sometimes applies its trade restrictions on an extraterritorial basis, applying them to both US and foreign firms doing business with China in violation of global trading rules. Does the US move to overt industrial policy require new trading rules and the revitalisation of the WTO dispute settlement mechanism to enforce these rules[35]? Without these changes, the open trading order is likely to be undermined by wasteful beggar-thy-neighbour industrial policies that encourage onshoring, nearshoring and friend shoring and that further fragment the global

---

35 A cynic might remark that in the era of the Washington Consensus and a neo-liberal order, we were in fact both protectionist and promoting our own interests when speaking of global trade. Our cynic would accuse us of saying 'do as we say, not as we do'. The response of others was often that we hid strategies pursuing our particular advantage in deals covered with the ideology of free trade.

economy. Such fragmentation will drive up costs, restrict the development options of emerging economies and slow global growth. Such fragmentation will also thwart the global cooperation necessary to speed and scale the transition to a sustainable green future. The climate challenge is a global one that requires coordinated global action supported by new global trade and investment rules and a new international order.

References

Autor, D., D. Dorn and G. Hanson (2016) 'The China Shock: Learning from Labor Market Adjustments to Large Changes in Trade', *NBER Working Paper* 21906, National Bureau of Economic Research, available at https://www.nber.org/papers/w21906

Breznitz, D. (2011) *Innovation and the State*, Yale University Press

Cohen, S.S. and J. Zysman (1987) *Manufacturing Matters: The Myth of the Post-Industrial Economy*, New York: Basic Books

Gerschenkron, A. (1962) *Economic Backwardness in Historical Perspective*, Cambridge, MA: Belknap Press

Hufbauer, G. and E. Jung (2021) 'Scoring 50 years of US industrial policy, 1970, 2020', *PIIE Briefings* 21-5, Peterson Institute for International Economics, available at https://www.piie.com/publications/piie-briefings/scoring-50-years-us-industrial-policy-1970-2020

Meckling, J., N. Kelsey, E. Biber and J. Zysman (2015) 'Winning Coalitions for Climate Policy', *Science* 349(6253): 1170-71

Meckling, J. (2021) 'Making Industrial Policy Work for Decarbonization', mimeo, available at https://dx.doi.org/10.2139/ssrn.3802719

Putnam, R.D. (1988) 'Diplomacy and Domestic Politics: The Logic of Two-Level Games', *International Organization* 42(3): 427-460

Tyson, L. and J. Zysman (1983) *American Industry In International Competition: Government Policies and Corporate Strategies*, Cornell University Press

Tyson, L. and J. Zysman (2021) 'America's Vital Chip Mission', *Project Syndicate*, 27 July, available at https://www.project-syndicate.org/commentary/us-semiconductor-strategy-by-laura-tyson-and-john-zysman-2021-07

Zysman, J. (1983) *Governments, Markets, and Growth*, Cornell University Press

6 Green industrial policy: the necessary evil to avoid a climate catastrophe

Alessio Terzi

1 Introduction[36]

Industrial policy is a term that is often interpreted differently depending on the audience. The fact that it cuts through a variety of economic policy tools, ranging from innovation programmes and tax policy, to trade and foreign direct investment (FDI), makes the matter even more complex. It lends itself to easy misinterpretation. At its core, it refers to *"any type of selective intervention or government policy that attempts to alter the structure of production toward sectors that are expected to offer better prospects for economic growth than would occur in the absence of such intervention"* (Pack and Saggi, 2006). This might include sectors/technologies in which leadership might have geopolitical, security and military implications. The concept builds on two fundamental elements: (i) production in some sectors is more desirable than in others (Hausmann *et al*, 2007), and because of this, (ii) governments should make an active effort to nudge the production structure in that direction.

It is important to note that, irrespective of simplistic characterisations (eg capitalism vs socialism) or standard economic modelling of markets under perfect conditions, practically all countries, including the United

---

36 The views expressed here are the author's and do not necessarily represent those of the institutions to which he is affiliated.

States, the UK, France, China, Japan, Taiwan and South Korea, engage in various forms of industrial policy, and always have (Rodrik, 2009; Terzi *et al*, 2022).

Nonetheless, it is true that over the past few decades there has been a generalised reduced use of industrial policy, which has moved to the margins of mainstream economics. As this principle became embedded in policymakers' minds, it was framed under the narrative that governments cannot pick winners in a market economy, and rather they are at high risk of being captured by interest groups (Rodrik, 2014a). And of course, narratives eventually shape policies (Shiller, 2019).

Moreover, industrial policy was seen as harmful to the pursuit of a more globalised world economy, which to some extent became a leading objective in and of itself (Rodrik, 2011). In the service of a rules-based global trade order, richer nations of the West sided against a preponderant role of governments in altering production in a certain direction, rather allowing comparative advantages to manifest themselves freely. If that meant the relocation of manufacturing to China and away from the US and Europe, this was to be welcomed in the face of the associated gains from trade and specialisation (Figure 1).

Figure 1: Manufacturing, share of world total (%)

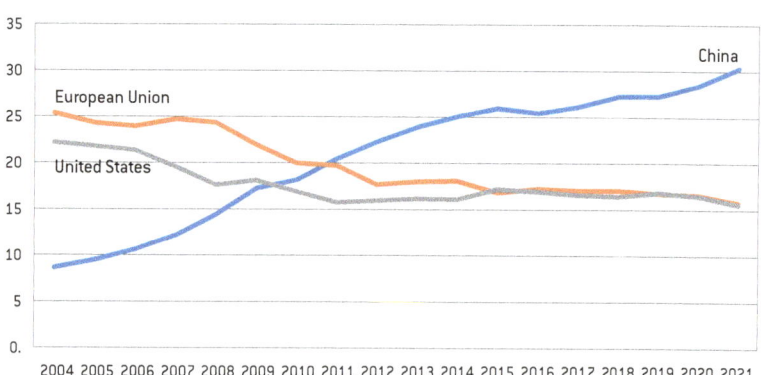

Source: World Bank.

The idea that industrial policy was unhelpful was to some extent codified in the so-called 'Washington Consensus', or else the idea that a small government (together with open current and capital accounts) was instrumental in achieving rapid development. As such, the resistance to industrial policy was exported to the Global South, in particular during macroeconomic adjustment programmes (Boccaletti, 2021).

Over the last few years, however, what has facetiously been called "*the policy that shall not be named*" has returned to the main stage of economic policy (Cherik and Hasanov, 2019). There are several reasons for this. First, and most prominently, China has been making extensive use of industrial policy, experiencing meteoric growth in the process. Moreover, the fact that the country's access to the World Trade Organisation in 2001 did not prod it to abandon such practices effectively invalidated the argument for others to favour the safeguarding of a level playing field at global level. Second, COVID-19 required a large degree of government intervention in the economy, including for the stockpiling and provision of personal protective equipment and the fast development and production of vaccines. And, of course, in the moment at which global supply chains came to a grinding halt because of COVID-19-induced restrictions, there was a sudden realisation of the central role that microchips play in today's economy, from cars to military applications. Lack of access to them could be weaponised, because artificial intelligence and the digital economy will play a crucial role in defining military supremacy in the twenty-first century.

Finally, the returning appeal of industrial policy is due to climate change, defined as the greatest market failure the world has ever seen (Stern, 2006), and thus questioning the narrative that market forces should be left largely unfettered. In this chapter, we focus narrowly on the latter aspect, namely what comes under the name of 'green industrial policy', aimed at accelerating decarbonisation.

2 Green industrial policy and its intended consequences

If global warming is an externality problem, no matter how big, then the standard textbook solution to it should be to price emissions, in a way reinserting them into the market economy. Carbon pricing must be a crucial element in any credible pathway towards net zero (Tagliapietra, 2020). However, even the High-Level Commission on Carbon Prices, put together to identify the optimal price of carbon to achieve fast decarbonisation, eventually concluded that carbon pricing alone will not be sufficient to address climate change (Stern and Stiglitz, 2017). This is because there are other market imperfections that work against speedy decarbonisation (Stern and Stiglitz, 2017).

An example of this could be technological path dependency, meaning that innovation tends to build on pre-existing knowledge, which generates a bias towards fossil fuels (Aghion *et al*, 2019). Another example could be risk aversion combined with lack of perfect information about the technology that will prevail in a green economy, leaving firms in a wait-and-see mode (Rodrik, 2014a). Due to the same problem, firms are particularly wary of investing in green technologies that are far from marketable, such as decarbonised steel and cement production, carbon capture and storage, and carbon-free aviation (Gates, 2021). Finally, for political-economy reasons, it could very well be that the optimal level of carbon pricing cannot be achieved, in part because of the large redistributive implications it would have[37]. When that is the case, a more active role of government can be envisioned, including by means of industrial policy, which has been shown to complement carbon pricing, increasing the speed of the transition (Acemoglu *et al*, 2012).

There is another reason related to climate change that, in my view, drives the current push for industrial policy: effectively reaching net zero will require a complete restructuring of production, consumption,

---

[37] John Van Reenen, 'The Case for Green Industrial Policy', *ProMarket*, 14 February 2023, https://www.promarket.org/2023/02/14/the-case-for-green-industrial-policy/.

transport, housing, agriculture and more because we live in a fossil-fuel civilisation. In other words, the green transition has historical resemblances to an industrial revolution (Terzi, 2022a). When that is the case, comparative advantages will be reshuffled across companies and countries, based on the (general purpose) technologies that will become the bedrock of the future green economy. It should thus come as no surprise that governments will use all policy tools available to try and develop an edge in the key technologies of the future, and secure the long-term prosperity of their country, as they did in the early phases of past industrial revolutions (Beckert, 2015; Rodrik, 2011).

This competitive argument in favour of industrial policy would not apply in a first-best world in which decarbonisation was planned in an optimal way at the global level, and where positive and negative spillovers between countries could be internalised. However, the urgent need to tackle catastrophic climate change will not lead to the end of geopolitics. Decarbonisation policies must rather be designed in a way that is incentive-compatible with a world in which policies will primarily be designed at the national level[38], and where nation states will continue to scramble for economic and military primacy. In this context, green industrial policy in the service of national interest should be seen as suboptimal but necessary.

Terzi *et al* (2022) discussed the design characteristics an effective industrial policy should have in order to minimise the risks that it will not deliver its intended effects at home. The remainder of this chapter will instead focus on the unintended effects if it does indeed succeed, particularly on other countries.

---

38 The European Union is perhaps a notable exception in this respect, having substantial policy competence with respect to climate and environment issues.

3 Unintended consequences

First, it is important to realise that even mainstream experts are generally in favour of R&D subsidies or tax credits. However, the use of such active industrial policy at a multi-billion-dollar scale will effectively plant the seed for the defensive side of industrial policy, meaning trade and investment restrictions, which is the type normally considered negative or protectionist (Poitiers *et al*, 2023). This is almost inevitable, particularly in a post rules-based world trade order (Terzi, 2022b): if billions worth of taxpayers' money is being used, the political-economy forces pushing for restricting it to domestic firms and jobs will be strong. The US for instance is openly celebrating how the Inflation Reduction Act (IRA) is "*prioritising American jobs*"[39].

Effectively, this means that a more active use of (green) industrial policy at home is bound to spark an international subsidy race. To some, this is a good result because it will fast-track decarbonisation and the development/deployment of new green technologies[40]. The reality is however that only countries with deep pockets and wide access to financial markets will be able to engage in it, as already well noted by Kleimann (2023). These are likely to be high-income countries, but it is not limited to those and encompasses also a small set of large and rapidly emerging economies, including China and India. At a rough estimation, it will encompass most G20 economies, with the notable exception perhaps of Argentina and South Africa. The others will suffer its consequences or do the only thing they can with

---

39 Aime Williams and Derek Brower, 'US Makes 'No Apologies' for prioritising American jobs, Clean Energy Tsar tells EU', *Financial Times*, 24 February 2023, https://www.ft.com/content/cb0a8ddf-6b32-49d8-8870-d1384580e9c9.

40 Arvind Subramanian, 'Global Cooperation Is Not Necessary to Fight Climate Change', *Project Syndicate*, 10 November 2022, https://www.project-syndicate.org/commentary/multilateral-cooperation-climate-change-unnecessary-inflation-reduction-act-by-arvind-subramanian-2022-11, and Gernot Wagner, 'The Clean-Energy Race Is On', *Project Syndicate*, 15 August 2022, https://www.project-syndicate.org/commentary/inflation-reduction-act-global-clean-energy-race-by-gernot-wagner-2022-08.

no immediate costs for the public coffers, ie increase trade barriers to try and protect domestic production along the lines of 'infant industry protection'. These are likely to be less-developed economies and some emerging markets, which are far from the technological frontier and will hardly benefit from having to develop innovation at home rather than exploit technology transfers associated with imports, especially of capital (Aiyar *et al*, 2023).

3.1 Investment and production

In terms of investment, there is likely to be a wave of re-shoring as a result of the ramp up of active and defensive industrial policy, accompanied by national security concerns in an increasingly fractured geopolitical world. Up to now, much of the focus in the media has been on whether the IRA would draw European firms and their production plants to the US[41]. As Europe will set up its own response, in equilibrium, what will be lured will mostly be investment that could have otherwise taken place in third countries, especially emerging markets.

The active use of subsidies to attract production and FDI, combined with trade and investment barriers, means that production will relocate closer to demand. Note that OECD countries currently command 60 percent of world demand (Figure 2). This number goes down to roughly 45 percent for G7 countries only, and 62 percent if China is added to the G7, ultimately reflecting the great degree of income inequality between a small group of larger, richer economies and the rest (Milanovic, 2019).

---

41 Sam Fleming, Alice Hancock and Javier Espinoza, 'Can the EU Keep up with the US on Green Subsidies?' *Financial Times*, 31 January 2023, https://www.ft.com/content/85b55126-e1e6-4b2c-8bb2-753d3cafcbe5.

Figure 2: Gross national expenditure, share of world (%)

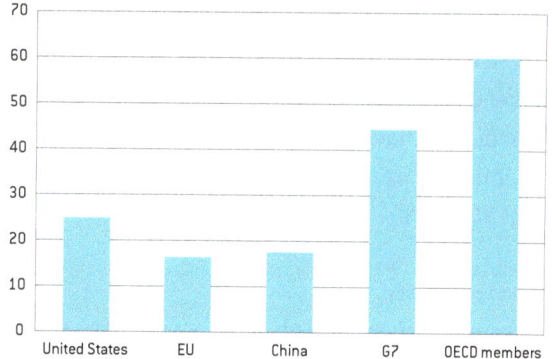

Source: World Bank. Note: Gross national expenditure (formerly known as domestic absorption) is the sum of household final consumption expenditure, general government final consumption expenditure, and gross capital formation. Underlying data are in constant 2015 prices, expressed in US dollars.

As these reflections will apply to a variety of sectors, including electric vehicles, solar panels, green hydrogen, wind energy, heat pumps and possibly also raw materials that are critical for the green transition, they will ultimately imply less trade[42]. Most of this trade is of the standard manufacturing type, requiring limited advanced education and therefore suitable to propel growth in less-developed economies that want to move away from agrarian societies (Rodrik, 2014b).

3.2 Development and global income convergence
Effectively, industrial policies and in particular those with local content provisions, will reduce global trade, which is fundamental for rapid development. To understand why, it is worth going back to the so-called *Growth Report* (World Bank, 2008). In 2008, a group of 19 policymakers, mostly from developing economies, headed by two Nobel economics laureates, put together a report analysing the

---

42 Martin Wolf, 'The New Interventionism Could Pose a Threat to Global Trade Receive Free Protectionism Updates', *Financial Times*, 14 February 2023, https://www.ft.com/content/3bc33cc4-1ee9-42ce-bcc2-2ba2a483e8ce.

experiences of 13 countries that had managed to sustain high GDP growth since the 1950s. Drawing on the input of over 300 academics, on top of the personal hands-on experiences of the policymakers, the report sifted out the common traits of successful cases. Of the 13 episodes of 'miracle' development, which came with sharp reductions in extreme poverty, from China to post-war Japan, and including South Korea, Indonesia, Malaysia, Brazil and Taiwan, literally all relied on a fast expansion of exports. This is for two reasons. First, low trade barriers give access to markets where demand is large or rapidly expanding, whereas demand at home in a poor country is limited by definition. Second, exports loosen the current-account constraint, allowing countries to obtain hard currency, import foreign advanced machinery and move up the value chain.

The implication is that an aggressive use of green industrial policy in countries that can afford it will come to the detriment of the global income-convergence process. This was already running out of steam (Rodrik, 2016), so effectively industrial policy will compound this problem.

To sum up, even if inspired by the genuine desire to tackle a global challenge like climate change, strong use of green industrial policy will ultimately contribute to deglobalisation. Combined with the fact that production and investment will locate closer to where demand is found, widening inequalities between countries can be expected or, at the very least, a halt to the so-called *"great income convergence"* (Baldwin, 2016).

3.3 Prices and innovation

A variety of factors already distort prices at global level, but the use of policy tools to distort prices even more and twist production in a certain direction could easily imply that citizens at home will pay more for a set of products than they would have otherwise. This is something that has already been seen when trade tension and barriers increased during the Trump Administration (Cerutti *et al*, 2019). Ultimately, this is the other side of the coin to the so-called 'gains from trade' that classical economists Adam Smith and David Ricardo were already describing three centuries ago. We could define them as losses from protectionism.

At the same time, however, inflationary losses from protectionism will be counteracted by the speed at which innovation proceeds in green sectors, notably walking down cost curves at a fast clip. This leads us to the aspect that deserves the closest attention: the degree to which active (and especially defensive) industrial policy leads to a slowdown in the rate of innovation at the technological frontier. This is particularly crucial because catastrophic climate change can be avoided only if the speed of the development and deployment of green technology and innovation ramps up enormously (Terzi, 2022b).

This concern might be overstated, however. Taking a long-term perspective, it is not trade that has generated the acceleration in innovation associated with industrial revolutions (Mokyr, 2016). And therefore, unsurprisingly, for economies at the technological frontier, gains from trade are comparatively small relative to overall cumulative rates of growth[43]. In fact, it could very well be that investment in and urgency of innovation picks up as a result of great-power rivalry – accelerations of innovation have happened typically at times of geopolitical confrontation (Moretti *et al*, 2019). To an extent, the US Defense Advanced Research Projects Agency (DARPA), which is now celebrated as the mother of many crucial inventions, including the internet, GPS, touch screens and voice recognition, is the product of US industrial policy in response to the Soviet Union launch of the Sputnik

---

43 Looking at the US for instance, it is estimated that the 12 bilateral free trade agreements (FTAs), plus two regional FTAs (the North American Free Trade Agreement and the Dominican Republic-Central America-United States Free Trade Agreement), resulted in the US economy being one half of a percent bigger than what it would have been without the agreements in place (Russ, 2021). To put this into perspective, since the NAFTA came into effect in 1994, US real GDP has grown by 89 percent.

(Mazzucato, 2013). The Apollo Project, often given as a commendable example of public-sector-driven innovation, generating waves of secondary innovation for decades, was only possible because of the space race with the Soviet Union during the Cold War (Mazzucato, 2021).

However, what should instead not be overlooked is that competition plays a crucial role in fostering innovation, and as such should be safeguarded even in the face of increasing trade barriers (Aghion *et al*, 2023). This, incidentally, is why competition policy should not be loosened in the name of industrial competitiveness and creating national champions (Terzi *et al*, 2022). And state aid should be deployed only with great care.

4 Policy implications

It should be evident that the use of industrial policy will come with some significant downsides, especially for less-developed countries. What is particularly ironic is that for a long time a more forceful use of industrial policy in the rich world has been a trope of left-wing thinkers, which would prioritise to an equal extent the rapid development of the Global South. Now that industrial policy is starting to be used forcefully, it will come to the detriment of the latter.

This consideration is not meant to discourage the use of industrial policy. Overall, the pursuit of a green transition powered by national interest is suboptimal, but is the only path likely to obtain it at a fast enough speed. To a certain extent, this comes to the benefit of the Global South in that many poorer nations are likely to be impacted most and earliest by extreme weather events associated with unfettered global warming (Carleton *et al*, 2020). However, this benefit is indirect, and will therefore likely go missed in global negotiations, which are instead set to become more tense in the face of more evident direct costs for poorer nations (Kleimann, 2023; Terzi, 2022c).

Policymakers must be aware of these negative effects so that the renewed interest in industrial policy does not lead to an excessive enthusiasm with this policy tool, which, as the title of this chapter suggests, should at best be considered a necessary evil to avoid catastrophic climate change.

In particular, in the face of what will represent a scaling down of international cooperation, policymakers should avoid as much as possible measures that risk harming innovation. International scientific cooperation and migration policies, for example, are conducive to the attraction of talent and must be ringfenced as much as possible, so they do not fall prey to broader protectionist reflexes (Neufeld, 2022).

On the international front, countries should be mindful of the repercussions of their national industrial policies. International negative spillovers are to a degree inevitable, but in principle allies and like-minded countries should be spared them as much as possible. This is particularly so in an increasingly fractured geopolitical scenario, if foreign policy alliances are to remain solid. Even just from a political-economy perspective, one cannot expect to impose economic damage on a trade partner on one hand, and expect deep political or security cooperation on the other. Moreover, the national security argument for industrial policy does not really hold relative to trusted partner countries, while the general principle of gains from trade and comparative advantages do.

Instead, in order to prevent allied countries from being forced to engage in a wasteful subsidy war or to raise trade barriers, blunting the positive effect of national industrial policies at home, international economic agreements should be sought. This idea may not be new, but rather responds to the logic of growing regionalisation, which many, including US Treasury Secretary Janet Yellen[44] and European Central Bank President Christine Lagarde (Lagarde, 2022), see as the natural response to safeguard what can be saved as the world moves away from the multilateral trade order (Evenett, 2022). It is in this spirit that the EU and the US should, for example, seek an agreement on sourcing

---

44 Remarks by Secretary of the Treasury Janet L. Yellen on Way Forward for the Global Economy, 13 April 2022, https://home.treasury.gov/news/press-releases/jy1425.

green minerals, which could potentially extend to the G7 as a whole, and then extend to partnerships with Chile, Australia and other like-minded nations.

Building on this idea, and in an effort to expand alliances, nations pursuing aggressive industrial policies at home should reinforce their international climate finance and climate-linked aid to less-developed economies, in particular to fast-track the rollout of green technologies in the Global South, in line with the bilateral agreements with South Africa, Indonesia and Vietnam as part of the international Just Energy Transition Partnerships.

In such as scenario, it is possible to imagine that firms that have developed a technological edge in green sectors will be on the benefitting end of these large decarbonisation investment projects, extending even further the benefits of industrial policy for home-based companies. However, they will also provide local (green) jobs and some much-needed technological transfer to the Global South in a win-win fashion (Tagliapietra and Veugelers, 2021). Benefits to lower-income countries will also come from the fact that these green technologies will be available at a cheaper and more developed stage, also thanks to industrial-policy efforts in richer economies.

All in all, a more aggressive use of industrial policy at home should warrant more active engagement outside national borders to engage partner countries, establish broad economic alliances and mitigate the international economic and political fallouts from industrial policy, and to prevent a green transition pursued in the name of national interest from ending up isolating a country at global level, straining much-needed strategic alliances, and creating lost decades of development for the world's poorest.

References

Acemoglu, D., P. Aghion, L. Bursztyn and D. Hémous (2012) 'The Environment and Directed Technical Change', *American Economic Review* 102(1): 131-66

Aghion, P., R. Bénabou, R. Martin and A. Roulet (2023) 'Environmental Preferences and Technological Choices: Is Market Competition Clean or Dirty?' *AER: Insights* 5(1): 1-20

Aghion, P., C. Hepburn, A. Teytelboym and D. Zenghelis (2019) 'Path dependence, innovation and the economics of climate change', in R. Fouquet (ed) *Handbook on green growth*, Edward Elgar

Aiyar, S., J. Chen, C.H. Ebeke, R. Garcia-Saltos, T. Gudmundsson, A. Ilyina ... J.P. Trevino (2023) 'Geo-Economic Fragmentation and the Future of Multilateralism', *Staff Discussion Notes* No. 2023/001, International Monetary Fund

Baldwin, R. (2016) *The Great Convergence*, Cambridge, Massachusetts: Harvard University Press

Beckert, S. (2015) *Empire of Cotton: A Global History*, New York: Vintage

Boccaletti, G. (2021) *Water: A Biography*, New York: Pantheon

Carleton, T.A., A. Jina, M.T. Delgado, M. Greenstone, T. Houser, S.M. Hsiang ... A. Tianbo Zhang (2020) 'Valuing the Global Mortality Consequences of Climate Change Accounting for Adaptation Costs and Benefits', *NBER Working Paper* 27599, National Bureau of Economic Research

Cerutti, E., G. Gopinath and A. Mohommad (2019) 'The Impact of US-China Trade Tensions', *IMF Blog*, 23 May, International Monetary Fund, available at https://blogs.imf.org/2019/05/23/the-impact-of-us-china-trade-tensions/

Cherif, R. and F. Hasanov (2019) 'The Return of the Policy That Shall Not Be Named: Principles of Industrial Policy', *IMF Working Papers* 19(74), International Monetary Fund

Evenett, S.J. (2022) 'What Endgame for the Deglobalisation Narrative?' *Intereconomics* 57(6): 345-51

Gates, B. (2021) *How to Avoid a Climate Disaster: The Solutions We Have and the Breakthroughs We Need*, New York: Random House

Hausmann, R., J. Hwang and D. Rodrik (2007) 'What You Export Matters', *Journal of Economic Growth* 12(1): 1-25, available at http://link.springer.com/10.1007/s10887-006-9009-4

Kleimann, D. (2023) 'Climate versus trade? Reconciling international subsidy rules with industrial decarbonisation', *Policy Contribution* 03/2023, Bruegel

Lagarde, C. (2022) 'A new global map: European resilience in a changing world', speech at the Peterson Institute for International Economics, 22 April, available at https://www.ecb.europa.eu/press/key/date/2022/html/ecb.sp220422~c43af3db20.en.html

Mazzucato, M. (2013) *The Entrepreneurial State: Debunking Public vs. Private Sector Myths*, London: Anthem Press

Mazzucato, M. (2021) *Mission Economy: A Moonshot Guide to Changing Capitalism*, London: Allen Lane

Milanovic, B. (2019) *Capitalism, Alone: The Future of the System That Rules the World*, First edition, Cambridge, Massachusetts: Belknap Press

Mokyr, J. (2016) *A Culture of Growth: The Origins of the Modern Economy*, Princeton, NJ: Princeton University Press

Moretti, E., C. Steinwender and J. Van Reenen (2019) 'The Intellectual Spoils of War? Defense R&D, Productivity and International Spillovers', *NBER Working Paper* 26483, National Bureau of Economic Research

Neufeld, J. (2022) 'Immigration Powers American Progress', Institute for Progress, 8 February, available at https://progress.institute/immigration-powers-american-progress/

Pack, H. and K. Saggi (2006) 'Is There a Case for Industrial Policy? A Critical Survey', *World Bank Research Observer* 21(2): 267-97

Poitiers, N., A. Sapir, S. Tagliapietra, R. Veugelers and J. Zettelmeyer (2023) 'The EU Net Zero Industry Act and the risk of reviving past failures', *First Glance*, 9 March, Bruegel, available at https://www.bruegel.org/first-glance/eu-net-zero-industry-act-and-risk-reviving-past-failures

Rodrik, D. (2009) *One Economics, Many Recipes: Globalization, Institutions, and Economic Growth*, Princeton, NJ: Princeton Univerity Press

Rodrik, D. (2011) *The Globalization Paradox: Democracy and the Future of the World Economy*, New York: W.W. Norton

Rodrik, D. (2014a) 'Green Industrial Policy', *Oxford Review of Economic Policy* 30(3): 469-91

Rodrik, D. (2014b) 'The Perils of Premature Deindustrialization', *Project Syndicate*, 11 October, available at https://www.project-syndicate.org/commentary/dani-rodrikdeveloping-economies--missing-manufacturing

Rodrik, D. (2016) 'Premature Deindustrialization', *Journal of Economic Growth* 21: 1-33

Russ, K. (2021) 'Yes, US Trade Agreements Led to Economic Gains, Especially in Services, New Report Says', *Trade and Investment Policy Watch*, Peterson Institute for International Economics, available at https://www.piie.com/blogs/trade-and-investment-policy-watch/yes-us-trade-agreements-led-economic-gains-especially

Shiller, R.J. (2019) *Narrative Economics: How Stories Go Viral and Drive Major Economic Events*, First edition, Princeton, NJ: Princeton Univerity Press

Stern, N. and J.E. Stiglitz (2017) *Report of the High-Level Commission on Carbon Prices*, Carbon Pricing Leadership Coalition

Stern, N. and J.E. Stiglitz (2021) 'The Social Cost of Carbon, Risk, Distribution, Market Failures: An Alternative Approach', *NBER Working Paper* 28472, National Bureau of Economic Research

Stern, N. (2006) T*he Economics of Climate Change: The Stern Review,* Cambridge University Press

Tagliapietra, S. (2020) *Global Energy Fundamentals: Economics, Politics, and Technology*, Cambridge University Press

Tagliapietra, S. and R. Veugelers (2021) 'Fostering the Industrial Component of the European Green Deal: Key Principles and Policy Options', *Intereconomics* 56(6): 305–10

Terzi, A. (2022a) 'A Green Industrial Revolution Is Coming', *VoxEU*, 28 June, available at https://cepr.org/voxeu/columns/green-industrial-revolution-coming-0

Terzi, A. (2022b) *Growth for Good: Reshaping Capitalism to Save Humanity from Climate Catastrophe*, Cambridge, Massachusetts: Harvard University Press

Terzi, A. (2022c) 'The Green Revolution Will Not Be Led by International Treaties, but by Persistent Voters', *LSE Business Review*, 15 March, available at https://blogs.lse.ac.uk/businessreview/2022/03/15/the-green-revolution-will-not-be-led-by-international-treaties-but-by-persistent-voters/

Terzi, A., A. Singh and M. Sherwood (2022) 'Industrial Policy for the 21st Century: Lessons from the Past', *Discussion Paper* 157, European Economy, Publications Office of the European Union, available at https://data.europa.eu/doi/10.2765/538421

World Bank (2008) *Commission on growth and development The Growth Report: Strategies for Sustained Growth and Inclusive Development*, Washington DC

7 Industrial strategies for the green transition

Chiara Criscuolo, Antoine Dechezleprêtre and Guy Lalanne

1 Introduction[45]

Governments have been using industrial policy, to varying degrees and in different forms, since the industrial revolution, but until recently these policies had a bad reputation. Among various criticisms, they were seen as instruments that allowed governments to pick winners or support losers, and that were plagued by so-called government failures, eg asymmetry of information, meaning governments do not have sufficient information to select the right projects, technologies or sectors, and are prone to policy capture by rent-seeking players.

Since the 2008 great financial crisis, and even more so since the COVID-19 pandemic and subsequent geopolitical crises, industrial policies have however made a full comeback. The urgency of global societal challenges, and in particular the need to reach climate neutrality by 2050, have heightened the need for government intervention.

There is now wider recognition of the role of industrial policies, as, in a world of imperfect markets, imperfect government intervention might still be welfare-enhancing.

- For example, the inefficient sectoral allocation revealed by the great financial crisis justified intervention to favour reallocation.
- In a period of multifaceted structural change, there is a major need

---

[45] The opinions expressed in this chapter are those of the authors and do not necessarily reflect the official views of the OECD.

for public impetus and guidance, combined with large-scale private investment. This is particularly the case for the investment needed to transition to climate-neutral economies, which the IEA has estimated at $4.2 billion per year by 2030 (IEA, 2021).
- Similarly, the development of new general purpose technologies (eg artificial intelligence) and green technologies with potentially large spillovers requires new rules, new governance frameworks and high-level domestic and international coordination and cooperation. Some of these new (digital) technologies are also characterised by network externalities, which might provide governments with a justification to support the development of these technologies early on, in order to secure global leadership positions. The COVID-19 pandemic and the geopolitical crisis have highlighted how short-run and potential long-term disruptions in global value chains might call for industrial policy interventions – as a complement to trade and competition measures – to ensure the goals of economic resilience and strategic autonomy.
- Finally, industrial policy is being called on in support of other challenges linked to the slowdown of productivity growth (OECD, 2015), coupled with the increase in productivity dispersion and wage inequality (Andrews *et al*, 2016; Berlingieri *et al*, 2017; OECD, 2021b). In particular, Rodrik and Sabel (2019) have highlighted the potential role of industrial policies in reducing geographical and wage inequalities by providing 'good jobs' and supporting the provision of skills to make productivity more inclusive. The importance of focusing on good jobs, opportunities and skill provision – initially triggered by the impacts of globalisation – is becoming ever more relevant, given the potential costs associated with the digital and green transitions.

The world is thus witnessing the development of a new wave of industrial strategies that combine horizontal and targeted instruments, and demand- and supply-side measures. The objectives of these strategies go beyond productivity growth and innovation to include sustainability, resilience and strategic autonomy. Beyond traditional sectoral or place-based orientations, these new industrial strategies focus increasingly on specific technologies or missions. Examples include the US Chips and Science Act and the Inflation Reduction Act, the EU's proposed Net Zero Industry Act and China's 13th Five-Year Plan for Economic and Social Development (2016-2020).

Building on the conceptual framework developed in Criscuolo *et al* (2022a), several of its applications to country- or sector-specific contexts (Anderson *et al*, 2021; Cammeraat *et al*, 2022; Dechezleprêtre *et al*, 2023), and work on the role of innovation and industrial policies to accelerate the development and diffusion of low-carbon technologies (Cervantes *et al*, 2023), this chapter summarises the main lessons learned for the design of effective industrial strategies, with a focus on policies to reach climate neutrality. In fact, the discussion today is no longer about whether industrial policies should exist, but how they should be best designed and implemented.

This chapter emphasises that effective policy design is crucial and should leverage complementarities across different policy instruments within industrial strategies, which Criscuolo *et al* (2022a) defined as a consistent and articulated group of policy instruments aimed at achieving policy objectives. To encompass a broad set of instruments and ensure that many complementarities are taken into consideration, they delineate industrial policy as including "*all interventions intended to improve structurally the performance of the domestic business sector.*" This definition covers both manufacturing and non-manufacturing, and includes horizontal and targeted policies.

These new industrial strategies, if well designed, can help achieve diverse objectives and contribute to addressing societal challenges. Indeed, industrial strategies, through a combination of several policy instruments, including carbon pricing, can support the urgently needed innovations and the adoption of new technologies and business models to achieve climate neutrality, while helping firms and workers adapt to the green and digital transitions, including by focusing on the skills needed to thrive in the new environment. For this, governments might need to be bold and invest in sizeable programmes.

This will not come without significant challenges, not least because of the multiple goals new industrial strategies are asked to achieve, from climate neutrality to strategic autonomy. As the Tinbergen rule (Tinbergen, 1956) highlights, this will require at least as many independent policy instruments as there are policy targets, but also coordination of policies managed by different agencies within countries and, especially when dealing with societal challenges such as climate change, coordination and cooperation across countries.

The rest of the chapter is organised as follows: the next section focuses on the need for green industrial strategies. Section 3 describes the role of innovation and technology diffusion incentives. Section 4 highlights the importance of framework conditions for green industrial strategies, while section 5 focuses on the role of competition. The last section concludes.

2 Green industrial strategies are needed

2.1 Industrial decarbonisation faces a number of market and government failures
Countries representing more than 90 percent of the world economy have adopted or announced targets on climate neutrality by mid-century. Reaching this objective requires rapid deployment of zero-carbon energy sources and production processes across all economic sectors, while reducing emissions unrelated to energy consumption, for example from the agriculture sector.

Some of the carbon-free technologies necessary to reach net-zero emissions already exist, but their cost needs to be reduced so they become fully competitive with carbon-based alternatives and can be deployed rapidly and at scale (IPCC, 2022). Other technologies, such as green hydrogen, are still in their infancy and need to be further developed. According to the IEA, half of the global reductions in energy-related CO_2 emissions up to 2050 will have to come from technologies that are currently at the demonstration or prototype phase (IEA, 2021).

In heavy industry and long-distance transport, the share of emissions reductions from technologies that are still under development today is even higher. For example, the decarbonisation of manufacturing requires not only the adoption of technologies that are close to market, such as a massive increase in renewable electricity generation to enable the electrification of low temperature heat processes, but also the deployment of many technologies that are still far from maturity, notably bio-based products and green hydrogen (Anderson *et al*, 2021).

Despite the urgent need for low-carbon innovation, the current pace of innovation is not in line with the challenge of carbon neutrality. Over the past decade, climate-related frontier innovation, measured as the share of patent filings in climate-related technologies relative to all technology areas, has slowed (Figure 1). Following a period of strong growth between 2004 and 2011, innovation efforts in climate-related technologies declined around 2012, despite the signing of the 2015 Paris Agreement. Moreover, the decrease in low-carbon patenting affects nearly all relevant technologies except for energy storage (batteries), and can be observed across almost all major innovating countries, except Denmark.

Figure 1: Global low-carbon patenting efforts have declined

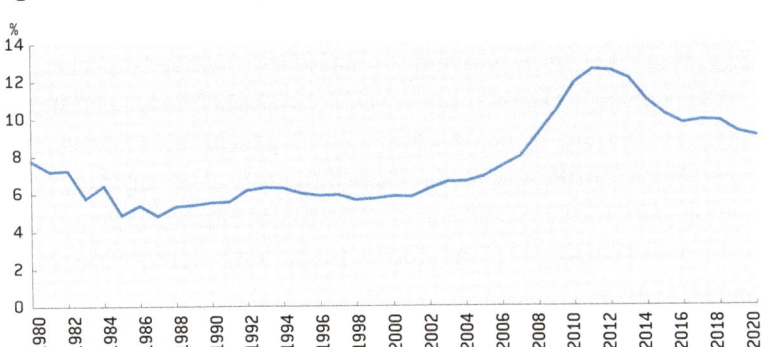

Source: OECD, STI Micro-data Lab: Intellectual Property Database, http://oe.cd/ip-stats, November 2022. Note: Data refers to families of patent applications filed under the Patent Cooperation Treaty (PCT), by earliest filing date.

Numerous barriers and market failures discourage low-carbon innovation.

A first obvious major market failure is related to the existence of large environmental externalities from greenhouse gas emissions. Because carbon remains largely unpriced at the global level (OECD, 2022b), the lack of economic incentives implies low financial returns for low-carbon innovations, limiting the market for these technologies and reducing incentives to develop them in the first place. There is ample empirical evidence that carbon pricing, by encouraging the diffusion of low-carbon technologies, affects innovation activity further up the technology supply chain, favouring R&D in clean technologies and discouraging it in conventional (polluting) technologies (Dechezleprêtre and Kruse, 2022; Calel and Dechezleprêtre, 2016).

Second, green innovations are characterised by the existence of significant knowledge spillovers, which have been shown to be 60 percent greater for low-carbon than for high-carbon technologies (Dechezleprêtre *et al*, 2014). For green innovation, learning-by-doing at the sector- or technology-level is also important. This occurs when the costs to manufacturers or users fall as cumulative output increases (Rubin *et al*, 2015), and accrues not only to the first movers but also, perhaps to a lesser extent, to other firms in the same sector or using the same technology. For example, production costs in renewable energy typically fall by around 15 percent each time the cumulative installed capacity doubles, with higher learning rates in earlier stages of deployment. The presence of learning-by-doing provides a strong justification for deployment subsidies. In the renewable electricity domain, these subsidies (in the form of feed-in tariffs and auctions) have been instrumental in inducing the massive cost reductions observed in the last couple of decades (Nemet, 2019).

Third, imperfections in the capital market, such as reluctance to take on risk and lack of information on the potential value of new innovations, also limit the amount of private capital available for low-carbon R&D. Small firms developing clean innovations face particularly high financial constraints, as shown by Howell (2017). Additional factors include systemic barriers to change and innovation, barriers to competition, lack of co-operation within an innovation system, prevailing norms and habits, and technology lock-in and path dependence (Aghion, 2019).

However, government failures, including a preference for incumbents, lack of policy predictability and stability, and regulatory barriers, may also act as barriers to low-carbon innovation. In particular, climate policy uncertainty is associated with significant decreases in investment, particularly in pollution-intensive sectors that are most exposed to climate policies (Berestycki *et al*, 2022).

2.2 These barriers call for the use of coherent industrial strategies
This complex set of market failures and policy objectives calls for a carefully designed strategy relying on a consistent and articulated group of policy instruments, corresponding to the definition of mission-oriented industrial strategies (Larrue, 2021; Criscuolo *et al*, 2022a).

Mission-oriented innovation policy can be defined as a *"co-ordinated package of research and innovation policy and regulatory measures tailored specifically to address well-defined objectives related to a societal challenge, in a defined timeframe. These measures possibly span different stages of the innovation cycle from research to demonstration and market deployment, mix supply-push and demand-pull instruments, and cut across various policy fields, sectors and disciplines"* (Larrue, 2021). Even though this definition is designed for innovation policies, it is straightforward to extend it to industrial strategies more generally. For instance, mission-oriented industrial strategies are motivated primarily by the societal benefits they can provide and the need to coordinate multiple stakeholders around complex challenges, such as the green transition.

Mission-oriented strategies are becoming increasingly popular in order to address societal challenges, including the green transition and more generally the United Nations' Sustainable Development Goals

(OECD, 2021a). By improving sustainability, mission-oriented strategies can also be understood as contributing to the long-run resilience of industry.

Mission-oriented strategies differ from other types of strategies in that they are "*transformation-oriented*" (Weber and Rohracher, 2012), ie they address the direction of innovation rather than its level, and require coordination across policy domains and across stakeholders (including consumers, governments and research institutions).

Green industrial strategies must therefore feature a variety of industrial policy instruments. Alongside investment incentives, policy instruments on the demand side and governance categories are also required. Criscuolo *et al* (2022a) defined a taxonomy of industrial-policy instruments (Figure 2), which identifies the channels through which policy instruments operate and highlights potential complementarities between them. In addition to keeping with the traditional distinction between horizontal and targeted policies, the taxonomy distinguishes between demand-side instruments and two types of supply-side instrument: those that primarily improve firm performance (such as tax credits, grants, loans or loan guarantees and public support for training within firms) and those that affect industry dynamics (framework instruments including the tax system, capital and labour market policies, competition and trade policies). Green industrial strategies require all these categories of instruments.

This framework can shed light on the design of industrial strategies for the green transition, for example by helping to understand the complementarities between innovation and technology adoption support on one hand and demand-side instruments on the other. The latter can contribute to transformative industrial change by affecting the demand for products through their price, availability or public demand, and have become increasingly common, particularly in transformative mission-oriented strategies. The underlying rationale is the creation of demand to support scaling-up, and in turn lowering costs through learning-by-doing. In the context of targeted industrial strategies, demand-side policies are particularly interesting as they may be less distortive than targeted supply-side policies.

Figure 2: Taxonomy of industrial policy instruments

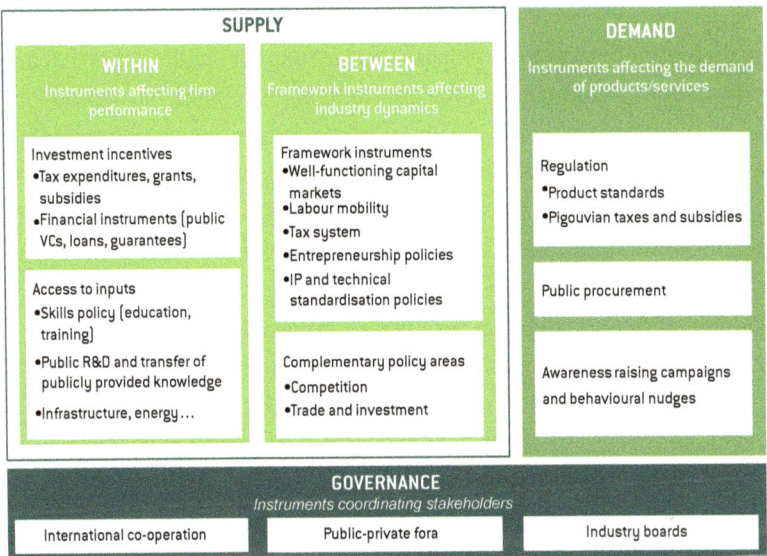

Source: Criscuolo *et al* (2022a). Note: Examples based on the main channel through which policy instruments work.

This framework highlights the need for coherent policy packages adopted as part of industrial strategies. For example, although innovation policies have a major role to play in carbon-neutrality strategies, they are insufficient on their own. While innovation policy can help facilitate the creation of new environmentally friendly technologies, it provides little incentive to adopt these technologies, unless R&D activities manage to make clean technologies competitive with high-carbon alternatives on economic grounds. Until then, incentives for adoption need to be provided by demand-side policies, which can make low-carbon options more attractive economically. However, demand-side policy cannot supplant the need for innovation policy, given the presence of barriers and market failures at the R&D and demonstration stages.

These instruments are thus not substitutes but can instead be mutually reinforcing. Carbon pricing, in particular, is also not sufficient on its own. Carbon prices ensure there will be a demand for new low-carbon technologies. However, they are unlikely to help for technologies that are far from market and require long development timelines. As any technology-neutral instrument, carbon pricing tends to favour technologies that are closest to market and with the shortest payback time. It needs to be complemented by technology-specific support, which, by lowering the cost of future green technologies, can build the case for stronger carbon pricing in the future. The Dutch climate policy package is a good example of an approach that combines a strong commitment to raising carbon prices – through a carbon levy on industrial emissions – with ambitious technology support provided by the Sustainable Energy Transition Incentive Scheme (see section 3.1; Anderson *et al*, 2021).

The digital transformation could be a key enabler for reaching climate goals, thanks to technologies including smart meters, sensors, artificial intelligence (AI), the internet of things (IoT) and blockchain, along with digitally-induced changes in business models and consumption. In the energy sector, demand-side management can help balance the renewables-based electricity system. Digital solutions are equally important on the supply side, for example by accelerating low-carbon innovation with simulations and deep learning. Already, around 20 percent of patents protecting climate change mitigation technologies have a digital component (Amoroso *et al*, 2021). However, digital technologies consume large amounts of energy, implying higher direct energy demand and related carbon emissions, which warrant further efficiency improvements. This suggests that the digital and green transformations need to be tackled jointly through coherent industrial strategies.

Preliminary estimates from the Quantifying Industrial Strategies (QuIS) project, based on evidence from nine countries (Figure 3; Criscuolo *et al*, 2022b; Criscuolo *et al*, 2023) show that green industrial policies, while not negligible, comprise on average 15 percent of industrial policy expenditures (or an average of 0.24 percent of GDP). In addition, green industrial policies are on the rise, as their weight increased by about 10 percent from 2019 to 2021, and is expected to grow even more in the near future. Post-pandemic recovery plans, which are still being ramped up, include in many countries a much higher share of green expenditures (O'Callaghan *et al*, 2021; OECD, 2022; Aulie *et al*, 2023). Similarly, digital industrial policies represent an even lower share of industrial policy expenditures (3 percent on average). Countries' priorities are in fact still dominated by a sectoral approach (Figure 3): policy instruments for specific industries still represent close to 30 percent of expenditures on average, mainly targeting manufacturing, energy and transportation. Country profiles are nevertheless diverse, with, for instance, green expenditures as high as 34 percent in some countries and almost non-existent in others, and digital going from as low as 0 percent to 8 percent.

Figure 3: Industrial policy priorities in nine selected OECD countries*, industrial policy expenditures by eligibility criteria in 2021, % of total industrial policy subsidies and tax expenditures

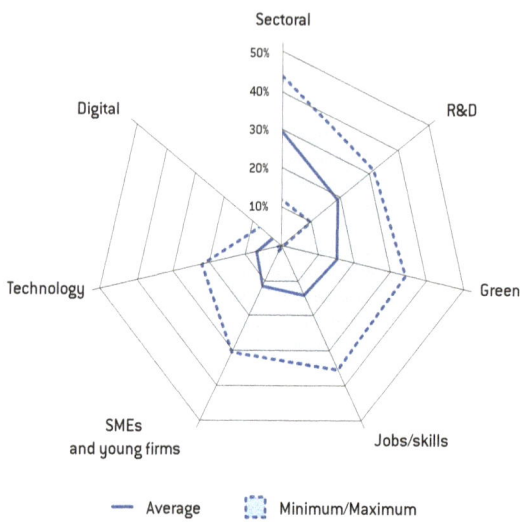

Source: Criscuolo *et al* (2023). Note: * QuIS covers Canada, Denmark, France, Ireland, Israel, Italy, the Netherlands, Sweden and the United Kingdom. Structural policies (ie excluding COVID-19 emergency support). Categories are not mutually exclusive, as policies can be tagged in several categories. Additionally, some policies do not fulfil any of these eligibility criteria. Hence, the numbers in this figure do not add up to 100 percent.

3 Innovation and technology diffusion incentives are the foundation for green industrial strategies

Bringing about the necessary cost reductions to make carbon-free technologies competitive with their high-carbon alternatives should be the primary objective of climate-neutral strategies. This would also help accelerate the diffusion of available technologies, which is critical to reach medium-term carbon emissions reductions. For these reasons, innovation and industrial policies – with a focus on both the development and deployment of low-carbon technologies – should underpin strategies to reach carbon neutrality. Given the wide range of barriers discouraging low-carbon innovation, the theoretical justifications for policy intervention are sound and well established.

Innovation and industrial policies can also complement carbon prices, which are often difficult politically to implement. In fact, technology support policies are more popular among voters and citizens than other climate change policies (including carbon pricing, bans or regulations), making them an attractive option from a public acceptability point of view (Dechezleprêtre *et al*, 2022). In addition, by reducing clean technology adoption costs and boosting the growth of new carbon-efficient firms and sectors, such policies can facilitate the adoption of more ambitious emissions reduction targets, including among emerging economies, where the bulk of future emissions growth is projected to take place.

3.1 Evidence suggests that specific R&D support instruments are required
Public expenditures on research, development and demonstration of low-carbon technologies are a key element of the toolkit available to governments to achieve climate neutrality. However, low-carbon public R&D spending has remained broadly flat as a percentage of GDP over the last 30 years (Cervantes *et al*, 2023).

In addition to public R&D spending on low-carbon technologies, governments can support financially the innovation activities of firms through direct and targeted instruments (eg research grants) or via horizontal and untargeted instruments (R&D tax credits). Horizontal R&D support has indisputable advantages, including its low administrative cost and technological neutrality, but by construction, it cannot be directed and likely benefits mostly technologies that have the greatest short-run returns. As such, tax credits may not be the best policy tool to promote new technologies that are far from the market and require long development timelines. Climate neutrality will require innovation in breakthrough technologies, which cannot be incentivised through horizontal support. Support for an emerging technology justifies a stronger focus on targeted instruments for

R&D, complementing horizontal instruments. Therefore, support for low-carbon R&D undertaken by business should primarily be direct, rather than horizontal. Technology neutrality – even between various low-carbon technologies – tends to favour technologies with the shortest payback time and is therefore not neutral in practice.

For example, the main technology support instrument in the Netherlands is the Sustainable Energy Transition Incentive Scheme (SDE++), which subsidises the additional costs associated with adopting a low-carbon technology. The instrument is allocated to applicants in increasing order of subsidy requirement per tonne of CO_2 reduction. While this allocation design is economically efficient and ensures least-cost decarbonisation in the short run, it favours technologies that are close to the market at the expense of more radical alternatives that are still at an earlier stage of development, such as green hydrogen (Anderson *et al*, 2021).

An analysis of countries' hydrogen strategies provides a worrying example (Cammeraat *et al*, 2022). The ambitious hydrogen production targets at the 2030 horizon included in national hydrogen strategies mostly rely more on financial support for the deployment of new large electrolysers than on direct support for innovation. Between 2008 and 2019, several countries increased public R&D spending on hydrogen, but others cut public spending on R&D by more than half. The focus of public support at the deployment stage is evident in firms' filings of intellectual property rights: while patenting activity on hydrogen production technologies is growing at a very slow pace, the number of hydrogen trademarks has taken off, suggesting that companies are focusing on commercialisation rather than on innovation, and anticipate a growing hydrogen market pulled by government subsidies. This calls for greater targeted support for R&D in green hydrogen.

3.2 Financial instruments also have a role to play
Recent evidence on venture capital (VC) funding for green start-ups shows that, conditional on receiving VC, these firms are less likely to

secure seed funding compared to non-green start-ups, suggesting that in the early phases of product or service development they might be perceived as riskier than their non-green counterparts (Bioret *et al*, 2023). Holding patents also increases the likelihood of being awarded a grant or of receiving VC more for green firms than for non-green firms, suggesting that grant providers and investors potentially wait for green technologies to be de-risked through patent applications before supporting the companies that hold them. The relationship between cumulative grants or cumulative VC received and subsequent innovation is substantially lower for green firms relative to non-green, which might suggest higher development costs for green products and services. Taken together, this evidence demonstrates the importance of reducing barriers to external funding to help high-risk companies raise funds. Low-interest or subsidised loans for young firms and greater mobilisation of government venture capital toward the green transition can help.

4 Framework conditions and demand-side support are also key components of green industrial strategies

Framework policies and demand-side policies complement innovation and technology diffusion policies and are important in enabling frontier firms (in terms of productivity, but also in terms of greenness) to invest and grow. These instruments not only play on strategic decisions within these firms but also directly affect the allocation of resources and their reallocation between firms, which is one of the main drivers of structural change.

This section illustrates the role of framework conditions using three examples: first, with the role of science and skills in enabling the green transition of the industry, then the role of regulations and standards in allowing the diffusion of green technologies, and finally how the carbon price is key to promote green investment and technology adoption. The next section focuses on the contribution of competition and business dynamics to structural change.

4.1 Education, skills and science policies

Education, skills and science policies are necessary to ensure that industry can rely on the right set of skills and that new research into low-carbon technologies is not performed at the expense of the development of other productivity-enhancing innovations.

Re-skilling and up-skilling displaced workers with green skills through active labour market policies and adult training is essential to address social concerns and contribute to reducing skill shortages in the future low-carbon industries. Cross-sector training programmes can ease labour market transitions from surplus to shortage sectors. Timely and transparent information on sectoral labour markets can help workers anticipate future labour needs and policymakers to monitor and accompany the changes. With a view to the longer run, education programmes need to incorporate new material and competences, so the next cohort of workers can cope with the impact of the low-carbon transition in the workplace.

Universities and research institutes play a key role in developing emerging green technologies. For instance, patents in automotive emerging technologies (particularly hydrogen, and to a lesser extent autonomous vehicles and electric vehicles) are more likely to cite university patents and the academic literature than patents in traditional combustion engine technologies (Figure 4). This result is confirmed when looking at the share of patents filed in collaboration between firms and academic institutions.

Figure 4: Emerging technologies are strongly linked with universities and scientific research, automotive technology patent citations, 2000-2019

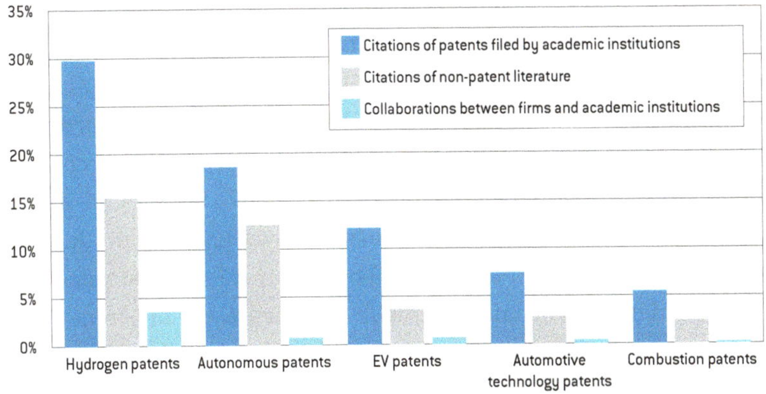

[Bar chart showing percentages for Hydrogen patents, Autonomous patents, EV patents, Automotive technology patents, and Combustion patents across three categories: Citations of patents filed by academic institutions, Citations of non-patent literature, and Collaborations between firms and academic institutions.]

Source: Dechezleprêtre *et al* (2023), based on STI Micro-data Lab: Intellectual Property Database, http://oe.cd/ipstats, June 2022. Note: A collaboration is defined as a patent family with at least two applicants, one being a firm and another a non-firm entity (eg universities, governments, hospitals). Patents filed by academic institutions only include patents for which the type of applicant (individual, company, government entity) is identified. A patent is labelled as citing an academic patent if at least one application in the patent family cited a patent filed by an academic institution. A patent family is labelled as citing the academic (non-patent) literature if at least one patent in the patent family cited a serial/journal/periodical citation, a chemical abstract citation, or a biological abstract citation. When labelling a patent family as citing the non-patent literature, the sample is restricted to those patent families that have at least one patent application at the EPO, USPTO or WIPO (PCT applications). This restriction is necessary as non-patent literature citations are only available for patents filed in one of these three offices.

4.2 Regulatory standards

Setting regulatory standards is another important complementary policy, which can help reduce uncertainty and facilitate coordination. Standardisation can strongly promote the diffusion of technologies with network externalities, such as carbon capture and storage (CCS; Anderson *et al*, 2021) or green hydrogen (Cammeraat *et al*, 2022).

For instance, defining liabilities would allow investors in CCS to more accurately price and potentially insure this risk. The industry, the financial sector and the different levels of government have to work together to explore potential risk-sharing solutions should such liabilities create a barrier to market development.

For hydrogen, standards are needed on the purity of hydrogen for passenger vehicles, on the gas composition for cross-border sales, on safety measures (such as materials used for hydrogen tanks) and on how to measure lifecycle environmental impacts from hydrogen production (IEA, 2019), and for blending hydrogen into the gas grid. As it is impossible to assess from hydrogen itself how it has been produced, accounting standards for the origin of hydrogen are needed to create a market for blue (out of natural gas with CCS) or green (out of renewable electricity through electrolysis) hydrogen.

Hydrogen can be produced on-site, but also in a centralised manner before being stored and transported via tanks or pipes, in a pure form or blended with natural gas. This wide variation in the modes of producing, storing and transporting hydrogen suggests that regulatory standards can facilitate the creation of a dynamic hydrogen market.

Harmonisation of standards and regulations related to the use of recycled products is necessary to promote the circular economy and, ultimately, address Scope 3 emissions (ie linked to the supply chain). This is of particular importance in the steel industry, where relabelling by-products of steel production at the European level (eg slag and fly ash) from 'waste' to 'product' with all due care to avoid pollution hazard, would reduce the administrative burden associated with purchasing scrap for companies while increasing import opportunities.

Standardisation faces a trade-off: advancing fast on a national basis or slower at the international level. For example, China has at time of writing adopted 93 standards for hydrogen infrastructure and applications. Even EU countries do not yet rely on EU standards. For example, Italy has adopted a national regulation on hydrogen fuelling stations. Most countries recognise that standards are important and should ideally be set at the international level, and international cooperation related to hydrogen is thus mostly about harmonising codes and standards.

4.3 Carbon pricing

Carbon pricing is a cornerstone of the policy toolbox for industrial decarbonisation. It is essential to have clear trajectories of gradually increasing carbon prices over the next decades to establish a level playing field and make the business case for a low-carbon transition. In this respect, the design of the Dutch carbon levy (Anderson *et al*, 2021) is particularly interesting, with an increasing price path and a levy base that phases in gradually over time. The levy adds a floating contribution on top of the EU ETS allowance price to yield a fixed price on Dutch emissions covered by the system. This price floor provides more certainty about future prices and protects investors against volatility of EU ETS allowance prices. Such a design can provide forward guidance to investors without immediately imposing new taxes on businesses in the context of high uncertainty about short- and medium-term demand and liquidity. Since expectations of future prices, rather than current prices, determine innovation, long term regulatory consistency is crucial for new technology development. Commitments to raise carbon prices in the future and clear carbon-price trajectories can already induce innovation even if current carbon prices are low. Carbon contracts-for-difference (CCfD), experimented on in Germany, can decrease uncertainty thanks to forward contracts on the price of abated greenhouse gases (Neuhoff *et al*, 2022).

Nevertheless, all carbon pricing instruments in the Netherlands (carbon levy, European carbon market, energy tax and energy surcharge) include competitiveness provisions which grant extensive preferential treatment to energy-intensive users, for instance in the chemicals, refineries and basic metals sectors. These can take various forms, including tax exemptions, regressive tax rates and free emissions allowances. This naturally erodes the carbon pricing signal, reduces the cost-effectiveness of the policy instrument and generates equity concerns as small firms typically face much higher energy and carbon prices than large incumbents (Anderson *et al*, 2021).

In this respect, strong financial support for low-carbon technology adoption should be seen as an alternative, not a complement, to the provision of generous exemptions to energy-intensive industry, and should allow governments to gradually remove such preferential treatment, which stands in the way of long-term decarbonisation. The convergence of climate policy ambitions at EU level and beyond – notably among large emitters from the developed and developing world alike – as well as the progress made towards the introduction of a carbon border adjustment mechanism, are other justifications for removing these exemptions.

5 Competition and business dynamism are key for structural change

Competition policy is closely linked to industrial strategies, favouring an efficient allocation of production factors between firms, and thereby contributing to aggregate productivity and structural change.

At the same time, industrial policy also has an impact on competition.

- First, industrial policy, by promoting technology adoption, innovation and entrepreneurship, can foster competition by supporting business dynamism.
- Second, targeted industrial policies, by giving an explicit advantage to some firms over others, might compromise competitive neutrality principles, while horizontal industrial policies are less likely to have a detrimental effect on competition (see OECD, 2009).

In general, targeted industrial policies should be competitively neutral. In case competitive neutrality is not feasible to achieve the desired objective, interventions should be narrow, temporary and monitored closely (OECD, 2020). Inclusiveness and technology-neutrality are essential to ensure that in practice industrial policies do not discriminate unduly between firms. This issue is even more meaningful for instruments that are by essence discriminatory, such as incentives provided on a competitive basis (grants, loan or equity financing).

However, even if they might be at risk of hurting competition, targeted industrial policies that are designed to fix market failures or to address externalities do not necessarily affect competition negatively. By increasing the returns for a given project, they may even enable more firms to enter into that market (Aghion *et al*, 2015a).

Both theory and evidence suggest the existence of significant complementarities between industrial and competition policies. Competition promotes the most efficient firms and provides incentives for innovation, while industrial policy increases the ability to innovate and protects the rights of innovators, thus guaranteeing the returns to innovation and investment. For example, Acemoglu *et al* (2018) highlighted the fact that R&D support might not be effective in the absence of efficient exit policies. Interestingly, Aghion *et al* (2015b) showed that there is a complementarity between competition and intellectual property rights (patents) in fostering innovation. Indeed, with stronger patent rights, the incentives to escape competition are higher.

Besides innovation, competition is also a major driver of technology adoption and of organisational and managerial improvements, since competitive pressures boost returns to adoption (Andrews *et al*, 2016).

Finally, most of the arguments developed in this section also apply to international trade, which can contribute to increasing competition on domestic markets and expanding the size of the market for domestic firms. For instance, comparative advantage is an important lever to decrease the cost of green hydrogen, which should be produced where renewable energy is more abundant and cheaper (Cammeraat *et al*, 2022). Importantly, reconciling green investment support and trade rules is necessary (Kleimann, 2023).

5.1 The example of the automotive sector
Ongoing trends in the automotive sector, such as the major investment required for the shift to connected, automated, shared and electric

(CASE) vehicles, the network externalities linked to the increasing role of data or the potential increase in market segmentation could reduce competition in the medium run. High upfront investment needs, network externalities and high economies of scale required in this sector might indeed lead to a higher level of concentration in this industry. This could be reinforced by the evolution towards increasingly segmented markets.

Dechezleprêtre *et al* (2023) showed that the automotive sector experienced very significant growth in mergers and acquisitions (M&As) before the COVID-19 crisis. Given the likelihood of a new wave of M&As after the crisis, the level of competition and contestability in the ecosystem may decrease in the near future, thereby threatening innovation and the benefits for consumers.

Nevertheless, M&As and concentration are also an effective way to acquire new knowledge, to integrate new technologies, know-how and talents in the products, and to benefit from economies of scale or scope. M&A is often cited as a strategy to acquire external knowledge (Cassiman *et al*, 2005; Phillips and Zhdanov, 2012). If this is indeed the case, the patent portfolio of target firms should reflect the technologies of interest for acquiring firms. As transactions within the automotive sector can have other motives, such as industrial synergies or entry in a new market, target firms outside the automotive sector are more likely to be bought for their technologies.

Compared to firms that are not the target of a merger or an acquisition, target firms outside the automotive sector have a much higher proportion of patents in autonomous vehicle technologies (Figure 5). However, they have significantly lower shares of patents related to combustion engines. Target firms in the automotive sector tend to have higher shares of patents in combustion and electric engine technologies.

Figure 5: Automotive sector, patent portfolio of selected firms, by technology, 2016-2019

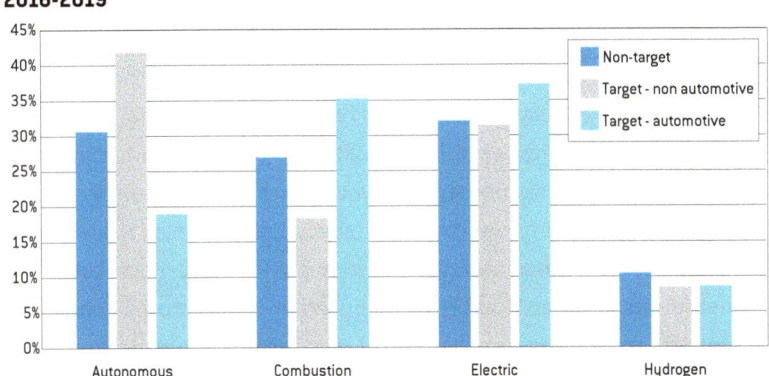

Source: Dechezleprêtre *et al* (2023), based on Zephyr data. Note: This figure covers the deals in the following categories: 'genuine acquisition', 'further acquisition', 'minority stakes' and 'joint venture'. Non-target firms correspond to firms having filed patents in at least one of the four selected technologies.

In this context, it is important to find new ways to support collaboration between firms, while preserving competition and a level playing field (eg industrial alliances in the EU). This calls for:

- Ensuring that competition authorities have adequate tools to monitor and enforce merger control. As acquisitions of young firms often remain below applicable thresholds, analyses (Crémer *et al*, 2019; Shapiro, 2019; Digital Competition Expert Panel, 2019; Kamepalli *et al*, 2020; Argentesi *et al*, 2020; Motta and Peitz, 2021) have suggested reassessing them in order to review potentially problematic mergers. Although this literature mainly focuses on acquisitions by large digital platforms, its conclusions may also apply to the automotive ecosystem, which is becoming more digital and prone to network effects.
- Ensuring that young and fast-growing firms can choose between several exit strategies. Being bought by a larger firm should remain a possibility, but young ventures should also be able to opt

for initial public offerings (IPO) or private equity funding. The development of financial markets is therefore key to allow for the growth of promising firms and to limit market concentration in the medium run. This seems to be particularly relevant for the European automotive ecosystem, which is often a target of cross-border transactions (Dechezleprêtre *et al*, 2023). Publicly provided financial instruments can also support young and fast-growing firms, especially in downturns when capital markets are more risk averse.

- Finally, competition can also be fostered by limiting market segmentation. This can notably be achieved by international cooperation on regulatory and technical standards, for instance on autonomous vehicles (eg homologation; see Fernandez Llorca and Gomez, 2021) and emissions. Technical standardisation must nevertheless balance the risk of premature standardisation against the need to provide clarity to investors and facilitate investments (see Cammeraat *et al*, 2022, on hydrogen). In addition, clear data governance rules are needed to facilitate the deployment of connected and autonomous vehicles.

6 Conclusion

Industrial policy has made a comeback and is seen as a way to achieve an increasing number of goals. Industrial strategies are indeed necessary to deal with urgent societal challenges, such as climate change. As many of the technologies required to reach carbon neutrality are still in the labs and innovation in green technologies seems to have reached a plateau, there is a strong and urgent need to stimulate these innovations and, more generally, to transform economies towards net-zero emissions, leaving no one behind. Green industrial strategies, which still represent a small share of industrial policy, even if they are growing, are therefore required to speed up the green transition.

Green industrial strategies rely on important pillars, such as incentives for innovation and technology diffusion or carbon pricing, but deserve a more encompassing approach that takes into consideration other aspects of industrial policy. In particular, this chapter stresses the importance of education, skills and science policies, regulatory standards and competition and business dynamism, which are shown to be highly complementary to green technology support and carbon pricing. In order to succeed, these policies need to be coherent and provide clear trajectories and long-term consistency.

Industrial and competition policies have often been considered as antagonistic, but major complementarities exist between industrial and competition policies. For green industrial strategies to succeed, they need to go hand in hand with competition policies to continue to foster business dynamism, business entry and the efficient allocation of resources.

The chapter also indicates fruitful avenues for future research. First, the chapter summarises the results of novel efforts aimed at quantifying industrial strategies. This is the first step of a long journey, the final goal of which is to evaluate industrial strategies. Second, the chapter focuses on industrial strategies for the green transition, but, as highlighted in the chapter, achieving climate neutrality and succceding in the green transition requires relying on a sustainable digital transition and the buy-in of voters. For this reason, an important area of work could be on how industrial strategies can best support an inclusive twin transition.

References

Acemoglu, D., U. Akcigit, H. Alp, N. Bloom and W. Kerr (2018) 'Innovation, Reallocation, and Growth', *American Economic Review* 108(11): 3450-3491, available at https://doi.org/10.1257/aer.20130470

Aghion, P., C. Hepburn, A. Teytelboym and D. Zenghelis (2019) 'Path dependence, innovation and the economics of climate change', in R. Fouquet (ed) *Handbook on green growth*, Edward Elgar, available at https://doi.org/10.4337/9781788110686.00011

Aghion, P., J. Cai, M. Dewatripont, L. Du, A. Harrison and P. Legros (2015a) 'Industrial Policy and Competition', *American Economic Journal: Macroeconomics* 7(4): 1–32, available at https://doi.org/10.1257/mac.20120103

Aghion, P., P. Howitt and S. Prantl (2015b) 'Patent rights, product market reforms, and innovation', *Journal of Economic Growth* 20(3): 223-262, available at https://doi.org/10.1007/s10887-015-9114-3

Amoroso, S., L. Aristodemou, C. Criscuolo, A. Dechezleprêtre, H. Dernis, N. Grassano ... A. Tübke (2021) *World Corporate Top R&D investors: Paving the way for climate neutrality*, European Commission Joint Research Centre and Organisation for Economic Co-operation and Development, available at https://doi.org/10.2760/49552

Anderson, B., E. Cammeraat, A. Dechezleprêtre, L. Dressler, N. Gonne, G. Lalanne ... K. Theodoropoulos (2021) 'Policies for a climate-neutral industry: Lessons from the Netherlands', *OECD Science, Technology and Industry Policy Papers* No. 108, Organisation for Economic Co-operation and Development, available at https://doi.org/10.1787/a3a1f953-en

Andrews, D., C. Criscuolo and P. Gal (2016) 'The Best versus the Rest: The Global Productivity Slowdown, Divergence across Firms and the Role of Public Policy', *OECD Productivity Working Papers* No. 5, Organisation for Economic Co-operation and Development, available at https://doi.org/10.1787/24139424

Argentesi, E., P. Buccirossi, E. Calvano, T. Duso, A. Marrazzo and S. Nava (2020) 'Merger Policy in Digital Markets: An Ex-Post Assessment', *Journal of Competition Law & Economics* 17(1): 95-140, available at https://doi.org/10.1093/joclec/nhaa020

Aulie, F., A. Dechezleprêtre, F. Galindo-Rueda, C. Kögel, I. Pitavy and A. Vitkova (2023), "Did COVID-19 accelerate the green transition?: An international assessment of fiscal spending measures to support low-carbon technologies", *OECD Science, Technology and Industry Policy Papers*, No. 151, OECD Publishing, Paris, https://doi.org/10.1787/5b486c18-en.

Berestycki, C., S. Carattini, A. Dechezleprêtre and T. Kruse (2022) 'Measuring and assessing the effects of climate policy uncertainty', *OECD Economics Department Working Papers* No. 1724, Organisation for Economic Co-operation and Development, available at https://doi.org/10.1787/34483d83-en

Berlingieri, G., P. Blanchenay and C. Criscuolo (2017) 'The great divergence(s)', *OECD Science, Technology and Industry Policy Papers* No. 39, Organisation for Economic Co-operation and Development, available at https://doi.org/10.1787/953f3853-en

Bioret, L., A. Dechezleprêtre and P. Kelly (2023) *The New Green Economy: Venture Capital, Innovation and Business Success in Cleantech Startups*, Organisation for Economic Co-operation and Development, forthcoming

Calel, R. and A. Dechezleprêtre (2016) 'Environmental Policy and Directed Technological Change: Evidence from the European Carbon Market', *Review of Economics and Statistics* 98(1): 173-191, available at https://doi.org/10.1162/rest_a_00470

Cammeraat, E., A. Dechezleprêtre and G. Lalanne (2022) 'Innovation and industrial policies for green hydrogen', *OECD Science, Technology and Industry Policy Papers* No. 125, Organisation for Economic Co-operation and Development, available at https://doi.org/10.1787/f0bb5d8c-en

Cassiman, B., M.G. Colombo, P. Garrone and R. Veugelers (2005) 'The impact of M&A on the R&D process', *Research Policy* 34(2): 195-220, available at https://doi.org/10.1016/j.respol.2005.01.002

Cervantes, M., C. Criscuolo, A. Dechezleprêtre and D. Pilat (2023) 'Driving low-carbon innovations for climate neutrality', *OECD Science, Technology and Industry Policy Papers* No. 143, Organisation for Economic Co-operation and Development, available at https://doi.org/10.1787/8e6ae16b-en

Crémer, J., Y.-A. De Montjoye and H. Schweitzer (2019) *Competition policy for the digital era*, European Commission, Directorate-General for Competition, available at https://ec.europa.eu/competition/publications/reports/kd0419345enn.pdf

Criscuolo, C., L. Díaz, G. Lalanne, L. Guillouet, C.-É. van de Put, C. Weder and H. Zazon Deutsch (2023) 'Quantifying industrial strategies across nine OECD countries', *OECD Science, Technology and Industry Policy Papers* No. 150, Organisation for Economic Co-operation and Development, available at https://doi.org/10.1787/5f2dcc8e-en

Criscuolo, C., N. Gonne, K. Kitazawa and G. Lalanne (2022a) 'An industrial policy framework for OECD countries: Old debates, new perspectives', *OECD Science, Technology and Industry Policy Papers* No. 127, Organisation for Economic Co-operation and Development, available at https://dx.doi.org/10.1787/0002217c-en

Criscuolo, C., G. Lalanne and L. Díaz (2022b) 'Quantifying industrial strategies (QuIS): Measuring industrial policy expenditures', *OECD Science, Technology and Industry Working Papers* No. 2022/05, Organisation for Economic Co-operation and Development, available at https://doi.org/10.1787/ae351abf-en

Dechezleprêtre, A., L. Díaz, M. Fadic and G. Lalanne (2023) 'How the green and digital transitions are reshaping the automotive ecosystem', *OECD Science, Technology and Industry Policy Papers* No. 144, Organisation for Economic Co-operation and Development, available at https://doi.org/10.1787/f1874cab-en

Dechezleprêtre, A., A. Fabre, T. Kruse, B. Planterose, A. Sanchez Chico and S. Stantcheva (2022) 'Fighting climate change: International attitudes toward climate policies', *OECD Economics Department Working Papers* No. 1714, Organisation for Economic Co-operation and Development, available at https://doi.org/10.1787/3406f29a-en

Dechezleprêtre, A. and T. Kruse (2022) 'The effect of climate policy on innovation and economic performance along the supply chain: A firm- and sector-level analysis', *OECD Environment Working Papers* No. 189, Organisation for Economic Co-operation and Development, available at https://doi.org/10.1787/3569283a-en

Dechezleprêtre, A., R. Martin and M. Mohnen (2014) 'Knowledge spillovers from clean and dirty technologies', *CEP Discussion Papers* CEPDP1300, Centre for Economic Performance, London School of Economics and Political Science, available at http://eprints.lse.ac.uk/60501/

Digital Competition Expert Panel (2019) *Unlocking digital competition*, HM Treasury, available at https://assets.publishing.service.gov.uk/government/uploads/system/uploads/attachment_data/file/785547/unlocking_digital_competition_furman_review_web.pdf

Fernandez Llorca, D. and E. Gomez (2021) *Trustworthy Autonomous Vehicles*, JRC Science for Policy Report, European Commission Joint Research Centre, available at https://doi.org/10.2760/120385

Howell, S. (2017) 'Financing Innovation: Evidence from R&D Grants', *American Economic Review* 107(4): 1136-1164, available at https://doi.org/10.1257/aer.20150808

IEA (2021) *Net Zero by 2050: A Roadmap for the Global Energy Sector*, International Energy Agency, available at https://dx.doi.org/10.1787/c8328405-en

IEA (2019) *The Future of Hydrogen: Seizing today's opportunities*, International Energy Agency, available at https://www.iea.org/reports/the-future-of-hydrogen

IPCC (2022) *Climate Change 2022: Mitigation of Climate Change. Contribution of Working Group III to the Sixth Assessment Report of the Intergovernmental Panel on Climate Change*, Cambridge University Press

Kamepalli, S., R. Rajan and L. Zingales (2020) 'Kill Zone', *NBER Working Paper* 27146, National Bureau of Economic Research, available at https://doi.org/10.3386/w27146

Kleimann, D. (2023) 'Climate versus trade? Reconciling international subsidy rules with industrial decarbonisation', *Policy Contribution* 03/2023, Bruegel, available at https://www.bruegel.org/sites/default/files/2023-02/PB%2003%202023.pdf

Larrue, P. (2021) 'The design and implementation of mission-oriented innovation policies: A new systemic policy approach to address societal challenges', *OECD Science, Technology and Industry Policy Papers* No. 100, Organisation for Economic Co-operation and Development, available at https://dx.doi.org/10.1787/3f6c76a4-en

Motta, M. and M. Peitz (2021) 'Big tech mergers', *Information Economics and Policy* 54: 100868, available at https://doi.org/10.1016/j.infoecopol.2020.100868

Nemet, G. (2019) *How Solar Energy Became Cheap: A Model for Low-Carbon Innovation*, Routledge, available at https://doi.org/ISBN 9780367136598

Neuhoff, K., N. May and J. Richstein (2022) 'Financing renewables in the age of falling technology costs', *Resource and Energy Economics* 70: 101330, available at https://doi.org/10.1016/j.reseneeco.2022.101330.

O'Callaghan, B., N. Yau, E. Murdock, D. Tritsch, A. Janz, A. Blackwood ... L. Heeney (2021) *Global Recovery Observatory*, Oxford University Economic Recovery Project, available at https://recovery.smithschool.ox.ac.uk/tracking/

OECD (2022a) *Assessing environmental impact of measures in the OECD Green Recovery Database*, OECD Policy Responses to Coronavirus (COVID-19), Organisation for Economic Co-operation and Development, available at https://doi.org/10.1787/3f7e2670-en

OECD (2022b) *Pricing Greenhouse Gas Emissions: Turning Climate Targets into Climate Action*, OECD Series on Carbon Pricing and Energy Taxation, Organisation for Economic Co-operation and Development, available at https://doi.org/10.1787/e9778969-en

OECD (2021a) *Industrial Policy for the Sustainable Development Goals: Increasing the Private Sector's Contribution*, Organisation for Economic Co-operation and Development, available at https://dx.doi.org/10.1787/2cad899f-en

OECD (2021b) *The Role of Firms in Wage Inequality: Policy Lessons from a Large Scale Cross-Country Study*, Organisation for Economic Co-operation and Development, available at https://doi.org/10.1787/7d9b2208-en

OECD (2020) *COVID-19: Competition policy actions for governments and competition authorities*, Organisation for Economic Co-operation and Development, available at https://www.oecd.org/daf/competition/COVID-19-competition-policy-actions-for-governments-and-competition-authorities.pdf

OECD (2015) *The Future of Productivity*, Organisation for Economic Co-operation and Development, available at https://doi.org/10.1787/9789264248533-en

OECD (2009) *Competition Policy, Industrial Policy and National Champions*, Organisation for Economic Co-operation and Development, available at http://www.oecd.org/daf/competition/44548025.pdf

Phillips, G. and A. Zhdanov (2012) 'R&D and the Incentives from Merger and Acquisition Activity', *Review of Financial Studies* 26(1): 34-78, available at https://doi.org/10.1093/rfs/hhs109

Rodrik, D. and C. Sabel (2019) 'Building a Good Jobs Economy', *Harvard Kennedy School Faculty Research Working Paper* RWP20-001, available at https://scholarship.law.columbia.edu/cgi/viewcontent.cgi?article=3612&context=faculty_scholarship

Rubin, E., I.M.L. Azevedo, P. Jaramillo and S. Yeh (2015) 'A review of learning rates for electricity supply technologies', *Energy Policy* 86: 198-218, available at https://doi.org/10.1016/j.enpol.2015.06.011

Shapiro, C. (2019) 'Protecting Competition in the American Economy: Merger Control, Tech Titans, Labor Markets', *Journal of Economic Perspectives* 33(3): 69-93, available at https://doi.org/10.1257/jep.33.3.69

Tinbergen, J. (1956) *Economic Policy: Principles and Design*, North-Holland, available at http://hdl.handle.net/1765/16740

Weber, K. and H. Rohracher (2012) 'Legitimizing research, technology and innovation policies for transformative change', *Research Policy* 41(6): 1037-1047, available at https://doi.org/10.1016/j.respol.2011.10.015

8 A more globally minded European green industrial policy

Ricardo Hausmann and Ketan Ahuja

"I want Europe to be the first climate neutral continent in the world by 2050," proclaimed Ursula von der Leyen, President of the European Commission, in the context of discussions about the European Green Deal in December 2019. The goal at the time sounded bold and inspiring. To back it up, the European Commission announced ambitious targets for 2030: a 55 percent emissions reduction from 1990 levels, which corresponds to a 40 percent reduction from 2019 levels. To achieve this, Europe is adopting a set of directives and policies, including an expansion of its carbon trading mechanism to include air and shipping transport, and the adoption of the Carbon Border Adjustment Mechanism (CBAM). In addition, in the context of the recovery from COVID-19, it is putting on the table €750 billion (€360 billion in loans and €390 billion in grants) in NextGenerationEU funds to support decarbonisation and digitalisation processes.

If the plans are successful and all goals are achieved, the EU will have reduced global emissions by 2050 by a paltry 9 percent. Obviously, this is too little to do much to change the course of global warming.

Moreover, decarbonisation is only one half of Europe's green industrial policy equation. The other half, to *"make sure that the future of industry is made in Europe,"* featured prominently in Ursula von der Leyen's State of the Union speech in 2022 (Von der Leyen, 2022). In Europe's post-COVID-19 economy, wracked by supply-chain disruption, strategic competition over critical minerals, and an uncomfortable dependence on Russian oil and gas and Chinese solar panels, it is easy to see where von der Leyen is coming from. Europe's policy prescriptions though – to mine its own minerals and make its own green hydrogen and solar panels – are harder to understand.

Both of Europe's goals suffer from the wrong framing, because they neglect the global dimensions of global warming and the future of industry. On decarbonisation, Europe's goal must obviously be to reduce global emissions. Reducing Europe's emissions to zero does very little, unless Europe can bring the other 91 percent of emissions along with it. On the future of industry, Europe's goal should be first to maximise the global value of the clean economy, and then to claim as much as it can.

To be fair, many of the current European policies and policy proposals are sensitive to the international dimension. Europe's CBAM attempts to create a level playing field that applies the same price to carbon emissions embodied in industrial production, whether they take place domestically or abroad[46]. Similarly, the proposed Critical Raw Materials Club appears to aim in part at developing critical mineral supply chains and deposits around the world, and the Green Deal Industrial Plan affirms a commitment to open trade in principle (European Commission, 2023).

But 'Europe First' policy goals – decarbonising the European continent and making what Europe needs domestically – mean that Europe might not consider valuable approaches and instruments because of a lack of a framework to justify them. Here, we reframe the goals of Europe to include these global dimensions, and draw out some of the implications.

---

46 See European Commssion press release of 14 July 2021, 'Carbon Border Adjustment Mechanism: Questions and Answers', https://ec.europa.eu/commission/presscorner/detail/en/qanda_21_3661.

The silent prologue to 'Europe First' goals

'Europe First' goals (to be the first net-zero continent and to make the future of industry in Europe) suppose a set of unspoken assumptions on how the whole will respond to its parts. We should bring these assumptions into the light to see how realistic they are.

Europe aims to be the first net-zero continent. One implicit assumption is that by promoting the technological innovations needed to reduce emissions, it will bring the costs of clean technologies down for everyone and hence accelerate global decarbonisation. Maybe, but maybe not. Europe trying to decarbonise faster than the rest of the world could increase the relative price of scarce resources including lithium, copper and cobalt, and hence slow everyone else's decarbonisation efforts. It might also cause Europe to try to do things in Europe that can be more efficiently done elsewhere, such as capturing solar and wind energy, and hence become uncompetitive and decline economically, with uncertain effects on global emissions. Europe could also end up protecting its domestic market in ways that may reduce the incentives others have to decarbonise in order to meet Europe's emission standards.

By making the future of industry in Europe, Europe hopes to supply the world with what it needs to make its own energy transition, and thereby profit from the rest of the world as it attempts to decarbonise. But it is equally likely that Europe's industrial policy could be zero sum: by attempting to localise supply chains domestically, Europe could disrupt efficient allocation of capital, undermine economies of scale and needlessly transfer wealth to shareholders of companies by engaging in subsidy races with other industrial nations.

For a guide on how to make industrial policy zero sum, Europe just needs to look across the Atlantic. In late 2017, Amazon announced it would create a second headquarters somewhere on the North American continent. Over 200 municipal economic development agencies across the US lined up to lavish tax breaks, subsidies and funding on one of the world's largest companies in the hopes of attracting its 50,000 workers.

More than a year later, Amazon selected Washington DC and New York (its presumptive frontrunners from the start), having extracted offers of over a billion dollars in state funds for its shareholders. Getting drawn too far into a subsidy race with Europe's strategic competitors to localise clean industries could have the same effect.

All of this is to say that the general equilibrium effects of a 'Europe First' industrial policy are opaque. Green industrial policy in Europe takes place under conditions of fundamental uncertainty: not only are there obvious uncertainties over which technologies are likely to win in the search for a cleaner future, but there are also many degrees of freedom on how the world might respond to Europe First efforts, making it hard to know whether they will really benefit Europe. Better to start with the right goals: to reduce global emissions, and to maximise the global clean economy (while claiming as much of it as Europe can).

What is industrial policy?

Part of Europe's challenge is that it is not always clear what industrial policy means. Economists have long questioned whether industrial policy should exist at all. As the traditional argument goes, governments should not pick winners: they should let the market allocate resources across industries to reflect consumer preferences and technological possibilities. Governments rarely have superior information to justify interfering in the market, and even when they do, they shouldn't make matters worse by adding government failures (such as rent seeking) onto market failures.

But before there can be market regulation, there must be a market. A cardinal function of government is to co-create markets alongside changing technology and social relations. Industrial policy is about creating the ingredients needed for an industry to thrive in the first place: the focus is on the rich web of (often vertical-specific) public goods that modern industries need. Cars require roads, traffic lights, rules and cops. Air travel requires airports, air traffic controllers, safety regulations, overflight rights and visas. Electricity systems require standardised voltage and frequency. In other words, every technology presumes a set of public goods that are relatively specific and that need to be provided for an industry to thrive. This may involve creating product standards for market players to adhere to, inspecting product safety and quality so customers have the confidence to buy, adapting infrastructure to product needs, training the workers industries will require, and coordinating research ecosystems, companies and investors around particular technology or industry roadmaps. Governments need to engage deeply with industry to supply the public goods needed for industries to take off.

Industrial policy can also involve internalising learning externalities, solving coordination problems and de-risking private investment. Without intervention, market outcomes in these cases may be inefficient because the incentives faced by certain activities are weak relative to the benefits that society may obtain from them. This is the general case in favour of subsidies. R&D subsidies may compensate for learning externalities. Advance market commitments may solve coordination problems. Grants de-risk investment. But over-emphasising subsidies may shift the focus away from the public goods that industries need in order to thrive.

Industrial policy's cardinal rule is never to stray too far from an industry's inherent economics, or a region's underlying comparative advantage, while helping to accumulate the capabilities needed to evolve that comparative advantage in purposeful directions. Put differently, industrial policy can do many things, from promoting good jobs, to reviving the Rust Belt, to bringing production home, so long as it does not try to step beyond what is economically possible given the state of technology, or a region's production costs relative to those of its competitors. States that do so at scale risk grave public waste and self-defeating policies.

China knows this only too well. Chinese industrial policy is currently the envy of the western world, which admires, loathes, fears and attempts to emulate it all at the same time. But three generations ago, in an attempt to wean itself off imported steel and develop its hinterlands, China planned a 'Great Leap Forward' consisting of small-scale backyard steel furnaces that waged misguided war against the technology and economics of large-scale modern steel production. This is not, of course, to compare Europe's highly considered green industrial policy with China's tragic decision. But efforts by many developed countries with high labour costs to recreate relatively small-scale domestic solar manufacturing industries may not, ultimately, be any more successful.

A framework for green growth

A rigorous framework for green growth in Europe starts with the observation that Europe can best pursue its dual economic and environmental goals not by focusing only on decarbonising its own economy, but on helping the world decarbonise. This involves helping the world produce the goods and services it needs to decarbonise, wherever they can most efficiently be produced.

A seismic shift in comparative advantage will take place as local energy resources start to matter in the production of energy-intensive industrial commodities again. Throughout the history of human civilisation, industry has been located close to sources of energy. This changed in the twentieth century, as cheap-to-transport fossil fuels made it possible for energy-intensive industrial production to take place pretty much anywhere.

But decarbonisation implies a move from cheap-to-transport fossil fuels to green sources of energy – sun, wind, hydro and geothermal – that are unevenly distributed and very hard to move. A megawatt of solar energy costs a small fraction of what it takes to transform it into green hydrogen or ammonia and ship it to Europe. Better use it where it hits. The local availability of renewable energy will increasingly drive an economy's comparative advantage. Places rich in hard-to-transport renewable power have a generational opportunity to produce the energy-intensive building blocks of the world's economy, including fertilisers, steel, aluminum, chemicals and fuels.

Europe's green industrial policy should recognise and work with this economic reality, rather than attempt to fight it. Europe is a large net importer of energy: it lacks the renewable resources to engage in zero-carbon energy-intensive industrial production. Producing basic industrial commodities such as green hydrogen, steel or ammonia with German sunshine and wind will be less efficient than doing it with German knowhow and Namibian sun and wind.

None of this means that Germany needs to deindustrialise the Mittelstand. Fortunately for Europe, energy costs matter less for more complex forms of production that are further downstream from many of the energy-intensive inputs. Energy costs make up a greater proportion of the cost of raw aluminum than they do of the aluminum-encased laptops on which we are writing this chapter. And increasing the size of the global green economy will increase overall demand for the green products and services in which Europe does have a comparative advantage, such as carbon accounting services, engineering, procurement, construction and complex electrical equipment.

Europe is already seeing these dynamics play out in the way that surging natural gas prices have rendered sectors of European heavy industry uncompetitive, from ammonia to steel to basic chemical production. Natural gas is substantially more transportable than hydrogen or renewable electricity, but much less so than oil. As a consequence, the spot price of natural gas in the European market (TTF) is, at the time of writing, some 20 times the price at Henry Hub, coming down from much higher multiples. Definitely, the law of one price does not apply to natural gas and it will apply much less to green hydrogen. Trying to keep energy-intensive nodes of the value chain in Europe is unlikely to succeed. Instead, these nodes should relocate to places that are potentially more efficient in capturing green energy. Part of the mechanism through which Europe will achieve net zero is by relocating – outside of Europe – production steps that can be more effectively decarbonised elsewhere. European green industrial policy shouldn't try to fight this reality: it should instead plan an orderly transition into the green industries of the future in which it is likely to retain or enhance its comparative advantage.

This dynamic applies in the same way for manufacturing of clean-energy technologies. Industry dynamics and Europe's economic structure give Europe an advantage in producing some clean-energy technologies, but make it less well equipped to produce other technologies. Manufacturing of wind turbines and lithium batteries appears to be easier to localise in high-wage industrial economies.

Other technologies such as solar panels exhibit extraordinary economies of scale and labour forms a relatively high share of total production costs, meaning that it will always be most efficient to produce the world's solar panels in only a few places with low labour costs. The US Department of Energy's Solar Office has accordingly concluded that:

"to reestablish domestic solar manufacturing in the U.S., companies that produce and sell solar components will require financial support to offset the 30 – 40% higher cost of domestic solar production… These tax credits should be enacted for at least a decade… Renewal for some time thereafter… could be required to maintain US competitiveness" (US Department of Energy, 2022).

Europe, it seems, should not follow the US's lead and create large subsidies for domestic production of solar panels. Doing so would fight comparative advantage, rather than work with it.

Coordinate international value chains to maximise shared value

A globally-minded European green industrial policy would therefore put production where it makes sense to put it, and only engage in strategic competition over the parts of the value chain in which Europe realistically has a comparative advantage.

How should Europe determine in which parts of the value chain it could have a comparative advantage? Bottom-up technoeconomic cost modelling is one approach widely used in firms and industrial strategy offices. Another approach (that is less familiar to industrial strategy offices) is to apply economic complexity analysis to emerging clean supply chains (Hausmann *et al*, 2014). This enables researchers to predict which industries might thrive in certain places based on whether the industries are similar to existing activities that already succeed in that place.

Where parts of clean value chains should be located abroad, European industrial policy should coordinate with partner countries to help build out these value chains. Europe's ultimate aim, after all, is to help the world decarbonise, not to bring its own emissions to zero the fastest. To do so, it must create the infrastructure to scale the building blocks of the clean economy wherever it makes sense to scale them, whether these building blocks are critical minerals, green steel or manufacturing supply chains.

Of course, this doesn't mean that Europe should bankroll the green transition for everyone else. European industrial policy should aim to maximise the size of the clean economy, and take a fair share of it for Europe. Crucially, Europe's return depends on the total size of the pie, not just on its share of the pie. Attempting to take too much of a green value chain can be counterproductive. To understand this point, just look at Bolivia's lithium industry. Bolivia has the world's largest lithium reserves by some margin, but it produces no lithium: Bolivia's mining rules attempt to reserve such a high share of the industry profits for Bolivians that they scare away foreign investors that have the capital and knowhow to develop Bolivia's lithium industry. Europe's attempt to make all possible things at home might replicate a similar inefficiency, but on the manufacturing front.

In addition, it may prevent others from decarbonising. The global discussions in the context of the Paris Agreement and subsequent Conference of the Parties meetings have focused on what will be done to help finance the energy transition in developing countries, in order to reduce their carbon footprints. These talks include, *inter alia*, setting up the Global Environment Facility and the Clean Energy Finance

Facility. But many developing countries are already severely over-indebted, both fiscally and externally, and adding more debt to their books, even under soft terms, will crowd out other investment priorities. Ultimately, foreign financing only postpones payment. In the end, imports are paid with exports and if developing countries are not going to have a role as exporters in the new green economy, they will not be able to pay for the imports their economies will require. Helping these countries leverage their advantages so they can become efficient nodes in global green value chains is crucial to make sure that supply is elastic to the growing global demand for decarbonisation. However, all of the discussion of green development finance has been focused on funding the decarbonisation of developing countries themselves, not on helping them become important suppliers of the world's decarbonisation needs.

Helping Europe's partners to develop will also maximise Europe's economic returns, as it gives Europe's trading partners the resources they need to buy Europe's green technologies. Merely providing credit through development finance is not enough: it postpones the issue until the bill has to be paid. Europe's trading partners need revenues, not debt: they can get these revenues if Europe helps localise appropriate parts of green production there.

Just as vested interests and industry's political economy affects Europe, it also affects Europe's trading partners. In many developing economies, such as South Africa and India, powerful political interests sit behind the coal-based electricity system, and these forces resist the transition to green energy and decarbonised production. A globally minded industrial policy would develop economic constituencies and political economic forces behind green industries in Europe's trading partners (to counterbalance fossil-fuel interests that resist change). Seeding industries in these places around critical minerals, solar and wind, green hydrogen, green steel and other green technologies with European industrial policy would serve Europe's goal of helping the world decarbonise.

How should Europe earn a return from its industrial policy investments abroad? The answer to this lies in the recognition that every business has three constituents: workers, shareholders and customers. European workers can benefit if these industrial policy investments abroad lead to demand for products and services produced in Europe, for example through the design of projects, the sale of machinery and the provision of technical assistance. European shareholders can benefit when they earn a return on foreign direct investments through debt or equity. And European customers can benefit when they secure the lowest-cost sources of supply.

Flexibly and agnostically seeking to benefit the different constituents of the European economy – workers, customers and shareholders – can help inform how European industrial policy should address its thorniest industries. These are industries for which domestic production is uneconomical, where Europe is reliant on strategic adversaries for supply and where industry dynamics lead to extreme concentration. These include industries such as solar and also the energy-intensive segments of many value chains.

Recognising that industrial policy can promote these three different constituent groups can expand the parameter space for European industrial policy, and thereby enable it to create better strategies. Europe seems to be stuck: it shouldn't localise production domestically when doing so is uneconomic. At the same time, European energy security demands that it can't rely on China for its supply of solar panels, or try to protect its industry from more efficient producers of hard-to-move green energy. The solution is for Europe to channel its purchasing power into developing a supply chain outside of China in regions with lower labour or energy costs, and ideally with European participation in the technology and shareholding of the new supply chain. European industrial policy would thereby benefit European customers and shareholders, while recognising that European workers are better employed in tasks other than low-skilled labour or energy-intensive manufacturing.

Conclusion

Europe is in the process of aligning its considerable ingenuity, resources and ambition behind a green industrial policy that pursues the wrong goals: to become the first continent to decarbonise, and to build the future of industry in Europe. The right goals for European green industrial policy – to help the world decarbonise, and to maximise the value of the clean economy, while claiming Europe's share in it – are not far off. But the differences are significant, not just nit-picking: a green industrial policy framework that is more globally minded will be more adaptive, nuanced and accommodating of the real tradeoffs that Europe must confront.

Many proposals under the European green industrial policy umbrella are sensitive to these global dimensions. But in its actual implementation, European green industrial policy may end up splitting the difference. Its Carbon Border Adjustment Mechanism, for example, is seen both as a protectionist measure to defend European heavy industry, and an attempt to make global markets fairly price in carbon. Europe's REPowerEU plan aims to produce half of the EU's hydrogen domestically and import half of it from abroad, which seems like a compromise struck by policymakers keen to localise at least some production[47].

Promising all things to all people with industrial policy may be smart politics, but it is not smart economic strategy. Superior strategy involves confronting real inconvenient tradeoffs, choosing between dearly held goals, and letting go of good opportunities to pursue great ones. Baking the binding restrictions of green industrial policy in a global setting into European goals will make European green industrial policy stronger, not weaker, and more likely to benefit Europe's economy and the planet overall.

---

47 See European Commission press release of 13 February 2023, 'Commission sets out rules for renewable hydrogen', https://ec.europa.eu/commission/presscorner/detail/en/IP_23_594.

References

European Commission (2023) 'A Green Deal Industrial Plan for the Net-Zero Age', COM(2023) 62 final, available at https://eur-lex.europa.eu/legal-content/EN/TXT/HTML/?uri=CELEX:52023DC0062

Hausmann, R., C.A. Hidalgo, S. Bustos, M. Coscia, A. Simoes and M.A. Yildirim (2014) *The Atlas of Economic Complexity: Mapping Paths to Prosperity*, The MIT Press, available at https://doi.org/10.7551/mitpress/9647.001.0001

US Department of Energy (2022) *Solar Photovoltaics Supply Chain Deep Dive Assessment*, US Department of Energy Response to Executive Order 14017, 'America's Supply Chains', available at https://www.energy.gov/sites/default/files/2022-02/Solar%20Energy%20Supply%20Chain%20Report%20-%20Final.pdf

Von der Leyen, U. (2022) '2022 State of the Union Address by President von der Leyen', speech to the European Parliament, 14 September, available at https://ec.europa.eu/commission/presscorner/detail/en/speech_22_5493

9 Europe's green industrial policy

Simone Tagliapietra, Cecilia Trasi and Reinhilde Veugelers

1 Introduction

The transition of economies from brown to green represents the major socio-economic transformation of our time, often referred to as an industrial revolution against a deadline. Never in history has technological development been so crucial to tackle a global common good. The goal is clear: to facilitate a comprehensive decarbonisation process to avoid the most dramatic impacts of global warming, while simultaneously tackling the socio-economic issues that this transformation will unavoidably create.

With the European Green Deal, Europe has pledged to become the first climate-neutral continent by 2050. To get there, the European Union has committed to cut its greenhouse gas emissions by 55 percent by 2030 compared to 1990 and has also started to adopt the necessary legislation – the so-called 'Fit for 55' package – to turn this objective into reality (Tagliapietra and Veugelers, 2021).

But a strategy only based on climate targets and instruments would fall short if firms and citizens fail to adjust or reject the adjustment. The need to meet climate and environmental targets, while ensuring their economic and social sustainability, requires a transformation that generates enough benefits to compensate the losers. This puts industrial policy under the spotlight in the context of the European Green Deal's promise to be the EU's new growth engine.

Europe's focus on green industrial policy has gained momentum, notably since the adoption by the United States in August 2022 of the

Inflation Reduction Act (IRA). The IRA prompted fears of relocation of European clean-tech industries to the US, attracted by a combination of subsidies and protectionist local-content requirements. Regardless of how reasonable these fears are, this new geoeconomic context poses two challenges for Europe.

First, Europe is already lagging Asia and the US in the global race for digital technologies. It cannot afford to give up its position in the global race for clean technologies and miss out on the industrial growth opportunities from the green transition.

Second, for overall competitiveness and growth, the European economy is heavily reliant on carbon-intensive industries, such as the automotive industry. These sectors will undergo significant restructuring in the coming years, because of the transition to clean technologies – to electric vehicles, for example. A green industrial policy is therefore needed to ensure the success of the green transition and to help maintain and strengthen the EU's socio-economic model. This is why the EU has packaged the European Green Deal as its 'growth strategy' and why it has reacted nervously to the IRA by proposing its own Net Zero Industry Act (European Commission, 2023a).

In this chapter, we: i) outline a set of principles for an effective green industrial policy in Europe; ii) provide an overview of Europe's ongoing green industrial policy measures; iii) set out recommendations to deliver a more effective green industrial policy in Europe.

2 Principles for an effective green industrial policy in Europe

Green industrial policy is unique. Instead of solely focusing on the competitiveness of industries and companies, as is typical of traditional industrial policy, green industrial policy tackles the broader societal challenges arising from global warming. This sets it apart from climate-change policy, which usually has more narrow objectives aimed at reducing carbon emissions.

Similar to standard industrial policy, the selection of tools and projects for green industrial policy should be based on where the private and public returns from clean markets diverge the most. A green industrial policy should be developed in coordination with the instruments used for climate policy, and with industrial policy instruments more generally. For example, carbon pricing is an important instrument in the green industrial policy toolbox, which also includes subsidies, taxes, targets, regulations, and standards.

Green technologies, often still emerging, are complex and uncertain. Future uncertainty about climate and technology scenarios underlines the importance of learning and information sharing, and thus experimentation, risk taking, self-discovery on the market and industry-research-policy collaborations to share risks, costs and information.

Clean technologies are also characterised by inflated costs or benefits for those other than the producers (Martin and Verhoeven, 2022), if only because of the variety of climate policies worldwide. This calls for a more directed approach to supporting investments in clean technologies. In addition, a clean-tech investment push is necessary to counter the locking-in of fossil fuel-based technologies and their path-dependencies.

The difficulty in profiting from green technologies, and in developing new low-carbon technologies, lies in the hidden support provided to fossil-fuel products in different forms, from the absence of a carbon price to explicit subsidies. These mechanisms can skew the market in terms of production, technology adoption and innovation (Aghion *et al*, 2016; Aghion *et al*, 2019). The case for subsidising green technologies, in this sense, is broader and stronger than the general case. Environment-directed innovation policy. Needs to select 'clean' to address the greater knowledge spillovers and lock-in problems. This still leaves the questions of whether and how to choose between 'clean' technologies, and which winners to pick (eg focusing on individual clean technologies such as batteries or hydrogen). When choosing between clean technologies, the principle of divergence between expected social and private returns, and the greatest scope for reducing clean market failures, should guide the decision-making process. Choosing between clean technologies should also take into account the impact of any choice on other non-selected clean technologies. This calls for a good mix between vertical and horizontal instruments and putting time limits on support, and emphasises the importance of ensuring fair competition (Aghion *et al*, 2011).

The climate crisis requires urgent mitigation efforts and green industrial policy is no exception. More than other areas of industrial policy, the lack of risk-taking in clean-tech sectors can be particularly problematic overall. A green innovation policy portfolio with risks entails acceptance that there will be failures. This makes experimentation a key principle of green industrial policy, alongside close monitoring of the effectiveness of experiments and adaptability.

Finally, by addressing broader societal concerns, green industrial policy requires the involvement of a variety of stakeholders covering a larger set of private-sector areas. Public-private partnerships ought to be central in green innovation policy, much more than in climate policy and standard industrial policy. The extent of the transformation brought about by climate change means there is more need for the involvement of, and support from, civil society than in other areas of industrial policy.

3 Designing green industrial policy

Most of the challenges for green industrial policy deal with practical implementation rather than with theoretical justifications. This section lists a set of principles for green industrial policy design that draws especially on the insights of *"new industrial policy"* (Rodrik, 2014; see also Tagliapietra and Veugelers, 2021).

When introducing his new industrial policy perspective, Rodrik (2014) said industrial policy should be about institutionalised collaboration and dialogue between governments, the private sector and civil society, spanning multiple sectors, technologies and value chains (Figure 1), rather than about *"who gets how much"*.

Figure 1: The new industrial policy approach as a process of institutionalised collaboration and dialogue

Source: Bruegel based on Rodrik (2014).

To implement a new green industrial policy approach, it is important for governments to work with the private sector and civil society to identify constraints and opportunities, leveraging their knowledge and capacities to generate solutions, while addressing issues such as rent-seeking and political capture. This in turn requires accountability and a balanced set of incentives and penalties, with coherent, measurable and well-communicated targets to enable effective monitoring and evaluation.

Co-financing should be used to support projects that accelerate and consolidate existing scientific and industrial capacity, and new projects at the frontier of technologies and markets along the entire value chain, from research, development and diffusion, to manufacturing, distribution and sales.

Information problems and the elevated level of uncertainty can be dealt with by viewing green industrial policy as a continuous learning process through policy experimentation. To encourage risk-taking, policy should include milestones and should be adapted depending on lessons learned from regular monitoring and evaluation.

Finally, coordination between the many different stakeholders, policy governance areas, instruments and projects will require strong operational governance for successful green innovation policy.

4 An overview of Europe's current green industrial policy

The EU sets the framework for green industrial policies throughout the bloc through competition policy, trade policy, EU single market rules, climate policy, research and innovation policy, EU public investment and regional development policy. It has in place a wide range of policy tools, including public funding for green research, development and deployment of green technologies, green public procurement and clean energy standards (Table 1). This section summarises the financial tools available at EU level to support clean-tech innovation and deployment.

Table 1: Europe's main green industrial policy tools

	Innovation	Deployment	Framework conditions
EU level	• Horizon Europe European Research Council • European Innovation Council • European Institute of Innovation and Technology	• European Alliances • IPCEIs • EU Innovation Fund • European Investment Bank • EU Cohesion Funds • NextGenerationEU • Single market rules	• Trade and investment policy • Competition policy • Environmental standards • Climate policy • Energy policy • Development policy
National level	Regional level	• State aid • Investment programmes • Incentive programmes • Public procurement rules • Clean energy standards	• Energy policy • Environmental standards • Environmental taxation
Regional level	Regional level	• 'Smart' specialisation strategies • Regional investment budgets • Implementation of EU Cohesion policies	Regional regulations

Source: Bruegel.

4.1 Innovation

Horizon Europe is the EU's main funding programme for research and innovation[48]. Its budget is €95.5 billion for 2021 to 2027, of which €5.4 billion comes from NextGenerationEU[49]. Among other things, it seeks to tackle climate change and boost the competitiveness and growth of the EU. Horizon Europe also has a strong focus on green technologies. The programme defines a new partnership instrument, the Horizon Europe Missions, to catalyse cross-sectoral investments to find solutions to pressing challenges for society. In September 2020, Mission Boards proposed five Missions, of which four have a climate change/environment angle: A Climate Resilient Europe; Mission Starfish 2030: Restore our Ocean and Waters; 100 Climate-Neutral Cities by 2030 – by and for the citizens; Caring for Soil is Caring for Life.

The European Research Council (ERC)[50] was created in 2007 to fund frontier research through grants. Since its creation, it has funded more than 12,500 projects with an emphasis on early-stage researchers. The overall ERC budget from 2021 to 2027 is more than €16 billion. While ERC projects are selected for funding without thematic priorities, the research undertaken by many ERC grantees generates knowledge in support of the European Green Deal[51].

The European Innovation Council (EIC)[52] was created in 2017 to help companies grow and expand beyond European borders. It has a budget of €10.1 billion for 2021 to 2027. Money is provided to beneficiaries as grants and/or as equity investment. The EIC is split into two branches: the EIC Accelerator and the EIC Pathfinder. Although also a programme funding bottom-up proposals without thematic priorities, the EIC is

---

48 See: https://research-and-innovation.ec.europa.eu/funding/funding-opportunities/funding-programmes-and-open-calls/horizon-europe_en.
49 See: https://commission.europa.eu/strategy-and-policy/recovery-plan-europe_en.
50 See: https://erc.europa.eu/about-erc/erc-glance.
51 See https://erc.europa.eu/projects-statistics/frontier-research-european-green-deal.
52 See: https://eic.ec.europa.eu/about-european-innovation-council_en.

strong in the areas of clean energy, clean mobility and smart buildings[53].

The European Institute of Innovation and Technology (EIT)[54] was created in 2008. Its 2021 to 2027 budget is €2.9 billion from Horizon Europe. The EIT supports the development of pan-European partnerships between companies, research labs and universities, known as EIT Innovation Communities (Knowledge and Innovation Communities – KICs), which aim to find answers to global challenges. The EIT provides grants with a varying funding rate according to the life cycle of the KICs. Five out of the eight Communities at time of writing are strongly relevant to green industrial policy: EIT Climate-KIC: Innovation for climate action, EIT InnoEnergy, EIT Manufacturing, EIT Raw Materials and EIT Urban Mobility.

4.2 Deployment

The EU Innovation Fund (IF) was established under the EU emissions trading system (ETS) for the period 2021-2030 with at least 450 million carbon allowances. Assuming a carbon price of €75 per tonne, the Fund will provide around €38 billion of support over the period. Projects supported by the fund are expected to be implemented in collaboration with industry partners, research institutions and other stakeholders. As of March 2023, 52 projects had been signed, for a total contribution by the Fund of €2.94 billion: 58 percent of projects target energy-intensive industries, 21 percent renewable energy, 17 percent energy storage and 4 percent carbon capture and storage.

Industrial Alliances are a tool to promote public-private partnerships with an increasingly leading role in regulating and directing funds towards the strategic priorities identified by the European Commission. The aim is to maximise the job, growth and investment potential of new green technologies, and to prevent a technological dependence on

---

53 See https://eic.ec.europa.eu/news/green-deal-challenge-eic-supports-solutions-2021-12-15_en.

54 See https://eit.europa.eu/.

EU competitors. In practice, these Alliances are a network of industrial and innovation players (including SMEs), regional authorities, national authorities, the European Commission and the European Investment Bank. Out of the nine Industrial Alliances, at least three cover clean technology industries (Box 1).

Box 1: EU Industrial Alliances in the clean-tech supply chain

Launched in 2017, the *European Battery Alliance (EBA)* initiative is intended to support frontier innovation along the batteries value chain, from mining and processing of raw materials, production of advanced chemical materials, design of battery cells and modules and their integration into smart systems, to the recycling and repurposing of used batteries. This includes providing adequate training at EU and country level, re-skilling and upskilling, making Europe attractive for world-class experts in the field, and supporting the sustainability of EU battery cell manufacturing industry with the lowest environmental footprint possible.

Launched in 2020, *European Clean Hydrogen Alliance* aims to foster the deployment of hydrogen technologies up to 2030, bringing together renewable and low-carbon hydrogen production, demand in industry, mobility and other sectors, and hydrogen transmission and distribution. The main target is to reach a level of six gigawatts (GW) of clean hydrogen by 2024, and then 40 GW (EU) and 40 GW (non-EU) clean hydrogen by 2030. The Alliance covers about 750 projects in six main thematic areas of intervention, from renewable and low-carbon hydrogen production to industrial applications and energy.

Also launched in 2020, the *European Raw Materials Alliance (ERMA)* focuses on securing access to resources deemed strategic for the development of a green industrial value chain and on mobilising investment and innovation in this area. Its creation is in line with the recommendations of the Action Plan on Critical Raw Materials on reducing Europe's dependency on third countries, diversifying supply from both primary and secondary sources and improving resource efficiency and circularity, while promoting responsible sourcing worldwide.

Important Projects of Common European Interest (IPCEI) were introduced in 2014 in the context of a wider modernisation of state aid rules to facilitate the disbursement of aid targeted at identified market failures and objectives of common EU interest and considered the least distortive (so-called 'good aid'). To qualify for support under the IPCEI framework, a project must: i) contribute to strategic EU objectives; ii) involve several EU countries; iii) involve private financing by the beneficiaries, iv) generate positive spill-over effects across the EU, and v) be highly ambitious in terms of research and innovation. IPCEIs thus seek to bring together knowledge, expertise, financial resources and partners throughout the EU by supporting cross-border projects. As of March 2023, the European Commission has approved state aid in the context of five IPCEIs to support the development of a European clean-tech industry (Table 2).

Table 2: IPCEIs in the EU

Industry	Launch	Description and objectives	Countries	Public invest.	Private invest.
Micro-electronics	12/2018	(i) Energy efficient chips; (ii) Power semiconductors; (iii) Smart sensors; (iv) Advanced optical equipment; (v) Compound materials.	DE (€820 million), IT (€524 million), FR (€355 million), UK (€48 million)	€1.75 billion	€6 billion
Batteries	12/2019	IPCEI Battery I - (i) Raw and advanced materials; (ii) Cells and modules; (iii) Battery systems; (iv) Repurposing, recycling, and refining.	DE (€1250 m), FR (€960 m), IT (€570 million), PL (€240 million), BE (€80 million), SE (€50 million), FI (€30 million)	€3.2 billion	€5 billion
	01/2021	IPCEI Battery II - The project complements the first IPCEI in the battery value chain.	AT, BE, DE, EL, ES, FI, FR, HR, IT, PL, SK, SE	€3.2 billion	€5 billion
Clean Hydrogen	07/2022	IPCEI Hy2Tech - (i) the generation of hydrogen; (ii) fuel cells; (iii) storage, transportation, and distribution of hydrogen; (iv) end-users' applications, especially mobility sector.	AT, BE, CZ, DE, DK, EE, ES, FI, FR, EL, IT, NL, PL, PT, SK	€5.4 billion	€8.8 billion
	09/2022	IPCEI Hy2Use - complements a "Hy2Tech". The target is to build new electrolysis capacity of approx. 3.5 GW equivalent to 340,000 tons of renewable and low-carbon hydrogen per year.	AT, BE, DK, FI, FR, EL, ES, IT, NL, PL, PT, SK, SE	€5.2 billion	€7 billion
	09/2022	IPCEI Hy2Use - complements a "Hy2Tech". The target is to build new electrolysis capacity of approx. 3.5 GW equivalent to 340,000 tons of renewable and low-carbon hydrogen per year.	AT, BE, DK, FI, FR, EL, ES, IT, NL, PL, PT, SK, SE	€5.2 billion	€7 billion

Source: Bruegel.

The European Investment Bank (EIB) has positioned itself as the EU's *"climate bank"* since 2019. It adopted a new energy lending policy and sustainability strategy based on three pillars: i) end of lending for fossil-fuel projects from the end of 2021; ii) focus future financing on clean energy innovation, energy efficiency and renewables; iii) unlock €1 trillion of climate and environmentally sustainable investment in the decade to 2030. In 2022, the EIB allocated around €17.5 billion to the transport and industrial sectors. We estimate that €3.3 billion of this package was targeted at clean technology projects. In addition, the EIB provided €10.4 billion to projects in the energy sector, out of which €4.4 billion went to renewable energy-related projects. The EIB is also responsible for the implementation of around 75 percent of the EU guarantees allocated to the InvestEU programme. This is a tool with an EU budget guarantee of €26.1 billion to promote private investments in priority areas, distributed between four policy windows, including sustainable infrastructure (€9.9 billion) and research, innovation and digitisation (€6.6 billion).

Finally, it is worth mentioning that most state aid in the EU is paid out by EU countries. This state aid requires approval by the European Commission. In 2020, state aid approved for objectives related to environmental protection, renewable energy and energy savings amounted to €61.41 billion, with indications of levelling off compared to previous years (European Commission, 2022a).The Commission issued guidelines on state aid for climate, environmental protection and energy (CEEAG) in January 2022, to implement the European Green Deal objective of revising state aid rules to support a cost-effective and just transition to climate neutrality (European Commission, 2022b).

EU countries also have access under the NextGenerationEU Recovery and Resilience Facility (RRF) to loans and grants to support green investments, including for decarbonisation of industry and the strengthening of clean-tech supply chains.

Nevertheless, despite all these elements of green innovation policy at EU level, there remains a long way to go to achieve a green industrial policy, as outlined in section 2. Notably, strong governance that can ensure the consistency of green industrial policy is missing. Instead, the EU green industrial policy strategy seems more like a scattered collection of energy, climate, innovation and social policy initiatives, rather than a coherent industrial policy framework.

5 Recommendations for a more effective green industrial policy in Europe

The need to tackle climate change calls for a green industrial revolution. A new policy-driven approach should be based on strong governance, on formalised collaboration with the private sector and civil society, and on development of solutions that combine public and private knowledge and capacities. To design green industrial policy, a new industrial policy perspective is helpful. This should have much broader multi-dimensional objectives and should view policymaking as a process of partnership between the public sector, the private sector and society, rather than a top-down approach of allocating funds to a few winners.

The traditional EU strategy is not sufficient to turn the green transition into an industrial opportunity. The EU faces challenges in coordinating and achieving the necessary economies of scale because of the fragmentation of tools and funding sources, and because of nationalistic industrial policies. While some elements already reflect the new industrial policy approach, such as provision of support for industrial ecosystems encompassing all players operating in a value chain, much stronger measures are required to develop an effective EU green industrial policy.

5.1 Governing public-private collaboration and dialogue

Given the inherent complexities of both green industrial policy and the EU as policymaking machinery, strong governance is a prerequisite for effective EU green industrial policy. Only a leadership that is competent, independent and accountable to clear goals and milestones, and that encourages risk-taking, can coordinate the progress of different government groups, which are each responsible for distinct parts of green industrial policy.

5.2 Revamping EU-level subsidies for green innovation

While the EU should not copy the US IRA production subsidies, there may be a case for more EU subsidies for green R&D, innovation and early-stage deployment of next-generation green technologies, in which EU companies could build globally competitive positions. There may also be a case for building or maintaining within the EU minimum levels of capacity in certain areas critical for the green transition, to make the EU more resilient to natural or political shocks.

The EU should design such subsidies without harming the single market's level playing field. This justifies an EU-level approach, particularly for early-stage, high-risk projects, which are more vulnerable to market and eco-system failures. There should be more reliance on synergies, integration of knowledge spillovers, and cost and risk sharing, rather than on national subsidies. Current schemes are bureaucratically heavy and end up mostly supporting a few large incumbent firms that can propose and manage such projects, which typically take place in the EU countries that have sufficiently deep pockets to support them. While large firms can play anchor roles in such projects, it is important to ensure that smaller players and radically new clean eco-systems can find their place (Poitiers and Weil, 2022). Otherwise, the IPCEI format may fail to pick 'winning' clean eco-systems or particularly disruptive new green technology solutions, proposed by new young firms.

EU funding should also be deployed to improve EU strategic resilience. This involves support for new technological solutions for critical components that, without support, might make EU clean-tech production vulnerable to supply chain disruption. The EU should, for example, fund mission-oriented programmes to develop substitutes for certain critical raw materials. For these new early-stage projects, the EU approach should rely on an instrument other than IPCEIs. Novel support models that provide grants in a relatively non-bureaucratic way are crucial to unleash high risk/high return ideas[55]. Funding such grants could be the main purpose of the EU Sovereignty Fund proposed by the European Commission[56].

New joint borrowing may not be needed to fund such EU initiatives. As suggested by the European Commission (2023b), one option could be to re-shuffle EU budget money. Another option could be to make use of the additional grants that will be devoted to the new REPowerEU facility under the RRF, and to blend some of this money with EIB loans and guarantees[57].

Public funding can be more efficient when leveraging private investments in clean-tech public-private partnerships, with the size of the multiplier depending on the framework conditions that shape the private incentives for clean-tech investment. A green EU subsidy policy should thus be accompanied by monitoring of the barriers private firms face when investing in clean tech. These barriers can include lack of access to finance, excessive regulatory burdens, lack of access to public (procurement) and private markets, and lack of access to critical skills and components. Unless these barriers are addressed, additional public funding may not be as efficient. A further complementary policy instrument is carbon pricing. The EU ETS remains the critical cornerstone of any net-zero industry strategy.

5.3 Leveraging the single market as the most valuable tool

The single market is the EU's most valuable tool for EU green industrial policy. Single market rules can accelerate the roll-out of clean

---

55 See Tagliapietra and Veugelers (2021) on how to design such green subsidy programmes at EU level.

56 See European Commission press release of 15 September, 2022: https://ec.europa.eu/commission/presscorner/detail/en/statement_22_5543.

57 This will be financed through the frontloaded sale of emissions trading system allowances (40 percent) and the resources of the Innovation Fund (60 percent). The distribution of these extra resources will take into account cohesion policy, EU countries' dependence on fossil fuels and the increase in investment prices. See Regulation (EU) 2023/435.

technologies by avoiding regulatory costs associated with fragmentation, uncertainty, and bureaucracy. These include regulations that place time limits for decisions at each stage of permitting procedures, a measure that can accelerate developments in areas vital to decarbonisation, thus enlarging clean-tech markets more quickly. For example, in December 2022, EU countries agreed a temporary emergency regulation to fast-track permits for renewable energy infrastructure and grids (Council Regulation (EU) 2022/2577).

Similarly, tighter European standards can foster global competitiveness by demonstrating marketability and attracting investment into firms that comply with standards. One example, agreed by the EU in December 2022, is the introduction of stronger environmental sustainability requirements for all batteries sold in the EU[58]. Another option could be to develop regulatory sandboxes – frameworks for experimentation – to push for quicker development of clean technologies and fast-tracking of the necessary certifications required for placing them on the market[59]. Coordinated use of procurement can provide a larger, more integrated lead market for clean technologies. An efficient EU electricity market design could help to lower energy costs structurally, also for clean-tech manufacturers, with the related competitiveness benefits. Greater use of green public procurement would be particularly important in sectors in which public purchasers make up a large share of the market, including transport and construction (Rodríguez Quintero *et al*, 2019). By introducing sustainability requirements for clean technologies (for instance, by rewarding in tenders the use of electric cars that are produced to certain sustainability criteria, or based on certain innovation or environmental

---

58 See European Parliament press release of 9 December 2022: https://www.europarl.europa.eu/news/en/press-room/20221205IPR60614/batteries-deal-on-new-eu-rules-for-design-production-and-waste-treatment.

59 Such schemes already exist in EU countries, notably in Germany (see https://www.bmwk.de/Redaktion/EN/Dossier/regulatory-sandboxes.html). EU countries endorsed regulatory sandboxes in November 2020; see Council conclusions of 16 November 2020: https://www.consilium.europa.eu/media/46822/st13026-en20.pdf.

features), the EU could prioritise the deployment of clean technologies produced to European standards, without having any form of local content requirement[60].

5.4 Skills

The speed of manufacturing and roll-out of clean technologies is correlated closely with the simultaneous development of a qualified workforce to implement clean projects. Ensuring enough skilled workers is of prime importance for Europe, to avoid shortages and to ensure a prominent level of productivity for its clean-tech industry. This also is a crucial item when it comes to the just transition, as part of the workforce currently employed in carbon-intensive sectors can be re-skilled and re-employed in green-energy projects (IEA, 2022).

Recognising these factors, the EU has a European Skills Agenda (European Commission, 2020) intended to help individuals and businesses develop more and better skills in these sectors. It has earmarked sizeable funds to support worker training: the €61.5 billion European Social Fund Plus (ESF+), and the Just Transition Fund (JTF) and the RFF.

The European Commission (2023a) has stressed that the EU and its members can do more. For instance, as Europe seeks to develop pan-European clean-tech supply chains, it would be efficient to have integrated continuous monitoring at EU level of the supply of and demand for green skills and jobs. The EU single market for clean skills could be promoted by developing a Europe-wide strategy for clean-tech higher qualifications, and by easing intra-EU mobility of talent, linked also to Erasmus+ funding. Sector-level efforts should also be made through links

---

60 Environmental criteria in public procurement should be handled carefully, as they might expose officials to lobbying and electioneering (for instance, to protect local producers against competition; Blanchard *et al*, 2022). But this risk could be mitigated by using precise and easy-to-verify award criteria (eg CO_2 emissions of cars or carbon intensity of electricity) rather than imprecise and hard-to-verify criteria (eg environmental criteria related to the suppliers). This requires a clear categorisation of green criteria and adequate investment in the training of public authorities that must apply them (Sapir *et al*, 2022).

to European industrial alliances. The establishment in February 2023 of a large-scale skills partnership for onshore renewable energy[61] was a welcome first step.

6 Conclusions

In early 2023, the European Commission published a Green Deal Industrial Plan (European Commission, 2023a), intended to leverage the single market and improve the competitiveness of Europe's netzero industry. Its main plank was a proposal for a Net Zero Industry Act (NZIA) that serves three main purposes.

First, it identifies the net-zero technologies deemed of strategic importance, including renewable energy technologies, batteries, electrolysers and carbon capture and storage (CCS) technologies. Second, it defines a target for manufacturing capacity of at least 40 percent of the EU's annual deployment needs of these technologies by 2030. Third, it would establish a governance system resting on Net-Zero Strategic Projects (NZSPs) identified by EU countries, and a regulatory framework to facilitate their rapid implementation, including fast-track permitting and administrative procedures, evaluation of public procurement procedures against a 'sustainability and resilience' criteria, and a streamlined process for EU countries to grant aid to accelerate the green transition.

Yet, the design of the governance framework falls short. The NZIA would still rely on the dispersed assemblage of policy tools and initiatives, instead of delivering a systematic green industrial policy. Even more troubling is the how the proposed NZIA prioritises net-zero technology sovereignty and the pursuit of strategic autonomy over efficiency and the imperative of global decarbonisation. The US IRA is a wake-up call for the EU that a more coherent framework and public support is required for the manufacturing and deployment of clean technologies. However, rather than following the paths taken by others, the EU must

---

61 Under the Pact for Skills. See industriALL press release of 10 February 2023: https://news.industriall-europe.eu/Article/860.

leverage its strengths to meet the challenge of the green industrial transition, particularly by boosting the single market.

Policies should aim to improve the attractiveness of the single market as a location for green investment, with horizontal measures to enhance market functioning and specific measures in support of clean technologies. Examples of these measures include better regulation, better green procurement rules and EU-level financing to promote new or early-stage clean tech, in which EU firms can achieve sustainable competitive positions. Finally, a stronger governance model is needed to ensure better coordination and longer-term commitment.

References

Aghion, P., J. Boulanger and E. Cohen (2011) 'Rethinking industrial policy', *Policy Brief* 2011/04, Bruegel, available at https://www.bruegel.org/policy-brief/rethinking-industrial-policy

Aghion, P., A. Dechezleprêtre, D. Hemous, R. Martin and J. van Reenen (2016) 'Carbon taxes, path dependency, and directed technical change: Evidence from the auto industry', *Journal of Political Economy* 124(3): 1-51

Aghion, P., C. Hepburn, A. Teytelboym and D. Zenghelis (2019) 'Path dependence, innovation and the economics of climate change', in R. Fouquet (ed) *Handbook on green growth*, Edward Elgar

Blanchard, O., C. Gollier and J. Tirole (2022) 'The Portfolio of Economic Policies Needed to Fight Climate Change', *PIIE Working Paper* 22-18, Peterson Institute for International Economics, available at https://www.piie.com/sites/default/files/2022-11/wp22-18.pdf

European Commission (2020) 'European Skills Agenda for sustainable competitiveness, social fairness and resilience', COM(2020)274

European Commission (2021) 'Strategic dependencies and capacities', Commission Staff Working Document, SWD(2021 352 final

European Commission (2022a) *State Aid Scoreboard 2021*, available at https://competition-policy.ec.europa.eu/system/files/2023-04/state_aid_scoreboard_note_2021.pdf

European Commission (2022b) 'Guidelines on State aid for climate, environmental protection and energy 2022', 2022/C 80/01, available at https://eur-lex.europa.eu/legal-content/EN/TXT/HTML/?uri=CELEX:52022XC0218(03)

European Commission (2023a) 'A Green Deal Industrial Plan for the Net-Zero Age', COM(2023) 62 final

European Commission. (2023b) 'Proposal for a regulation of the European Parliament and of the Council on establishing a framework of measures for strengthening Europe's net-zero technology products manufacturing ecosystem (Net Zero Industry Act)', COM(2023) 161

IEA (2021) *The Role of Critical Minerals in Clean Energy Transitions*, International Energy Agency, available at https://www.iea.org/reports/the-role-of-critical-minerals-in-clean-energy-transitions

IEA (2022) *Skills development and inclusivity for clean energy transition*, International Energy Agency, available at https://www.iea.org/reports/skills-development-and-inclusivity-for-clean-energy-transitions

IEA (2023) *Energy Technology Perspectives 2023*, International Energy Agency, available at https://www.iea.org/reports/energy-technology-perspectives-2023

Rodríguez Quintero, R. C. Vidal-Abarca Garrido, H. Moons, M. Gama Caldas, O. Wolf, I. Skinner, A. van Grinsven, M. 't Hoen and H. van Essen (2019) *Revision of the EU Green Public Procurement Criteria for Transport*, JRC Science for Policy Report, European Commission Joint Research Centre

Kleimann, D., N. Poitiers, A. Sapir, S. Tagliapietra, N. Véron, R. Veugelers and J. Zettelmeyer (2023) 'How Europe should answer the US Inflation Reduction Act', *Policy Contribution* 04/2023, Bruegel

Martin, R. And D. Verhoeven (2022) 'Knowledge spillovers from clean and emerging technologies in the UK', CEP *Discussion Paper* CEPDP1834, Centre for Economic Performance, London School of Economics and Political Science

Mazzucato, M. (2013) T*he Entrepreneurial State. Debunking Public vs. Private Sector Myths*, London: Anthem Press

Poitiers, N. And P. Weil (2022) 'Opaque and ill-defined: the problems with Europe's IPCEI subsidy framework', *Bruegel Blog*, 26 January, available at https://www.bruegel.org/blog-post/opaque-and-illdefined-problems-europes-ipcei-subsidy-framework

Rodrik, D. (2014) 'Green industrial policy', *Oxford Review of Economic Policy* 30(3): 469-491

Sapir, A., T. Schraepen and S. Tagliapietra (2022) 'Green Public Procurement: A Neglected Tool in the European Green Deal Toolbox?' *Intereconomics* 57(3): 175-178, available at https://link.springer.com/content/pdf/10.1007/s10272-022-1044-7.pdf

Tagliapietra, S. And R. Veugelers (2021) 'Fostering the Industrial Component of the European Green Deal: Key Principles and Policy Options', *Intereconomics* 56(6): 305-310, available at https://www.intereconomics.eu/contents/year/2021/number/6/article/fostering-the-industrial-component-ofthe-european-green-deal-key-principles-and-policy-options.html

10 Smart green industrial policy

Ben McWilliams and Georg Zachmann

1 Industrial policy is back

Industrial policy is back in vogue. Governments worldwide are turning to it as a way to promote economic growth as their economies transition to climate neutrality. With the Inflation Reduction Act, the United States has sent a clear signal that it intends to pursue climate targets through a strong industrial policy. The European Union focuses more strongly on the use of carbon pricing, but is also responding with its own Net Zero Industry Act, which seeks to protect and expand the EU's clean technology industrial output. Governments are assuming a critical role through industrial policy in smoothly managing the transition from a fossil-fuel to a low carbon energy system. Bordoff and O'Sullivan (2022) predicted a wave of "*government intervention in the energy sector on a scale not seen in recent memory*".

But a European green industrial policy will not work only by throwing more euros at the problem. If the state is to assume a more dominant role in achieving decarbonisation and accelerating green technology innovation and deployment, green policymaking must be rethought. In this chapter we focus on the development of 'smart green industrial policy' focussed on the regional aspect.

1.1 Towards 'smart' green industrial policy
This chapter discusses the targeting of green industrial policy at the regional level. We argue that such targeting is essential for a government to maximise returns.

The logic of our argument is as follows:

1. Governments wish to use industrial policy for the development of priority low-carbon technologies (a policy decision that has already been made).
2. Regions have unique technological, knowledge and institutional capacities, and these are a crucial indicator of the ability of a region to absorb new specific knowledge and innovate (widely documented in literature).
3. It is possible to identify this *comparative advantage* at regional level (documented in literature).
4. Desirable green technological capacities can be mapped against existing comparative advantages by geography, allowing a policymaker to make positive, well-informed decisions about the likelihood of regions being successful in developing a new green technology.
5. By using the above, 'smart' green industrial policy should focus on removing bottlenecks to allow regions to grow their comparative advantage in the direction of new green technologies.

In section 2, we discuss a definition of green industrial policy suitable for today's political climate. In section 3, we provide a brief overview of the fact that governments are today actively in the process of selecting priority green technologies. In section 4, we provide theoretical and empirical evidence that regions have unique capabilities and potential development pathways. In section 5, we discuss metrics widely used in the literature for measuring these regional specialisation and comparative advantages. Existing energy factor inputs have driven regional industrial specialisation, but the advent of zero-carbon energy technologies will reshape the map, as we discuss in section 6. Public policy should utilise the information discussed in sections 3 to 6 to better target regional industrial policy at alleviating broad growth constraints that prevent development into nearby green technologies – which is the focus of section 7.

2 Contemporary green industrial policy

2.1 Defining industrial policy

The main objective of industrial policy is to increase the welfare of the population sustainably. This can be pursued by ensuring that a country can generate high value added. That is, a country should try to export many goods with a substantial mark-up on top of the initial production cost. This only works if a country is very efficient at producing desirable goods that competing exporters are unable/unwilling to offer more cheaply to global markets. The country is then said to have some form of market power. At the same time the welfare of the population depends on the cost of imports. If essential import goods are monopolised by certain exporters, the importing country's terms of trade will deteriorate.

Hence, industrial policy is both about generating own market power (eg supporting a highly efficient offshore wind industry) and breaking foreign market power (eg setting up Airbus to rival Boeing).

2.2 Defining green industrial policy

A future-proof industrial policy almost inevitably needs to have strong 'green' elements. Investments in production processes that lock in substantial carbon emissions are likely to become sunk, and the clusters around those investments, including the human skills, will lose value. Supporting this cannot be good industrial policy. By contrast, investments in low-carbon alternatives may be the first steps towards development of sustainable comparative advantages in relatively new fields – developing new skills that will see high demand in the future and pulling entire new value chains.

This implies a race between countries to host the growing sectors of the future. Using the revealed comparative advantage measure (RCA)[62],

---

62 Revealed comparative advantage is a computed index used in economics to determine the relative competitiveness of a country in a given class of goods or services. It is measured as the share of a class of goods or services in a country's total exports. This share is divided by the proportion of global exports of that class of goods or services.

Figure 1 indicates that current strength in exporting certain low-carbon products is strongly correlated to past strength. That means that developing competitive production and export advantages in new low-carbon products will provide a lasting advantage.

Figure 1: Correlation of the 2020 standardised RCA with the same technology's past standardised RCA

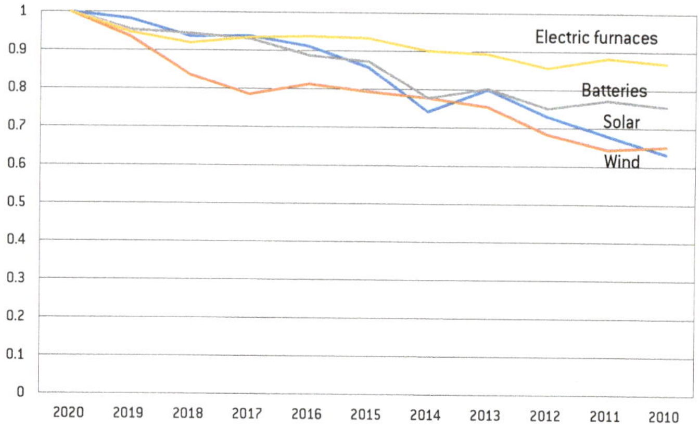

```
               Electric furnaces
               Batteries
               Solar
               Wind
```

Source: Bruegel based on UN COMTRADE database. Notes: the chart shows the correlation of RCA by country for each sector over time. Each data point shows the correlation of RCA across countries for a given sector and given year compared to the RCA by country in 2020 (the most recent data). All countries for which data is available were included; the exact number of countries for each correlation depends on each year/sector export data availability.

2.3 Goals for contemporary green industrial policy

2.3.1 Reducing greenhouse gas emissions
Traditional academic rationale for government support for the development of green technologies comes from positive societal spillovers that do not directly accrue into profit for investors or entrepreneurs. The first reason for this is a form of late-mover advantage: while pioneer companies take on the risk of failure, some of the valuable side

effects, including proving commercial potential, spill over to competitors. Second, falling costs of low-carbon technologies enable society to embark on lower-cost pathways to decarbonisation – think, for example, of government support in the early 2000s for solar PV and wind deployment in Europe and the United States. Third, there remains considerable uncertainty around carbon pricing and the extent of government commitment to climate targets (the Trump administration pulled out of the Paris Climate Accord, for example). Investors do not face a certain environment in which they can make green investments. The final reason is that in many cases, export markets for low-carbon products do not contain any serious climate policy, and hence pure market forces would make EU green-tech producers underinvest in low-carbon solutions (McWilliams and Zachmann, 2021).

2.3.2 As a growth strategy

In 2014, Rodrik proposed that the definition of green industrial policy be limited to only this first goal: developing innovative technologies that have the potential to reduce greenhouse gas emissions.

However, in the current political reality, green industrial policy is also being seen explicitly as a vehicle for growth: the European Green Deal, has been labelled "*our new growth strategy*" by European Commission president Ursula von der Leyen, for example. Domestic content requirements in the US Inflation Reduction Act highlight the US administration's focus on green industrial policy as a vehicle to create domestic jobs. President Biden commented that tax credits will "*create thousands of good-paying jobs*"[63].

2.3.3 To escape import dependencies

Finally, governments are also using green industrial policy as a political lever to position their own countries more strategically in a future

---

63 See https://www.whitehouse.gov/briefing-room/statements-releases/2022/08/04/remarks-by-president-biden-in-roundtable-with-business-and-labor-leaders-on-the-inflation-reduction-act/.

global energy order. The inevitability of the energy transition sees governments evaluating the potential strategic dependences that may emerge in future. Europe's experience of rapid energy decoupling from Russia in 2022, and the associated challenges, have strengthened the resolve that energy systems should not be overly dependent on external suppliers.

Consequently, a third aim for green industrial policy is identified as contesting or breaking foreign market power. Rhetoric around the US Inflation Reduction Act has clearly focused on competition with China, which is perceived to have excessive power over supply chains that will be critical in a decarbonised system, such as the production of solar cells and lithium-ion batteries. The EU Net Zero Industry Act lays out the context: *"net-zero technologies are at the centre of strong geostrategic interests"*, and the *"global technology race"*. The word 'strategic' occurs one and half times more often than 'climate' in the document, and three times more than the word 'carbon'.

3 Identifying green sectors for intervention

Beginning in the early 2000s, governments provided substantial support for the deployment of solar photovoltaic and onshore and offshore wind generation. Since then, there has been a clear government focus on supporting specific green technologies. The European Commission in July 2020 proposed a Hydrogen Strategy (European Commission, 2020), which was strengthened in 2022 to set fixed targets for 2030 for the domestic production and import of low-carbon hydrogen. The European Union operates an Innovation Fund that supports certain technologies deemed eligible for support. A Battery Alliance was launched in 2017, aiming to make Europe a global leader in sustainable battery production and use. The draft Net Zero Industry Act now lays out a range of technologies in which the EU aims to achieve 40 percent production capacity relative to deployment by 2030.

Bringing down the cost of low-carbon technologies and thereby enabling large-scale decarbonisation in the EU and beyond is the most tangible benefit. But mastering the technology, creating new production clusters and gaining a competitive edge in sectors that will become very large global markets certainly contribute to the boldness of interventions. Electric vehicles are expected to dominate the market for new passenger vehicles in less than a decade; renewable power generation investments are already larger than fossil-fuelled investments. For heating installations, energy-intensive industries and heavy road, maritime and air transport, low-carbon alternatives will also have to surpass the often technologically quite different incumbent fossil technologies in the next decade.

This is a real new deal as some incumbent strength (eg in internal combustion engines) will quickly depreciate, making space for entrepreneurial newcomers. As demand for these technologies might initially outpace supply, substantial margins might be available.

Though comparative advantages in green technologies are not as entrenched as those in many conventional technologies, the potential to develop certain sectors is not distributed evenly between regions. Desirable areas for development of green technologies can be mapped against existing regional comparative advantages. A region's existing specialisations can be a predictor of future potential specialisation (Bergamini and Zachmann, 2020).

A better understanding can thus be developed about the suitability of particular regions to develop capacities in any given direction. Such a strategy can build on academic demonstration, such as that by Bergamini and Zachmann (2020). Hausmann *et al* (2021) presented an empirical framework that allows policymakers to estimate potential comparative advantage, including for industries not currently present in a region.

BOX 1: Energy-intensive industries typically have low value-added
European energy prices have increased drastically since 2021. This has put the spotlight on the relatively high share of energy-intensive sectors in some European regions. This leads to the very uncomfortable policy question of whether energy-intensive production should be defended, (in)directly subsidising its energy use? For the most energy-intensive products this is hard to justify if viewed only in terms of value added and jobs. A few European sub-sectors require a lot of natural gas as a feedstock and/or energy to produce a product that has little value added as it is a globally traded commodity. Mertens and Müller (2022) found that if Germany were to import products with high gas intensity and import substitutability, industry could reduce gas demand by 26 percent, while losing only 3 percent of final sales, and less in value added. Hence, strong strategic reasons are needed to justify enabling these sectors to use scarce energy (and thus drive up the energy price for all other European industries) for these processes.

4 Regions are unique and this drives development

4.1 Conceptual consideration

Economic activity is distributed unevenly across geography. Different regions have different industrial and institutional structures, different educational, human and physical capital bases, and different access to production factor inputs, such as primary energy. The result is that agglomerations form, with similar firms co-locating in the same area, enabling knowledge spillovers. Areas evolve to become specialised in certain economic activities and develop location-specific advantages, including in transportation and energy infrastructure, access to particularly skilled labour, knowledge spillovers and economies of scale. Geographic regions develop comparative advantages in particular sectors, which grow over time. These specialisations are best understood at the regional, not national level. Consider Belgium, a small country, but with diverging specialisations between its chemical industry in Antwerp and automotive industry in Ghent and Brussels.

4.2 Uniqueness influences a region's ability to absorb new knowledge
A firm's ability to comprehend and absorb new knowledge is conditional on its own knowledge base (Cohen and Levinthal, 1990). For a given regional domain of knowledge and technical capacity, growth paths are then biased toward economic activities related to the region's existing skill base. This is a result of regions being better able to absorb new knowledge when it is more closely related to an existing domain. Tacit – as opposed to codified – knowledge is particularly important as it cannot be copied easily and is geographically restricted (Balland *et al*, 2018). Where external knowledge is unrelated, the existing industrial base will struggle to learn from it and develop economically. Political attempts to impose knowledge or technological capacity that is deemed strategically important, but unrelated to a given region, has been described as attempting to build *"cathedrals in the desert"* (Balland *et al*, 2018). Todtling and Trippl's (2005) summary of literature showed that knowledge spillovers are often spatially bounded, while knowledge spills over effectively only when complementarities exist among sectors (Boschma and Iammarino, 2009).

4.3 Empirical evidence from the literature
Boschma and Gianelle (2014) summarised the empirical literature, concluding that the ability to develop new growth paths is not equal in all regions, while trade profiles tend to remain constant because of increasing returns to scale and non-transferable tacit knowledge that is accumulated over time. Bergamini and Zachmann (2020) complemented this with regional patent data from the OECD to identify technological clusters at NUTS-2 level in the EU. In a second step, the authors used network proximity between existing technological base and 14 innovative green technologies to estimate the potential advantage regions may have in each tech.

Hidalgo *et al* (2007) showed that countries expand their mixes of exports around products in which they have already established a comparative advantage. Neffke (2011) found that Swedish regions diversify into industries that are related to their current portfolio of industries, and that industries which leave the region are typically located at the periphery of the existing technology portfolio.

On green technology specifically, Montresor and Quatraro (2020) performed patent-based empirical analysis for 240 NUTS regions, to show that relatedness to pre-existing knowledge makes a new green-tech specialisation more probable. An important contribution is the clarification that non-green tech specialisation is still important, and perhaps even more so, for developing green tech capabilities. To develop capacities for building hydrogen pipelines, it is helpful to have existing skills building natural-gas pipelines.

Boschma and Iammarino (2009) related the import and export structure of Italian provinces, to show that regions benefit particularly from extra regional knowledge when that knowledge originates from sectors that are related, but not too similar, to those present in the region. If cognitive proximity is too close, nothing is learned.

Box 2: Problems with picking winners

The key problem of industrial policy is the risk of 'picking winners': governments trying to decide in favour of which sectors/technologies/companies they are tilting the playing field. It is already intrinsically difficult to beat the market (where equity and finance providers should have a strong incentive to bet on the right horse). But governments not only typically lack the resources to make good choices, they are also politically more accountable to incumbent interests than to those unborn sectors and jobs. Moreover (hidden) distributional motives to favour specific regions/stakeholder groups over others can even inefficiently bias 'horizontal industrial policies'.

Following intervention, there is a risk of evaluating support given to incumbents overly positively, as the high indirect cost of withholding resources (skilled people, energy, finance) from new sectors is not properly accounted for.

5 Identifying regional comparative advantage

Regions typically do not become active in all industrial sectors at once. They specialise in several sectors in which they are particularly successful. Thereby, sectoral success in a region is driven by a complex combination of local knowledge, specific human capital, infrastructure, geography, input factor cost/availability, economic, industrial and institutional organisation. Some of these factors are relatively rigid, some are endogenous to past development and some can be shaped by policy. The combination of these factors can be said to determine a region's *comparative advantage*[64]. Every region, by definition, has a comparative advantage. It is a challenge to identify in which sectors this not directly observable advantage lies.

Bottom-up approaches mapping out specific regional factor endowments (eg based on regional labour surveys, energy cost and infrastructure statistics, etc) are possible. But as so many drivers determine a comparative advantage in a specific sector, and some factors are rather difficult to measure directly (and in an internationally comparable way), reliable bottom-up approaches are extremely challenging.

An alternative and/or complement is indirect approaches based on current outputs, rather than available inputs. Here, identifying comparative advantages can be approached empirically, in two steps:

1. Identifying the economic activities, and innovation efforts, currently present in a region;
2. Using known technological and knowledge linkages to project potential future specialisation.

---

64 The ability of a firm, region or country to produce a particular good or service at a lower opportunity cost than competitors. Opportunity cost is key to *comparative* rather than *absolute* advantage, and the idea that every economic actor in a system has *comparative* advantage at producing something.

5.1 Identifying current regional specialisation

Where market data is available, a typical step for translating this into comparative advantage is assessing export and import structure. The logic is that trade brings a region into direct competition with neighbouring and competitors further afield. Therefore, if a region is particularly successful at exporting a particular good, it is likely to be competitive in that sector. Export data has often been used to map national comparative advantage (eg by calculating the Balassa (1965) revealed comparative advantage index), for example by Hidalgo (2007), Boschma and Iammarino (2009), Zachmann (2016) and Hausmann (2021). However, trade data is typically not available at regional level[65] and so alternative indicators should be used to explore current regional specialisation.

Identifying current economic activities present in a region is relatively straightforward. For Europe, regional economic data is widely available for industrial output, employment, production and value added, but much of the data has only a (very) limited sectoral/product resolution. To have not only regional, but also sectoral and temporal granularity, more indirect sources might be needed.

Regional specialisation can be explored using labour-market data. For example, text mining of job vacancy descriptions and using artificial intelligence methods to develop up-to-date classifications can offer granular insights into regional specialisation trends (even slightly forward-looking).

Patent data is another source of information. A patent offers legal protection for new and innovative products or processes. Such data therefore can provide a very granular indication of technological and scientific data on a sectoral basis (see for example, Bergamini and Zachmann, 2020; Montresor and Quatraro, 2020). Data is publicly available for very specific locations and narrowly defined technological

---

65 Customs data might be in principle available at the zip-code level – but we have not seen them made accessible to research.

domains. Making them comparable internationally is not easy[66], but using relative frequency of technologies in specific regions gives an indication of a region's specialisation.

5.2 Exploiting linkages between sectors

Consistent with Hidalgo and Hausmann (2009), we can view the product space as a representation of the underlying economic factors that influence competitiveness. If a region specialises in producing semi-conductors, condensers and photovoltaic cells, this indicates the presence of economic factors that are conducive for such activities. There are relatively strong (and typically intuitive) linkages between specialisations. Turning this around, a region that specialises in a certain sector indicates that certain economic conditions are present, which also increase the likelihood of successfully specialising in related economic activities.

For export data, establishing the links between specialisations can be done relatively directly by exploiting the coincidence of revealed comparative advantages, eg through correlation or some regression analysis. Boschma and Gianelle (2014) proposed that relatedness between industries can be measured in different ways, including: industry classification codes, co-occurrence of products, input-output linkages and the intensity of labour reallocations between industries. As patent data classifications are much more granular and patents typically have more than one classification, Zachmann (2016) used the relative frequency with which two industry codes appear for the same patent to establish linkages between specialisations.

Building on the above, one approach to identify regional potential is to use predictive algorithms trained with historical data. That is, current specialisation on a regional level is regressed on past

---

[66] Patents are still not a perfect indicator of innovative activity. They measure only specific steps in the innovation process, and only apply in case entrepreneurs do apply for legal protection. Their quality can vary significantly, with some sectors, such as photovoltaic cells, being characterised by wider patent categories than others (Zachmann, 2016).

specialisation in the corresponding product space. The obtained coefficients allow extrapolation for any region of which technologies are more or less likely to emerge, based on past specialisation trends.

Box 3: From official statistics to big data

Pre-defined industrial and geographical classifications will not necessarily map well to a dynamic reality. For example, the 'Modifiable Areal Unit Problem' refers to the fact that clustering does not always take place at the geographic scale of available data (eg NUTS-2), and working at inappropriate scales can distort results. Second, industrial classifications are backward-looking and may constrain understanding of emergent sectors, including low-carbon tech applications, which may sit across multiple industries. Stich *et al* (2023) cited the fact that the NACE classification is over a decade old.

Recent, innovative attempts in the literature have been made to utilise big data and web scraping techniques for better identification of regional clusters. Stich *et al* (2023) scraped a dataset of archived webpages, which they interrogated using natural language processing techniques, to build a bottom-up classification of economic activities, alongside physical trading addresses that businesses report on their websites. They argued that their novel methodology can overcome traditional limitations, and successfully applied the methodology to the postcode region of Shoreditch, London. Papagiannidis *et al* (2017) applied a big-data mining methodology to identify regional clusters, applied to the northeast of England.

Making approaches based on very granular big data productive for industrial policy-making should allow for better targeting.

5.3 Interacting with industry

Finally, for all the quantitative and innovative analysis, having people on the ground engaging with local stakeholders will remain fundamental for regional policymakers to understand community specialisations and needs. In seminal work, Rodrik (2014) argued that the state should build on knowledge that resides in the private sector, in a pragmatic way. This requires significant communication between public and private sectors, with the state embedded but not 'in bed' with private interests (Tagliapietra and Veugelers, 2020). The challenge is for forums to be established in which policymakers can learn from entrepreneurs, but not fall prey to lobbying attempts and vested interests when designing policy.

6 The new energy map: evolving factors of production

Regions have unique comparative advantages, and empirical methods can reliably identify these. Maps of least resistance can be designed which plot the likely ability of any region to diversify into a desirable green technology.

One specific extension must be added to include the evolution of energy as a relative input cost. Europe's existing heavy industrial base has developed on the back of location-specific access to cheap fossil fuel-based energy. Bridge *et al* (2013) found that Europe's geographical pattern of industrialisation *"closely coincided with the geological distribution of coal beneath the ground"*.

Figure 2: Historically, ferrous metal facilities were built close to coal deposits

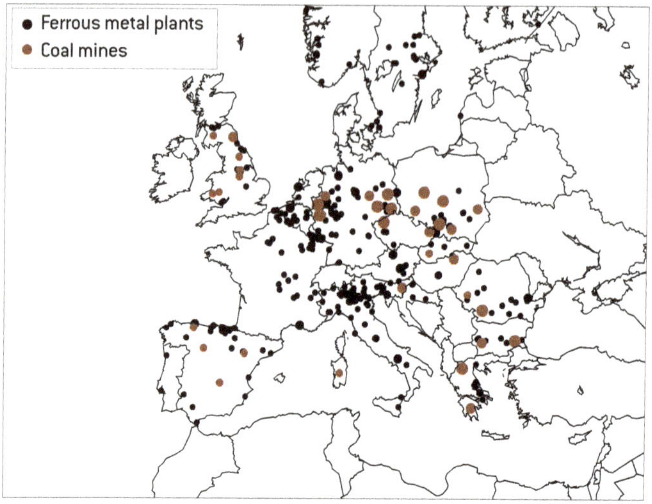

Source: Bruegel and Alves Dias *et al* (2018).

The energy transition implies that access to cheap fossil-fuel energy will no longer be a relevant factor for locational decisions. Instead, access to cheap, low-carbon energy will become important. McWilliams and Zachmann (2021) used the following framework to evaluate the extent to which the low-carbon evolution will change economic geographies, comprising three elements:

1. Location-specific differences in the cost of capturing clean energy;
2. The technological ability to cheaply transport this energy;
3. Existing 'sticky' agglomeration effects where investments, and policy support are drawn to existing capital and human investments.

Consequently, *maps of least resistance* must be adapted to include information about anticipated access to cheap, green energy, and the impact this will have on future competitiveness. The necessity of energy transformation can be considered an exogenous shock to a region's initial endowment. All else being equal, it will impact the comparative advantage and subsequent innovative capacity of a region.

Geography and endowments of renewable capacities (wind, sun, flowing water) are important, but government policy will also be heavily influential. Local regulations concerning land availability are fundamentally important for factor (1): *costs of capturing clean energy*. Policymakers play a central role in infrastructure development of electricity grids, and potentially hydrogen grids, which determine factor (2): *the ability to cheaply transport energy to a given region*. Policy may also choose to artificially reduce energy input costs through preferential industry tariffs or by flattening electricity costs across a country irrespective of location.

Existing and proven approaches can and should be used by policymakers to produce detailed *comparative advantage* maps. Onto this, desirable innovations can be contrasted against existing *comparative advantage*, as along with information on low-carbon energy input costs. Ideally, the industrial classification for calculating this *comparative advantage* should adapt over time as new low-carbon industrial processes develop that will not necessarily fit neatly into existing classifications. The use of more than one classification based on different techniques can provide a more holistic picture. The first steps toward such an approach have been undertaken by European governments under the Research and Innovation Strategies for Smart Specialisation (RIS3), as part of EU Cohesion Policy (Gianelle *et al*, 2020a), including initial priority visualisation[67].

Such information could be used as a tool for regional bottom-up approaches to identify relevant sectors to approach, and for national top-down approaches through which the most suitable regions are identified for supporting priority technologies.

---

67 See https://s3platform.jrc.ec.europa.eu/digital-innovation-hubs-tool.

7 'Smart' green industrial policy

7.1 One size-fits-all is not suitable
The primary consequence of regional uniqueness is that a one-size-fits-all industrial policy is not appropriate and should rather be tailored to regional needs. This follows from the fact that the leveraging of structural economic factors that are typically considered to drive growth will have different impacts in different areas. What matters for regional economic growth is the interaction of structural factors, not simply their aggregate volume (Zachmann, 2012).

7.2 Truly horizontal industrial policy is impossible
A regional economy cannot reach 'critical mass' in every domain, but must specialise. A local government cannot achieve all the specific capacities and infrastructure needed for all economic activity, so must specialise (Foray, 2017). Moreover, truly horizontal industrial policy is impossible. Each unique economic activity requires a set of specific inputs for success, many of which are influenced by public intervention. Public intervention, by definition, therefore, will not be neutral, but will have different impacts on different industrial bases (Hausmann and Rodrik, 2006). With information on regional *comparative advantage*, industrial policy can be tailored to put in place specific support that will best grow local knowledge.

7.3 Geographically targeted 'green bets'
Governments do not, and cannot, 'pick winners'. Instead, green industrial policy is built on the principle of making informed 'green bets', which at the individual level may or may not turn out profitable. What is desirable is that the aggregation of these green bets creates a portfolio which generates positive societal return. The public nature of industrial policy means intervention is centred on areas that lack private investment due to the largely socially externalised returns involved (see section 1).

To this understanding, smart green industrial policy adds the notion that policymakers target 'green bets' geographically. After the smart gambler picks a horse, he walks the length of the track to find the bookmaker offering the best odds on his choice. In similar fashion, when making green bets, governments should scour the range of geographically specific *comparative advantages*, to find the best odds of success. Alternatively, regional governments operating within a given *comparative advantage* should optimise public intervention to leverage domestic capacities.

7.4 Removing specific bottlenecks
Based on an evaluation of a regions *comparative advantage*, policymakers should look to remove and address bottlenecks that are slowing evolution into nearby green technologies. This does not entail simply providing subsidies to incumbent firms, which should only be a last-resort policy measure.

Instead, the goal for industrial policy is to facilitate organic growth toward green, innovative sectors. With defined technologies in mind, policies attempt to use industrial policy measures to smoothe the transition of industries and knowledge into said areas. This should be focused on bottlenecks that have public-good characteristics, which individual companies cannot solve, such as the provision of infrastructure. Regulatory measures, public spending on R&D, specific curricula at universities and colleges, public-private partnerships, support for commercialisation of research ideas, specific training of local workforces and encouragement of knowledge exchange between similar regions, can all be tailored to fit this design.

It is a challenge to identify bottlenecks that hold up development of individual technologies in certain regions. It is another challenge to implement smart policies to alleviate these bottlenecks. Smart specialisation has been a target for EU Cohesion Policy since 2014. In their review, Gianelle *et al* (2020a) concluded that regions put significant effort into defining priority areas for development, but then did not use this information to orient policy implementation. That is quite possibly because regional authorities lack the capacity, and know-how to do so. Bergamini and Zachmann (2020) provided a first step in this regard by empirically associating a variety of economic indicators with regional specialisation. Determining causality is an area for future policy-relevant academic research.

One temptation will be to subsidise an individual factor input cost. For example, policy could design industrial tariffs for electricity prices that provide lower prices for industries in a certain region. Governments might also consider subsidising the imports of new green fuels, such as hydrogen toward existing hubs. This approach only creates *artificial* specialisations in a region, dependent on government support, and are therefore not desirable. They will likely be driven for political reasons and are hence at risk of rent seeking. In cases where policymakers want to use such a tool, they should be explicitly limited in time.

7.5 Policy learning

The decision to embark on a revolutionary industrial policy programme of green technology development, that will reach into the billions of euros, must be accompanied by a rethink of, and improvements to, policy functioning. Significantly increased resources must also be made available to the public sector for more efficient distribution of the increased funds.

Government analytical capabilities should be developed for mapping out both regional *comparative advantage*, and *maps of least resistance*. Gianelle *et al* (2020b) argued that this will require the establishment of stable and accountable policy teams at the regional level, which are not vulnerable to political cycles, but accountable for the implementation of smart green industrial policy design.

The innovative and experimental nature of smart green industrial policy means active learning is important. Failures can be celebrated, but the public sector must learn from them. Built-in *ex-ante* and *ex-post* evaluation of policy is key. Each intervention should be accompanied by clear guidelines that will be used to evaluate its success at predefined time periods.

8 Conclusion

Industrial policy is set to play a critical role in the decarbonisation efforts of the next decade, providing billions of euros in public support. The challenge of stimulating innovative green technological development, whilst boosting domestic growth and reducing strategic import dependences, is significant. It is imperative that the public sector develops better competences for more efficient distribution of limited funds.

In this chapter, we have focused on one element: the idea that industrial policy should be focused on alleviating constraints, thus allowing regional *comparative advantages* to flourish and grow into nearby desirable green technologies. A wide literature base has shown that regions have unique potential growth pathways, and emerging analysis is demonstrating proven techniques for identifying these specialisations at decomposed granularities.

An area for future research remains the type of policy intervention that can best alleviate bottlenecks at regional level. We warn against firm-specific support, or artificially lowering the prices of certain energy inputs. Instead, support should focus on removing bottlenecks which have some public good nature, such as infrastructure provision. The targeting of this support to regional specificities will ensure that public support is efficient and provides the best chance for countries to successfully develop competences in the green technologies of the future.

References

Alves Dias, P., K. Kanellopoulos, H. Medarac, Z. Kapetaki E. Miranda-Barbosa, R. Shortall ... E. Tzimas (2018) 'EU coal regions: opportunities and challenges ahead', *JRC Science for Policy Report*, Joint Research Centre, European Commission, available at http://dx.doi.org/10.2760/064809

Balland, P-A., R. Boschma, J. Crespo and D. Rigby (2018) 'Smart specialisation policy in the European Union: relatedness, knowledge complexity, and regional diversification', *Regional Studies*, 53(9): 1252-1268, available at https://doi.org/10.1080/00343404.2018.1437900

Balassa, B. (1965) 'Trade Liberalisation and "Revealed" Comparative Advantage', *The Manchester School* 33(2): 99-123, available at https://doi.org/10.1111/j.1467-9957.1965.tb00050.x

Bergamini, E. and G. Zachmann (2020) 'Understanding the European Union's regional potential in low-carbon technologies', *Working Paper* 07/2020, Bruegel

Bordoff, J. and M. O'Sullivan (2022) 'The New Energy Order', *Foreign Affairs*, 7 June, available at: https://www.foreignaffairs.com/articles/energy/2022-06-07/markets-new-energy-order

Boschma, R. and C. Gianelle (2014) 'Regional Branching and Smart Specialisation Policy', *S3 Policy Brief Series* No. 06/2014, European Commission Joint Research Centre

Boschma, R. and S. Iammarino (2009) 'Related Variety, Trade Linkages, and Regional Growth in Italy', *Economic Geography* 85(3): 289-311

Bridge, G., S. Bouzarovski, M. Bradshaw and N. Eyre (2013) 'Geographies of energy transition: Space, place and the low-carbon economy', *Energy Policy* 53: 331-340, available at https://doi.org/10.1016/j.enpol.2012.10.066

Cohen, W.M. and D.A. Levinthal (1990) 'Absorptive capacity: New perspective on learning and innovation', *Administrative Science Quarterly* 35: 128–52

European Commission (2020) 'A hydrogen strategy for a climate-neutral Europe', COM(2020) 301 final

Foray, D. (2017) 'The Economic Fundamentals of Smart Specialisation Strategies', in S. Radosevic, A. Curaj, R. Gheorghiu, L. Andreescu and I. Wade (eds) *Advances in the Theory and Practice of Smart Specialisation*, Academic Press, available at http://dx.doi.org/10.1016/B978-0-12-804137-6.00002-4

Gianelle, C., F. Guzzo and K. Mieszkowski (2020a) 'Smart Specialisation: what gets lost in translation from concept to practice?' *Regional Studies* 54(10): 1377-1388, available at https://doi.org/10.1080/00343404.2019.1607970

Gianelle, C., D. Kyriakou, P. McCann and K. Morgan (2020b) 'Smart Specialisation on the move: reflections on six years of implementation and prospects for the future', *Regional Studies* 54(10): 1323-1327, available at https://doi.org/10.1080/00343404.2020.1817364

Hausmann, R. and D. Rodrik (2006) 'Doomed to choose: Industrial policy as predicament', Center for International Development Blue Sky Conference Paper, September

Hausmann, R., D. Stock and M. Yildirim (2021) 'Implied Comparative Advantage', *Research Policy* 51(8), available at https://doi.org/10.1016/j.respol.2020.104143

Hidalgo, C., B. Klinger, A-L. Barabási and R. Hausmann (2007) 'The Product Space Conditions the Development of Nations', *Science* 317(5847): 482-487, available at https://www.science.org/doi/10.1126/science.1144581

Huberty, M. and G. Zachmann, (2011) 'Green exports and the global product space: Prospects for EU industrial policy', *Working Paper* 2011/07, Bruegel

McWilliams, B. and G. Zachmann (2021) 'Commercialisation contracts: European support for low-carbon technology deployment', *Policy Contribution* 15/2021, Bruegel

Mertens, M. and S. Müller (2022) 'Wirtschaftliche Folgen Des Gaspreisanstiegs Für Die Deutsche Industrie', *IWH Policy Notes* 2/2022, Leibniz-Institut für Wirtschaftsforschung Halle, available at https://www.iwh-halle.de/fileadmin/user_upload/publications/iwh_policy_notes/iwh-pn_2022-02_de_Gaspreisanstieg_Industrie.pdf

Montresor, S. and F. Quatraro (2020) 'Green technologies and Smart Specialisation Strategies: a European patent-based analysis of the intertwining of technological relatedness and key enabling technologies', *Regional Studies* 54(10): 1354-1365, available at https://www.tandfonline.com/doi/full/10.1080/00343404.2019.1648784

Neffke, F., M. Henning and R. Boschma (2011) 'How Do Regions Diversify over Time? Industry Relatedness and the Development of New Growth Paths in Regions', *Economic Geography* 87(3): 237-265

Papagiannidis S., E. See-To, D.G. Assimakopoulos and Y. Yang (2018) 'Identifying industrial clusters with a novel big-data methodology: Are SIC codes (not) fit for purpose in the Internet age?' *Computers & Operations Research*, 98: 355-366, available at https://doi.org/10.1016/j.cor.2017.06.010

Rodrik, D. (2014) 'Green Industrial Policy', *Oxford Review of Economic Policy* 30(3): 469-491, available at https://doi.org/10.1093/oxrep/gru025

Stich, C., E. Tranos and A. Nathan (2023) 'Modeling clusters from the ground up: A web data approach', *Urban Analytics and City Science* 50(1): 244-267

Tagliapietra, S. and R. Veugelers (2020) A Green Industrial Policy for Europe, *Blueprint Series* 31, Bruegel, available at https://www.bruegel.org/book/green-industrial-policy-europe

Tödtling, F. and M. Trippl (2005) 'One size fits all? Towards a differentiated regional innovation policy approach', *Research Policy* 34(2005): 1203-1219

Zachmann, G. (2012) 'Smart Choices for Growth', *Policy Contribution* 2012/21, Bruegel available at https://www.bruegel.org/sites/default/files/wp_attachments/1211_pc_gz_smart_choices_for_growth.pdf

Zachmann, G. (2016) 'An approach to identify the sources of low-carbon growth for Europe', *Policy Contribution* 16/2016, Bruegel, available at https://www.bruegel.org/policy-brief/approach-identify-sources-low-carbon-growth-europe

11 Industrial policy for electric vehicle supply chains and the US-EU fight over the Inflation Reduction Act

Chad P. Bown

1 Introduction[68]

In August 2022, President Joe Biden signed the United States Inflation Reduction Act (IRA) into law. The European Union celebrated the fact that the United States finally had an aggressive climate policy, applauding the administration's commitment to reduce emissions from 2005 levels by 50–52 percent by 2030[69]. But it found fault with a number of the IRA's details.

One of the EU's most important complaints was the law's discriminatory 'Buy American' (local content) incentives. The IRA's new tax credit for electric vehicles (EVs), for example, seemed initially to deem eligible only cars assembled in North America. If so, this rule would shut out a Volkswagen imported from Germany but not one

---

68 The author thanks Olivier Blanchard, Kim Clausing, Kristin Dziczek, Robert Lawrence, Marcus Noland, and Brad Setser for helpful comments and discussions, and Madona Devasahayam, Barbara Karni, and Melina Kolb for editorial assistance. Yilin Wang and Julieta Contreras provided outstanding research assistance. Nia Kitchin, Melina Kolb, and Oliver Ward assisted with graphics.

69 Model estimates from Bistline *et al* (2023) suggested that the IRA could help the United States reduce emissions from 2005 levels by 32–42 percent by 2030, a 6-11 percentage point improvement relative to the business as usual (non-IRA) projections.

manufactured in Tennessee. Over the next few months, the US Treasury Department wrote implementing regulations that tweaked key IRA provisions on EVs in ways that accommodated some of the EU's concerns. Doing so through implementing regulation, however, rather than reform of the statute, comes with its own consequences. And some of the trading partners' more fundamental concerns with the IRA could not be fixed through implementing regulations.

This chapter showcases the political-economic complexity of US and EU attempts to cooperate over clean-energy transition policy to address a global externality. EVs are but one example of the challenge facing partners with integrated supply chains, similar levels of economic development and shared worries over climate and other environmental problems, rising inequality, workers, social issues and democracy itself. The EV conflict laid bare the different ways in which the United States and the European Union prioritise economic efficiency, World Trade Organisation (WTO) rules, the approach to non-market economies and national security vulnerabilities that arise from depending on an authoritarian regime such as China for import sourcing of critical inputs.

The details matter for how the IRA and its implementing regulations affect incentives for international trade in EVs and their key inputs. This chapter explores those details, including the potentially transformative decision that leased vehicles could qualify for consumer tax credits under a separate and independent track of the IRA that did not have those discriminatory local content incentives. It also examines numerous other policies – including the considerable differences in US and EU import tariffs on EVs toward each other and toward third countries, such as China – that are also likely to affect EV trade patterns in ways that offset some effects of the IRA. In the pre-IRA policy landscape, for example, EU imports of EVs were increasingly dominated by sourcing from China, which had largely displaced US exports. Furthermore, the United States continued to import large numbers of EVs from Europe even after implementing the IRA. Whether this trend continues, of course, remains an open question.

Most importantly, this chapter explains what the United States did in passing the IRA, as well as its implementing regulations, and why it did it. Along the way it attempts to identify inefficiencies, tradeoffs, inconsistencies and potential unintended consequences of the US policy approach, especially as manifest in the implementing regulations announced in the eight months following the IRA's passage in August 2022.

The analytical framing is driven largely by economics. Because the analysis operates in a setting motivated by both enormous environmental externalities (climate) and growing externalities associated with national security concerns, it is limited to identifying channels and clarifying trade-offs. Without an explicit model or data, such an approach is admittedly modest. The goal is to provide a detailed explanation of the policy to provide a building block for more formal modelling that can generate informed normative recommendations for enhanced policy cooperation in light of continually shifting real-world political-economic constraints.

2 The US policy objectives for its electric vehicle tax credits

Reducing greenhouse gas emissions, including carbon dioxide, is critical to meeting the Paris Agreement objectives of limiting the rise in global temperatures. This massive environmental externality provides a clear motivation for the US federal government to intervene with policy.

In the climate crisis, the economically efficient, first-best policy is a Pigouvian tax equal to the social cost of carbon. The current US federal estimate of that cost is $51 per tonne of carbon dioxide emissions, though recent estimates indicate that an updated measure would be in the range of $185–$200 per tonne (Rennert *et al*, 2022; EPA, 2022). The US federal government has never introduced a carbon price or an economically equivalent cap and trade scheme[70]. It has largely turned

---

70 At the sub-federal level, states like California have introduced carbon pricing programmes (Clausing and Wolfram, forthcoming). OECD (2022) estimated that 32 percent of greenhouse gas emissions in the United States in 2021 were subject to some *"positive net effect carbon rate"* policy instrument.

instead to regulations mandating certain clean-energy standards.

Given the constrained policy environment in which it operated, the Biden Administration also focused on second-best policies, including subsidies, in the IRA, which was signed into law on 16 August 2022 (Table 1). In general, subsidies for the take-up of clean energy are a second-best solution because they encourage excessive consumption of energy overall[71].

---

71 In the absence of a market failure for clean energy, a subsidy will lead to excess equilibrium production and consumption of clean energy relative to the social optimum, even if the subsidy internalises the negative externality in the dirty energy market (by reducing demand for dirty energy, assuming clean and dirty energy are substitutes in consumption). One potential market failure for clean energy could result from learning-by-doing (increasing returns to scale). Bistline *et al* (2023) found that the learning-by-doing externality would need to be sizable for a subsidy to be equivalent to the first-best carbon tax.

Table 1: Key events affecting US policy on electric vehicles

Date	Event
15 November 2021	President Biden signs into law the Infrastructure Investment and Jobs Act (House: 228-206; Senate 69-30). The bipartisan legislation includes funding of up to $7.5 billion for EV charging stations.
19 November 2021	The US House of Representatives passes the Build Back Better Act (220-213), which includes tax credits for EVs. The bill never passes the Senate.
27 July 2022	Senator Joe Manchin and Senate Majority Leader Chuck Schumer announce an agreement to allow a vote on the Inflation Reduction Act (IRA) of 2022. It subsequently passes both the Senate (51-50) and House (220-207).
16 August 2022	President Biden signs the IRA into law. The North American assembly requirement in IRA Section 30D goes into effect immediately.
7 September 2022	The Congressional Budget Office releases revised estimates of the budgetary effects of IRA over 2022-31.
1 December 2022	In response to European complaints, during the state visit of French President Emmanuel Macron, Biden says his administration will make 'tweaks' to the IRA.
19 December 2022	The Treasury Department delays proposed regulation on critical minerals and battery components requirements for Section 30D tax credits in the IRA until March 2023.
29 December 2022	Treasury (Internal Revenue Service) clarifies that the IRA's commercial clean vehicle tax credits (Section 45W) are available to consumers who lease vehicles. Treasury also releases a Section 30D White Paper anticipating the direction of proposed guidance on critical mineral and battery component value calculations.
3 February 2023	Treasury reclassifies certain vehicles, making more models eligible for the Section 30D consumer tax credit.
10 March 2023	President Biden and European Commission President Ursula van der Leyen launch negotiations on a targeted critical minerals agreement that would enable relevant critical minerals extracted or processed in the European Union to count toward requirements for clean vehicles in the IRA's Section 30D.
28 March 2023	The United States and Japan sign a Critical Minerals Agreement that qualifies Japan as a 'free trade agreement' partner for the IRA's Section 30D critical minerals content requirements.
31 March 2023	Treasury proposes a rule for content requirements in the IRA's Section 30D, including general criteria for 'free trade agreement' partners that will go into effect 18 April.
12 April 2023	The Environmental Protection Agency proposes new regulations for vehicle emissions to ensure that two-thirds of new passenger cars will be all-electric by 2032.
18 April 2023	The content requirements of IRA Section 30D announced on 31 March 2023, go into effect.

2.1 The environmental policy objectives of US tax credits on electric vehicles

Transportation accounted for 38 percent of US carbon emissions in 2021, the largest single contributor to emissions (CBO, 2022a). Of this figure, 83 percent came from personal vehicles (58 percent) and commercial trucks and buses (25 percent); air transport made up another 10 percent. If the United States is to reach its overall goal, carbon dioxide emissions from transportation will have to fall.

Historically, US consumers have been relatively slow to switch from cars with internal combustion engines (ICEs) to EVs. In 2021, for example, only 5 percent of new vehicles sold in the United States were EVs, a much smaller share than in China (16 percent) or the EU (18 percent) (Figure 1).

Figure 1: The US lags the EU and China on electric vehicle sales

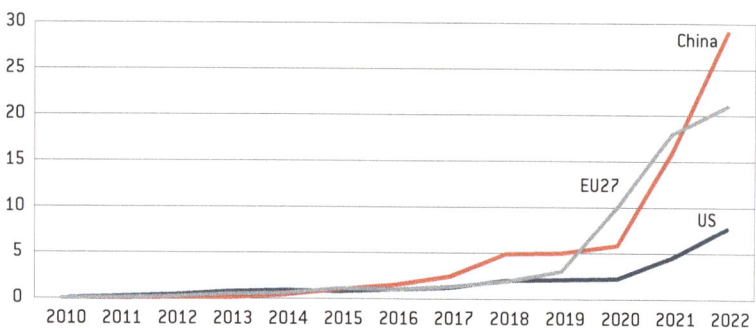

Source: International Energy Agency. Notes: Electric vehicles include battery electric vehicles and plug-in hybrids. Figures are based on number of vehicles, not their value.

Several factors explain why the share is small in the United States One is EV cost, relative to comparably performing ICE vehicles, especially since the gasoline used to power ICE vehicles has been inexpensive relative to many other countries. Another is consumer tastes. Many Americans prefer large vehicles that can drive long distances, which initial EVs could not easily do, especially given the lack of charging infrastructure in the geographically expansive United States[72]. This constraint on consumer EV take-up is often referred to as 'range anxiety'.

At the federal level, the United States provided consumer tax credits for EVs of up to $7,500 dating back to the American Recovery and Reinvestment Act (ARRA) of 2009. They were phased out once a manufacturer's US sales reached 200,000 units. By the summer of 2022, Nissan and Ford were getting close to reaching the cap, and Tesla, General Motors (GM) and Toyota had exceeded it and were no longer receiving subsidies[73].

To incentivise buyers to switch from ICE vehicles to EVs, the IRA modified existing federal consumer tax credits. It removed the 200,000 unit cap, making the tax credits available again to Tesla, GM and Toyota. The uncapped credits would be available for 10 years.

In an attempt to encourage automakers to build out a fleet of EV models for the mass market, the IRA initially limited the tax credit to lower-priced EVs and to individuals or households with lower earnings. These provisions were added out of concern that most of the limited EV take-up – and subsidies paid out by US policy under earlier tax credits – had gone to higher-income consumers who purchased expensive models, such as early Teslas. To the extent that these purchases would have been made without the tax credits, they were both costly to taxpayers and had insufficient impact on achieving US climate policy objectives[74].

2.2 Additional policy objectives of the tax credits

The IRA includes more than just consumer tax credits, as it also attempts to achieve other objectives. Understanding these requires

---

72 The bipartisan Infrastructure Investment and Jobs Act that was signed into law in November 2021 provided $7.5 billion of funding to address part of this challenge.

73 Jon Linkov, 'Toyota Becomes 3rd Automaker to Reach Electric Vehicle Tax Credit Limit', *Consumer Reports*, 7 July 2002, https://www.consumerreports.org/hybrids-evs/toyota-reaches-electric-vehicle-tax-credit-limit-a9709089660/.

74 For a review of the literature, see Sheldon (2022).

getting to grips with what the US government perceived as the initial, pre-IRA economic and policy equilibrium, as well as the domestic political-economic forces that would make the green energy transition policy sustainable and not subject to a political reversal of the sort that took place in 2017, when President Donald Trump pulled the United States out of the Paris Agreement.

The United States has a large, legacy ICE automobile industry. As ICE vehicles and EVs involve some different corporate players, as well as different inputs in their supply chains, a transition from one to the other puts hundreds of thousands of jobs at risk (Klier and Rubenstein, 2022; Hanson, 2023). Many of these at-risk jobs are in politically important swing states, such as Michigan and Ohio, where they affect communities that have suffered disproportionately large economic losses since 2001 – a period that coincides with the *"China shock"* (Autor *et al*, 2021). Whatever the source of the shock, the failure of workers and communities to adjust continues to play an outsized role in policy discussions – unsurprisingly, given the effectiveness with which Donald Trump weaponised it during the 2016 presidential campaign and while in office.

The US perception of the pre-IRA equilibrium was that it was dominated by China, which subsidised EVs. Beijing had prioritised the sector as part of its highly controversial 'Made in China 2025' industrial policy programme announced in 2015. China's supply-side policies for batteries were also alleged to discriminate in favour of indigenous firms[75]. Finally, its import tariffs were high, providing firms that produced locally protection from foreign competition (in game-theoretic terms, if the rivalry were modelled as a prisoner's dilemma, China was

---

75 See Trefor Moss, 'China's Road to Electric-Car Domination Is Driven in Part by Batteries', *Wall Street Journal*, 21 October 2017, https://www.wsj.com/articles/chinas-road-to-electric-car-domination-is-driven-in-part-by-batteries-1508587203; and Trefor Moss, 'Power Play: How China-Owned Volvo Avoids Beijing's Battery Rules', *Wall Street Journal*, 17 May 2018, https://www.wsj.com/articles/power-play-how-china-owned-volvo-avoids-beijings-battery-rules-1526551937.

already playing noncooperatively; if it were a Stackelberg game, China already had a first-mover advantage).

As a result, by 2022 China's EV exports to the world were booming, especially in volume terms (Figure 2, panel b), as Chinese exports tended to be in lower-priced models. US exports of EVs lagged considerably.

Figure 2: US electric vehicle exports are also trailing China and the EU

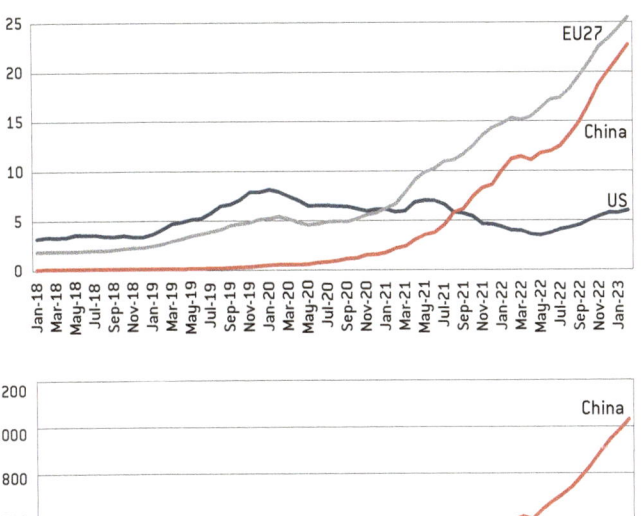

Source: US International Trade Commission Dataweb, Eurostat, China Customs. Notes: Figures show battery and fuel cell electric vehicles only. Trade values for the EU are converted to US dollars from euros using end-of-month $/€ spot exchange rates from FRED (DEXUSEU). For the EU, the CN codes are 87038010 and 87038090 in 2017–23 and 87039010 in 2016. For the US, the Schedule B code is 8703800000. For China, the HS code is 87038000. The code for both the US and China was created in 2017 and did not exist for electric vehicles prior to 2017.

In theory, the United States could have confronted China over concerns about its non-market economy and system of subsidies, negotiating rules to jointly limit such subsidies to cooperative and globally efficient levels[76]. It could have worked jointly with other major exporters, including the European Union and Japan, to address China together. However, the contemporary political reality of US-China tensions had taken that cooperative equilibrium off the table. From the US government's perspective, failure to intervene in the EV market risked another, automobile industry-specific 'China shock', with potentially devastating domestic political consequences.

Another important policy objective of the IRA is to improve the resilience of the EV battery supply chain by developing input sourcing for batteries outside of China, which dominates the supply chain for battery components, as well as lithium, cobalt, graphite, nickel and other critical materials (Leruth *et al*, 2022). Multiple concerns lay behind this goal. One is economic competitiveness. China has long used a variety of export-restrictions on inputs – including some critical minerals – to take advantage of its supply-side market power, thereby supporting its downstream, using industries relative to their foreign competitors (OECD, 2023).

A second is national security. As Biden Administration National Security Advisor Jake Sullivan would state in a major speech in April 2023[77], "*More than 80 percent of critical minerals are processed by one country, China. Clean-energy supply chains are at risk of being*

---

76 The United States did confront China unilaterally over a number of Chinese policy issues related to trade; the Trump Administration's trade war tariffs ultimately covered two-third of US imports from China. However, the approach was an ineffective way to address the subsidies issue (Bown, 2018). It was thus unsurprising that the 'Phase One' agreement that President Trump signed with China in January 2021 contained nothing that would address China's subsidies (Bown, 2021).

77 White House, 'Remarks by National Security Advisor Jake Sullivan on Renewing American Economic Leadership at the Brookings Institution', 27 April 2023, https://www.whitehouse.gov/briefing-room/speeches-remarks/2023/04/27/remarks-by-national-security-advisor-jake-sullivan-on-renewing-american-economic-leadership-at-the-brookings-institution/.

weaponised in the same way as oil in the 1970s, or natural gas in Europe in 2022. So through the investments in the Inflation Reduction Act and Bipartisan Infrastructure Law, we're taking action." With US-China geopolitical tensions worsening, the United States was unwilling to expose itself to the same sort of long-run energy dependencies that resulted in the OPEC-led supply shocks of the 1970s, which triggered backups at gas pumps, rationing and ultimately inflation, recession and political upheaval at home. Russia's weaponisation of energy supplies to the detriment of the European Union provided even more ammunition to policymakers worried that in a military conflict, China would do something similar in the future to restrict the supply of EVs or the ability to manufacture them domestically.

The final policy objective – and the one creating the biggest negative reaction from Europe – was to ease the US labour market transition from ICE vehicles to EVs. The IRA seeks to do so in several ways. First, consumption subsidies appeared initially limited to EVs assembled in North America. This feature of the law transformed the consumption subsidy into a subsidy to production, as it is paid only as long as the EV is both manufactured and sold domestically[78]. Second, the law includes a separate production tax credit for batteries and their inputs (as well as other sources of clean energy), which also affects the competitiveness of the EV supply chain in the United States.

Advocates for the local assembly provisions argued that the green transition would be sustainable in a democracy like the United States only if a political constituency of workers and domestic firms were created to support it. Consumer interests would never mobilise politically

---

78 The main competitiveness spillover was that the subsidy might impede the ability of foreign exporters to sell to the US market; that subsidy did not affect the direct cost of producing an EV for export. The IRA also does not 'pick winners' in terms of subsidising production. Because the subsidy flows through to producers through a consumer tax credit, consumers are still the ones choosing which EV models they want to purchase. This mechanism is different from the subsidies available in the 2022 CHIPS and Science Act, for example, which charges the Commerce Department with disbursing subsidies across semiconductor manufacturing investment projects.

in large enough numbers to support the lower prices that might arise through import competition.

A related argument is that political support for the United States remaining open at all remains tenuous (the national psyche remains scarred by the 'China shock', which President Trump so masterfully exploited politically). Policies like the IRA – even if discriminatory and inefficient – are needed to maintain a broader policy of trade openness elsewhere across the economy.

Numerous concerns with the IRA's objectives have emerged. An overarching worry is that using a single policy instrument to target multiple objectives reduces the chance that any one objective will be met.

One set of concerns is domestic. The IRA is a poorly targeted labour-market and community-adjustment policy. Although the geography of the North American EV supply chain may end up driven by the same forces as the ICE supply chain that emerged by the late twentieth century (Klier and Rubenstein, 2023), the plants and jobs are unlikely to end up in exactly the same communities as the ICE plants and where jobs are being wound down. Although there may be a political constituency of workers in the EV supply chain years from now to support a cleaner automobile sector, workers and communities that lose out as ICE supply chain plants are no longer needed may be nearly as unhappy about their jobs being replaced by EV jobs two or three states away as EV jobs overseas[79].

A second important domestic concern with the IRA is its fiscal implications. Targeting the climate externality with subsidies requires raising taxes elsewhere, which will generate additional inefficiencies (a carbon tax does not).

---

79 Other parts of the IRA unrelated to EVs do include place-based policies designed to facilitate new investment in the exact locations where economic activity driven by dirty energy would decline. The IRA also includes Low-Income Communities Bonus Credits for clean energy projects rooted in underserved communities, and the Davis-Bacon Act provides additional tax benefits if wages are high enough (under) and the work involves registered apprentices.

Even without those inefficiencies, the IRA is expensive for taxpayers, especially if take-up far exceeds initial estimates by the Congressional Budget Office (CBO, 2022b; Bistline *et al*, 2023; Goldman Sachs, 2023). If taxpayers end up unwilling to support the IRA fiscally over the long term, Congress could terminate the programme early, reducing the chance of achieving its most important objective of reducing carbon dioxide emissions.

An additional concern (discussed below) is whether the IRA approach will incentivise creation of an EV supply chain for the world outside of China. Two other worries involve how trading partners might respond to the international spillovers created by the US policy approach.

First, to the extent that the IRA displaces the legitimate market access expectations of trading partners exporting to the United States, there may be retaliation, which would impose other costs on the US economy. If the IRA leads to excessive US exports, trading partners may respond directly with tariffs (countervailing duties) to limit those exports. Rather than a cooperative equilibrium, in which governments agree to restrain their subsidies *ex ante* to socially efficient levels (and combine them with carbon taxes), the noncooperative equilibrium may end up with the same level of economic activity on EVs and carbon dioxide reductions but with excessive subsidies (which requires tax-raising elsewhere) and retaliation (which increases other costs).

Second, US subsidies may lead other countries to change their climate policies, especially out of concern over reduced industrial competitiveness. If the trading partner's initial emission reduction targets were insufficiently ambitious, this change could be positive for the environment. However, if it forces a trading partner (like the EU) to deviate from a potentially more efficient policy (such as carbon pricing), then it could be harmful, potentially offsetting some of the global externality (climate) benefits of the US policy.

Finally, the IRA did not include all of the important objectives of the Biden Administration's initial version of the legislation (the Build Back Better Act), which passed the House of Representatives in November

2021 but failed to pass the Senate[80]. One was a tax credit of $4,500 for vehicles assembled at unionised plants in the United States. The European Union lobbied heavily against this provision, in part because it would have discriminated against the US manufacturing facilities of European-headquartered car companies, many of which are located in right-to-work states where workforces are not unionised[81]. Canada complained vociferously as well, including in a letter sent by Deputy Prime Minister Chrystia Freeland and Trade Minister Mary Ng to a host of US senators that included explicit tariff threats if they passed the legislation[82]. The IRA stripped out the unionisation criterion and changed the requirement for US assembly to a requirement for North American assembly, making Canadian and Mexican plants eligible (Mexico also has plants for several European-headquartered automakers).

3 The effects of the IRA on electric vehicle supply chains

Multiple provisions of the IRA affect EVs. They include consumer tax credits for new clean consumer (Section 30D) and commercial (Section 45W) vehicles, and producer tax credits for other parts of the EV supply chain (Section 45X), which have received much less public attention[83].

---

80 House Committee on Rules, H.R. 5376: Build Back Better Act, 3 November 2021, https://rules.house.gov/sites/republicans.rules118.house.gov/files/BILLS-117HR5376RH-RCP117-18.pdf.

81 See Margaret Spiegelman, 'Mexico, EU, Japan, Others Voice Concern about Proposed US EV Tax Credit', *Inside, US Trade*, 1 November 2021, https://insidetrade.com/daily-news/mexico-eu-japan-others-voice-concern-about-proposed-us-ev-tax-credit; Joe Miller, 'German carmakers condemn Biden's electric-vehicle subsidy plans', *Financial Times*, 11 December 2021, https://www.ft.com/content/8b432548-9a7d-4669-b479-27fa6eb70bd9.

82 See David Ljunggren, 'Angry Canada Threatens to Impose Tariffs on US Goods over EV Tax Credit Plan', *Reuters*, 10 December 2021, https://www.reuters.com/world/americas/canada-threatens-impose-tariffs-us-goods-over-ev-tax-credit-plan-2021-12-10/.

83 Section 25 also includes a provision for previously owned clean vehicles.

3.1 Consumer tax credits for consumer vehicles

Consumer vehicles are defined as vehicles that weigh less than 14,000 pounds (6,350 kilogrammes). They include cars, pickup trucks and sport utility vehicles (SUVs). Even relatively heavy vehicles with batteries fall under the threshold with room to spare. Examples include the Audi RS e-tron (5,200 pounds/2,358kg) for cars, the Ford F-450 Crew Cab (8,600 pounds/3,900kg) for pickups and the GMC Hummer EV (9,000 pounds/4,082kg) for SUVs[84].

The consumer tax credit is restricted to vehicles for which final assembly takes place in North America. This requirement went into effect immediately on implementation of the law (16 August 2022). The sudden change left consumers who had placed orders but had not legally contracted for vehicle delivery in the lurch.

The consumer tax credit is up to $7,500, with eligibility determined by the inputs going into the batteries of the EV. Half of the tax credit eligibility ($3,750) is available for vehicles that include a battery recycled in North America or a battery that meets a critical minerals sourcing requirement. Critical minerals, defined in section 45X(c)(6), include lithium, cobalt and nickel (Tracy, 2022). Certain minimum thresholds have to be sourced from (extracted or processed in) the United States or a country with which the United States has a free trade agreement – a definitional issue that would turn out not to be innocuous. The minimal critical mineral threshold was 40 percent in 2023 – on a date (18 April) determined once Treasury issued guidance (31 March) – increasing by 10 percentage points a year up to 80 percent in 2027-32.

The other half of the tax credit eligibility is for vehicles meeting a battery components requirement. The components sourcing requirements are much more restrictive than for critical minerals: the threshold amount of material has to be manufactured or assembled in North America (this difference meant that other Treasury decisions – such as

---

84 See Matthew Guy, 'Weight, Weight: 5 of the Heaviest New Vehicles on Sale Today', *Driving*, 19 June 2022, https://driving.ca/car-culture/lists/weight-weight-5-of-the-heaviest-new-vehicles-on-sale-today.

where to draw the line in the battery supply chain between what was a critical mineral and what was a component – could matter substantially). The minimal battery components threshold was 50 percent in 2023 (once Treasury issued guidance), increasing by 10 percentage points a year until reaching 100 percent in 2029-32.

Also excluded under the law is sourcing from a *"foreign entity of concern,"* a designation that covers China, Iran, North Korea and Russia[85]. Beginning in 2024, a vehicle may not contain any battery components manufactured or assembled by a foreign entity of concern. Beginning in 2025, a vehicle's battery may not contain any critical minerals sourced from a foreign entity of concern.

Section 30D includes at least two other criteria that affect eligibility for a tax credit. The first is the limit on adjusted gross income (AGI), which cannot exceed $300,000 for married couples and $150,000 for individuals. The second is a price cap. Beginning in 2023, tax credit eligibility requires that the manufacturer's suggested retail price (MSRP) be less than $80,000 for SUVs, vans and pickup trucks, and less than $55,000 for vehicles under 14,000 pounds (on 3 February 2023, Treasury made more vehicles eligible for the consumer tax credit by shifting 'crossover' SUVs into the SUV category and out of the smaller vehicle category; GM's Cadillac Lyriq, Tesla's five-seat Model Y, Volkswagen's ID.4 and Ford's Mustang Mach-E and Escape Plug-in Hybrid were suddenly eligible thanks to the increase in the price cap to $80,000 from $55,000[86]).

Treasury and the Department of Energy needed to provide guidance in a number of areas. One was to define with which countries the United States has a 'free trade agreement', as the term was not formally

---

[85] Section 40207(a)(5) of the Infrastructure Investment and Jobs Act (42 USC. 18741(a)(5)) defines a *"foreign entity of concern"* as own owned by, controlled by, or subject to the jurisdiction or direction of a government of a foreign country that is a covered country (as defined in section 2533c(d) of title 10, United States Code).

[86] US Treasury press release of 3 February 2023, 'Treasury Updates Vehicle Classification Standard for Clean Vehicle Tax Credits Under Inflation Reduction Act', https://home.treasury.gov/news/press-releases/jy1245.

defined under US law. The United States has Congressionally ratified trade agreements with 20 countries, including major auto industry participants such as South Korea, Canada and Mexico. Its trade agreements with other countries (such as Japan) are more limited, including zero tariffs for only a limited set of products. The United States and the European Union do not have any sort of trade agreement beyond being members of the WTO. The Department of Energy was expected to determine whether part of a battery input was 'from' a foreign entity of concern – for example whether it would include subsidiaries or joint ventures in the United States or free trade agreement partners if the parent was headquartered in China or another foreign entity of concern[87].

These new criteria in Section 30D raised at least two questions. First, in the immediate term – before companies have a chance to adjust their supply chains – would they significantly limit the availability of car models eligible for the tax credit, even for vehicles assembled in North America? (As described below, the answer was yes). Second, over the long term, would these criteria be enough to shape economic activity and incentivise the shifting of supply chains?

3.2 Consumer tax credits for commercial vehicles

The IRA created a separate track for clean commercial vehicles. Section 45W provides a tax credit for businesses buying new EVs or fuel cell EVs (FCEVs), which could include a fuel cell stack powered by hydrogen rather than a battery. For businesses purchasing small commercial vehicles (weighing less than 14,000 pounds), eligibility requires battery capacity of at least 7 kilowatt-hours (kWh). For

---

87 For example, Jiyeong Go, 'Chinese Companies Expanding Footprint in Global Lithium Mines', FDI Intelligence, 29 August 2022, https://www.fdiintelligence.com/content/feature/chinese-companies-expanding-footprint-in-global-lithium-mines-81261; Scott Murdoch and Jaskiran Singh, 'China's Tianqi-Led Venture Bids for Australian Lithium Firm Essential', *Reuters*, 8 January 2023, https://www.reuters.com/markets/deals/igo-tianqi-lithium-jv-looks-beef-up-assets-with-essential-metals-bid-2023-01-08/.

vehicles weighing more than 14,000 pounds (such as buses and delivery trucks), eligibility requires battery capacity of at least 15 kWh.

In the commercial track, the maximum tax credits cannot exceed $7,500 for vehicles under 14,000 pounds and $40,000 for vehicles above 14,000 pounds. The actual tax credit amount is equal to whichever of the following is lowest: 15 percent of the vehicle purchase price for plug-in hybrid EVs, 30 percent of the vehicle purchase price for EVs and FCEVs, or the incremental cost of the vehicle compared with an equivalent ICE vehicle. Businesses cannot combine this tax credit with the clean vehicle tax credit for consumers; they can use one or the other.

Table 2 summarises crucial differences between Sections 30D and 45W. Equally important are all of the criteria not found in Section 45W, as made clear below. None of the eligibility requirements in Section 30D described above (limits related to North American assembly, critical minerals or battery components sourcing, MSRP or income levels) are included in Section 45W.

Table 2: Key requirements for qualifying for a tax credit under Sections 30D and 45W of the IRA

Requirement	Section 30D	Section 45W
Gross vehicle must weigh less than 14,000 pounds	X	X[a]
Vehicle must be used for business		X
Vehicle must be assembled in North America	X	
Manufacturer's suggested retail price cannot exceed $80,000 for SUVs, vans, and pickup trucks and $55,000 for smaller vehicles	X	
Annual adjusted gross income cannot exceed $300,000 for couples or $150,000 for individuals	X	
Credit of $3,750 is granted if critical minerals criterion is satisfied	X	
Credit of $3,750 is granted of battery components criterion is satisfied	X	
Vehicle must eventually include no critical mineral or battery components from 'foreign entity of concern'	X	

Note: [a] Vehicles with gross vehicle weight of more than 14,000 pounds are eligible for tax credits of up to $40,000 under Section 45W.

3.3 Production tax credits

Section 45X of the IRA provides for a tax credit for the production of battery cells, battery modules and battery components[88]. These provisions are additional and available only for production taking place in the United States. The tax credits are based on the capacity (in kilowatt hours) of the battery module or battery cell.

---

88 *Orrick*, 'Section 45X of the Inflation Reduction Act: New Tax Credits Available to Battery Manufacturers', 17 November 2022, https://www.orrick.com/en/Insights/2022/11/Section-45X-of-the-Inflation-Reduction-Act-New-Tax-Credits-Available-to-Battery-Manufacturers.

These tax credits could result in another $4,500 in tax credits per vehicle. For EVs eligible for the tax credit under Sections 30D or 45W, the additional $4,500 from Section 45X means that a single EV could potentially qualify for $12,000 in total subsidies (whether the consumer, the EV company, the battery company or the company making critical minerals or components will enjoy these subsidies needs to be determined empirically, but the combined benefit to consumers and firms in these markets clearly comes at the expense of the government and taxpayer). At the upper end of take-up, the cost to the US government for the production tax credit could total six times more than the Congressional Budget Office (CBO, 2022b) estimate[89].

While these tax credits may induce additional battery manufacturing investments into the United States, some of the subsidies may be transfers that do not have a marginal effect on investment facility decisions. EV companies had announced considerable new investment projects before July 2022 – when passage of the IRA seemed unlikely – and thus may subsequently receive subsidies for investments they had already committed to. As of January 2022, for example, plans were already afoot to build 13 large-scale EV battery plants in the United States[90].

4 The European response to the Inflation Reduction Act

The IRA was signed into law in August 2022. The European Union's political reaction was relatively slow to materialise. In contrast, in early September 2022, the trade minister from South Korea was already in Washington demanding action on behalf of Korean auto companies. He objected vociferously to the unexpected cutting off from consumer tax credits of Hyundai's popular Ioniq models, which were being

---

89 Christine McDaniel, 'The Cost of Battery Production Tax Credits Provided in the IRA', *Forbes*, 1 February 2023, https://www.forbes.com/sites/christinemcdaniel/2023/02/01/the-cost-of-battery-production-tax-credits-provided-in-the-ira/.

90 Dasl Yoon, 'EV Battery Maker's Sales Pitch to the West: We're Not Chinese', *Wall Street Journal*, 26 January 2022, https://www.wsj.com/articles/ev-battery-makers-sales-pitch-to-the-west-were-not-chinese-11643198401.

assembled in South Korea until their US plant was operational in 2025[91].

Once Europe fully understood the details of the IRA though, its public reaction was fierce. Bernd Lange, the head of the European Parliament's Trade Committee, called for a WTO dispute, which Thierry Breton, the European Commissioner for Internal Market, indicated could lead to retaliation[92]. There were threats of a subsidy war. In a state visit to Washington in early December, French President Emmanuel Macron said the IRA risked *"fragmenting the West."*

The ferocity of the criticism from Europe stunned Washington. To the extent that the United States had been motivated by nondomestic factors, it was the threat of China that it used to mobilise its legislation. It had not realised just how damaging its policy was to the political and economic interests of some of its key allies. The European political response was also remarkable, given the United States' massive political, economic and military support to Europe and its coordination with European and NATO allies following Russia's February 2022 invasion of Ukraine and its subsequent conduct of a brutal war[93].

The Biden Administration responded in various ways. The White House agreed to a high-level task force with the European Commission President's office[94]. It also placed the IRA on the formal agenda of the

---

91 See Bown (2022) and Christian Davies and Song Jung-a, 'South Korea complains of growing friction with US over high-tech trade', *Financial Times*, 18 September 2022, https://www.ft.com/content/9074c4ce-61f6-45c1-823f-84efe2af4d3e.

92 See Riham Alkousaa, 'Lawmaker Says EU Should Complain to WTO over US Inflation Reduction Act', *Reuters*, 3 December 2022, https://www.reuters.com/business/lawmaker-says-eu-should-complain-wto-over-us-inflation-reduction-act-2022-12-04/.

93 Europe's aggressive response risked alienating Washington, given the shift in the political climate in the United States in the wake of the November 2022 election, in which Republicans won control over the House of Representatives, potentially jeopardising continued military support for Ukraine and Europe.

94 White House, 'Statement by NSC Spokesperson Adrienne Watson on Launch of the United States–EU Task Force on the Inflation Reduction Act', 25 October 2022, https://www.whitehouse.gov/briefing-room/statements-releases/2022/10/25/statement-by-nsc-spokesperson-adrienne-watson-on-launch-of-the-us-eu-task-force-on-the-inflation-reduction-act/.

semi-annual US-EU Trade and Technology Council (TTC) meetings held in early December 2022 in Maryland. Biden's US Trade Representative Katherine Tai also suggested that Europe consider subsidies of its own[95].

Finally, during the state visit of French President Macron in December, President Biden indicated there would be flexibility[96]. The administration ultimately showed considerable and unexpected flexibility when the Treasury Department, the US government agency in charge of implementing key discretionary elements of the IRA, issued regulations on 29 December 2022 and 31 March 2023 (as discussed below).

Domestic political constraints meant that the administration could do relatively little to ease the pain of the IRA on its allies. The IRA was not a bipartisan piece of legislation. After the November 2022 midterm elections, when with Republicans took control of the House of Representatives, prospects for legislative reform became even less likely than they were before the election.

4.1 Europe's perspective

The IRA provoked a tremendous reaction in Europe for a number of reasons. For EVs, the problems were obvious. Under the new law, as of 16 August 2022, an EV manufactured in Europe would no longer be eligible for the consumer tax credit offered on EVs manufactured in North America. The difference created incentives for multinational companies to locate their production facilities in North America instead.

---

95 Andy Bounds and Aime Williams, 'Top US trade official urges EU to join forces on subsidies amid Green Deal tensions', *Financial Times*, 2 November 2022, https://www.ft.com/content/0e52d609-5cfe-453c-9baf-b33b66e941e9.

96 *"For example, there's a provision in it that says that there is the exception for anyone who has a free trade agreement with us. Well, that was added by a member of the United States Congress who acknowledges that he just meant allies; he didn't mean, literally, free trade agreement. So, there's a lot we can work out."* White House, 'Remarks by President Biden and President Macron of France in Joint Press Conference', 1 December 2022, https://www.whitehouse.gov/briefing-room/speeches-remarks/2022/12/01/remarks-by-president-biden-and-president-macron-of-france-in-joint-press-conference/.

There was also much more. The EU was caught off guard when the details of the new legislation were abruptly revealed in late July 2022. It had hoped that its efforts to work with the Biden Administration and establish the TTC in 2021 would prevent these sorts of policies from emerging with little notice. Failing to include Congress in the TTC proved to have been a mistake, as industrial policy often takes the form of legislation (given Treasury's rule-writing function under the IRA and the fact that industrial policy is being implemented through the US tax code, it would also be helpful if the Treasury Department, not only the US Trade Representative, the Commerce Department, and the State Department, were part of the TTC).

In terms of the EU's own policies, the IRA was problematic for reasons that went well beyond the EV sector. The European Green Deal and Fit for 55 involved first-best carbon taxes, phasing out free allowances, a carbon border adjustment mechanism and other potentially WTO–consistent policies as part of its clean energy transition (the IRA suddenly made apparent the fact that the United States was not interested in solutions consistent with traditional WTO rules). For Europe, an extremely important policy question was how much of its own original clean energy transition plan would remain feasible. Would the EU remain politically able to implement a sizable carbon tax, phase out free allowances and impose other policies that make dirty energy consumption in the bloc more expensive for industry?

The IRA's tax credits for batteries and other sources of clean energy make consumption of US energy cheaper, jeopardising the EU's industrial competitiveness. This fear was the major concern facing the EU that even the fixes to the EV tax credits (discussed below) would not be able to address.

Not only did the IRA put economic pressure on the European Union to move away from the first-best policy (taxing carbon at its high social cost), the new pressure to subsidise posed separate threats to the internal structure of the EU itself. The Treaty on the Functioning of the European Union (TFEU) has rules prohibiting member states from providing subsidies to companies; these rules are part of the fabric that maintains harmony within the union (Kleimann *et al*, 2023). The IRA may thus create a wedge between EU countries that can subsidise and those that lack fiscal resources and cannot. If EU countries now feel political-economic pressure to subsidise, their response to the IRA may be to not only discriminate against the United States and other countries; they may also end up discriminating against each other.

The timing of the IRA was also problematic, given the macroeconomic environment in Europe in 2022. Russia's war on Ukraine, its weaponisation of gas supplies flowing through the Nord Stream 1 pipeline and the European policy decision to wean itself off Russian energy, created political problems across the continent by straining European economies, creating high inflation and recessionary risk. Heavy industries in Europe – many concentrated in Germany – were already being forced to rethink their business models, given the loss of access to relatively inexpensive Russian natural gas. Adding early fuel to the fire was a September 2022 *Wall Street Journal* report that Tesla was putting on hold its plans to produce battery cells in Germany, potentially shifting more EV production to the United States to take advantage of the IRA's battery manufacturing tax credits[97]. Firms across the continent opportunistically threatened to leave for the United States unless Europe provided them with subsidies of its own. The problem was clearly not just the IRA though. Major German energy-intensive firms like chemical company BASF subsequently announced plans to relocate production not to the United States but to China[98].

---

97 Rebecca Elliott and Mike Colias, 'Tesla Shifts Battery Strategy as It Seeks US Tax Credits', *Wall Street Journal*, 14 September 2022, https://www.wsj.com/articles/tesla-shifts-battery-strategy-as-it-seeks-u-s-tax-credits-11663178393.

98 Patricia Nilsson, 'BASF outlines further cost-cutting and 2,600 job losses as it downsizes in Germany', *Financial Times*, 24 February 2023, https://www.ft.com/content/b0b2b2c2-ee63-4989-afab-6882feab4b73.

The EU was also concerned about the implications of the US policy actions for the WTO (the nondiscriminatory, rules-based trading system also formed the legal backbone of the European Union). Following four years of the Trump Administration's policies eroding rules-based trade, the hope had been that the Biden Administration might not only be different but that it might be a partner in rebooting efforts at multilateralism.

The IRA was perhaps the final nail in the coffin. By aggressively choosing subsidies – and a particularly discriminatory form of them – the United States clearly indicated that it had caved. At least for the moment, it was foregoing any rules-based effort to address what had been, at least rhetorically, joint EU-US concern over China's own large and discriminatory subsidies and industrial policy that was itself a major driver of the IRA[99].

The EU was also powerless to respond to the United States in a rules-based way. WTO dispute settlement was still dysfunctional. The United States continued to block appointments to the WTO's Appellate Body, disabling the EU's preferred (judicial) approach to send trade frictions off to be litigated[100].

4.2 Europe's own policies affecting electric vehicles

There has been some discussion in the EU about whether to respond to the IRA by deploying leftover funds from the €800 billion Recovery and Resilience Facility put in place following the COVID-19

---

99 Under the Trump Administration, the European Union, Japan and the United States formed a trilateral group to potentially consider new subsidies rules to address such concerns (Bown and Hillman, 2019).

100 WTO Director-General Ngozi Okonjo-Iweala discouraged litigation anyway, indicating in a Bloomberg interview that *"it's far better for them to speak to the United States and try to resolve this and see if there's any way to take account of their concerns than to come to the dispute-settlement system of the WTO".* Bryce Baschuk, 'WTO Chief Urges Talks to Resolve Green Subsidy Dispute', *Bloomberg*, 23 January 2023, https://www.bloomberg.com/news/newsletters/2023-01-19/supply-chain-latest-wto-urges-talks-to-resolve-subsidies-debate.

pandemic. As of April 2023, no new subsidy policy decision had been announced, however[101].

Most EU countries provide consumer tax credits for EVs, which average €6,000 (roughly $6,400) per vehicle (Kleimann *et al*, 2023; ACEA, 2022). The main difference is that the EU credits are nondiscriminatory (they do not include local content requirements or other limiting criteria found in Section 30D of the IRA). A US-assembled vehicle is eligible for EU member state tax credits just like a European assembled vehicle (this was the structure of the US tax credits in place after the ARRA in 2009 until passage of the IRA in August 2022).

Table 3 summarises important differences in tariffs on EVs by the United States, the EU and China. Several of these differences are noteworthy.

---

101 See, for example, Jan Strupczewski, 'Seven EU Countries Oppose New EU Funding as Response to US Subsidy Plan—Letter', *Reuters*, 27 January 2023, https://www.reuters.com/markets/europe/seven-eu-countries-oppose-new-eu-funding-response-us-subsidy-plan-letter-2023-01-27/.

Table 3: Tariffs on electric vehicles imposed by the US, EU and China in 2023

Economy	Applied MFN tariff (%)	Exceptions
United States	2.5	• Mexico: 0 percent (under the United States-Mexico-Canada Agreement [USMCA]) • Canada: 0 percent (under the USMCA) • South Korea: 0 percent (under the US-Korea Free Trade Agreement [KORUS]) • China: 27.5 percent (applied MFN tariff + trade war tariff) imposed since July 2018
European Union	10	• South Korea: 0 percent (under the EU-Republic of Korea Free Trade Agreement) • Japan: 3.8 percent (under the EU-Japan Economic Partnership Agreement) • Canada: 0 percent (under the EU-Canada Comprehensive Economic and Trade Agreement) • Canada: 0 percent (under the EU-Canada Comprehensive Economic and Trade Agreement)
China	15	• Applied MFN was 25 percent until July 2018, when it was lowered to 15 percent • United States: 40 percent tariff (applied MFN + retaliatory tariff) between July 2018 and January 2019 during the trade war, then reduced to 15 percent • South Korea: 13.5 percent (under Asia-Pacific Trade Agreement) • Japan: 15 percent (under Regional Comprehensive Economic Partnership)

Sources: US International Trade Commission, European Commission (CIRCABC), State Council of the People's Republic of China (China's tariff schedule, 2023), and trade war tariff announcements from China's Ministry of Finance and the United States Trade Representative. Notes: The HS code for battery EVs is 870380. MFN = Most favoured nation.

First, there is an important distinction in the argument that follows below relative to the earlier, Trump Administration argument for reciprocal tariffs in levels between the United States and its trading partners (Commerce Secretary Wilbur Ross famously argued that the United States and EU should have the same tariffs on ICE vehicles)[102]. Indeed, today's different US and EU tariff rates for ICE vehicles are the result of decades of reciprocal negotiating rounds under the General Agreement on Tariffs and Trade (GATT), in which the EU received lower tariffs on its ICE vehicle exports in exchange for the United States receiving lower tariffs on some other US export products. However, EVs are relatively new products for both sides; there have been no historical negotiations by the two economies over their tariff levels. This makes directly comparing US and EU EV tariff rates more relevant[103].

The European Union MFN import tariff for traditional consumer EVs (10 percent) is much higher than the US tariff (2.5 percent). One longstanding fundamental insight from economics is the equivalence of an import tariff and the combined effect of a consumption tax and a production subsidy. The EU's 10 percent import tariff on EVs is thus economically equivalent to EU member states offsetting some of their EV consumption subsidies with a 10 percent consumption tax, while simultaneously granting a 10 percent production subsidy for locally assembled EVs (the equivalent for the United States would be a 2.5 percent consumption tax and a 2.5 percent production subsidy). The US-EU differential is therefore equivalent to a 7.5 percent EU production subsidy. For a $50,000 vehicle, this would equate to a $3,750 production subsidy.

Second, US exports of EVs face further discrimination in the EU

---

102 Wilbur Ross, 'Most Favored Nation Rule Hurts Importers, Limits US Trade', *Wall Street Journal*, 25 May 2017, https://www.wsj.com/articles/most-favored-nation-rule-hurts-importers-limits-u-s-trade-1495733394.

103 For pickup trucks, the United States imposes a 25 percent import tariff; the EU import tariff is only 10 or 22 percent (depending on the cylinder capacity of the engine), and China's is 15 percent. Depending on the type of engine and the gross vehicle weight, pickup trucks could fall under several possible tariff lines in Harmonised System (HS) category 8704.

market because of the EU's free trade agreements (FTAs) with Korea and Japan – two other major EV manufacturers – as well as Mexico and Canada. The EU's FTAs with South Korea, Mexico and Canada already have a 0 percent duty on EVs in effect; the phase-in period for Japan's FTA means that the tariff will fall from its current level of 3.8 percent to 0 in 2026. The implication is that EU imports from these countries enjoy (or will enjoy) a 10 percentage point tariff preference into the EU market relative to the United States. Under the United States' FTAs, the tariff preference offered to South Korea, Mexico and Canada (2.5 percentage points) and Japan (none) is much smaller (or nonexistent). The United States and the EU could negotiate a trade agreement to reciprocally lower those bilateral tariffs to zero, but such a move is not currently on the policy agenda.

Third, the EU and US treat China, the other major exporter of EVs to the world, quite differently. In the EU market, imports from China face the same tariff as imports from the United States. In the United States, because of the trade war tariffs in effect since July 2018, EU exporters benefit from a 25 percentage point tariff preference into the US market relative to EVs manufactured in China.

These tariffs are likely to affect trade flows (Figure 3)[104]. The value of EU imports of EVs from China, for example, is nearly three times as high as EV imports from South Korea and 16 times as high as imports from the United States. Offshored production by Tesla, Volkswagen and MG – major US and European brands – dominates Chinese EV exports to the European Union[105]. Imports of EVs from Japan remain small; major exporters like Toyota have been relatively slow to move

---

104 In Figure 3, almost 90 percent of EU EV imports from rest of world were sourced from Mexico in 2022.

105 See Selina Cheng, 'Tesla Rival BYD Leads Push to Sell Chinese EV Brands Around the World', *Wall Street Journal*, 3 March 2023, https://www.wsj.com/articles/tesla-rival-byd-leads-push-to-sell-chinese-ev-brands-around-the-world-4e0b6d06; Peter Sigal, 'Europe Forecast to Import 800,000 Chinese-Built Cars by 2025', *Automotive News Europe*, 7 November 2022, https://europe.autonews.com/automakers/chinese-electric-car-exports-europe-soar.

to battery EVs, in part because they developed and stuck with plug-in hybrids[106].

Figure 3: The EU used to import electric vehicles from the United States but now mostly imports from China and South Korea

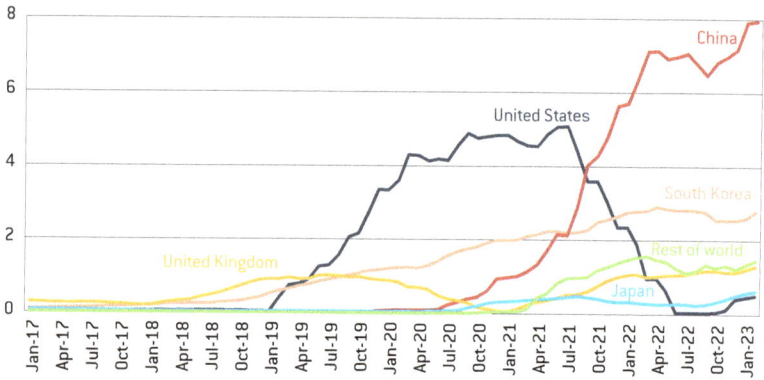

Source: Eurostat. Notes: The CN codes are 87038010 and 87038090 in 2017-23, 87039010 in 2016. Trade values are converted to US dollars from euros using end-of-month usd/euro spot exchange rates from FRED (DEXUSEU).

EU imports of EVs from the United States fell dramatically beginning in mid-2021. The decline was driven partly by Tesla shifting its exports to the EU away from its US facilities to its plant in China.

In late 2018, Tesla announced it would accelerate construction of its gigafactory in China in response to the trade war, after China's retaliatory tariffs made it too costly to export cars from the United States to China. US EV exports to China disappeared (Figure 4)[107]. After losing both

---

106   Eri Sugiura and Peter Campbell, 'Toyota was a hybrid pioneer with the Prius but struggles to leap to electric', *Financial Times*, 18 October 2022, https://www.ft.com/content/23707b53-0737-4271-bce2-65471005f34c.

107   *"Our vehicle sales in China have been negatively impacted in the past by certain tariffs on automobiles manufactured in the United States, such as our vehicles, and our costs for producing our vehicles in the United States have also been affected by import duties on certain components sourced from China"* (Tesla, 2020).

the Chinese and European markets, the only sizable recent US export growth for EVs has been to Canada[108].

Fourth, sales to the United States and Norway have dominated EU exports of EVs (Figure 5). EU exports to the United Kingdom resumed after a brief decline in the aftermath of Brexit. EU exports of EVs to China are modest.

Figure 4: Trade war tariffs wiped out US electric vehicle exports to China; exports to the EU have also suffered, but exports to Canada have grown

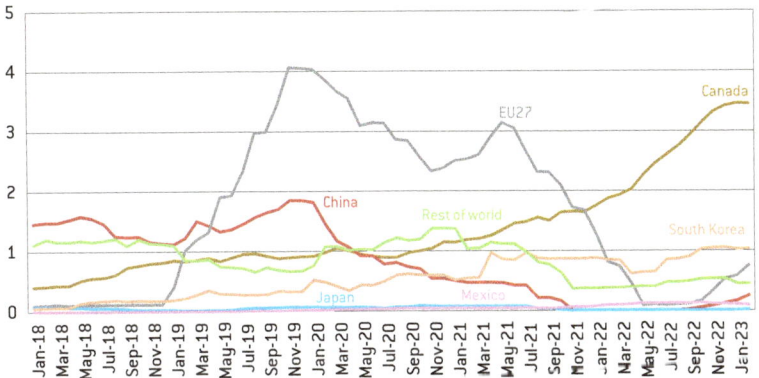

Source: US International Trade Commission Dataweb. Notes: The Schedule B code for electric vehicles is 8703800000. The code was created in 2017 and did not exist for electric vehicles prior to 2017.

---

108 Beginning in 2022, some lower US exports in the short run would also be partially attributed to an increase is US domestic demand for EVs driven by US policy - eg the consumer tax credits in the IRA as well as charging stations funded by the Infrastructure Investment and Jobs Act.

Figure 5: Major EU electric vehicle export destinations include the US, UK, and Norway

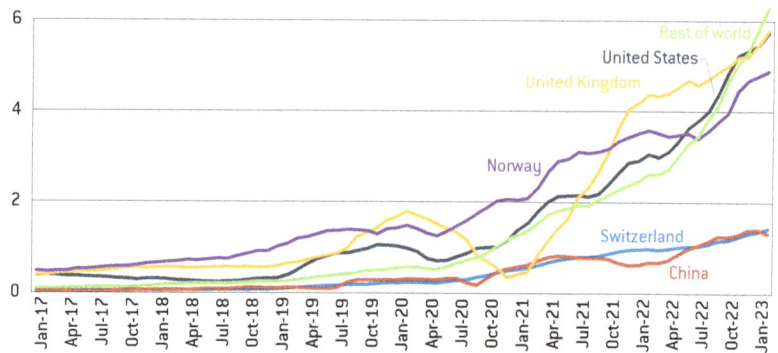

Source: Eurostat. Notes: The CN codes are 87038010 and 87038090 in 2017-2023, 87039010 in 2016. Trade values are converted to US dollars from euros using end-of-month usd/euro spot exchange rates from FRED (DEXUSEU).

5 The US policy response to European pleas and other announcements

On 29 December 2022, the Biden Administration quietly announced what may turn out to have been an economic bombshell. The Internal Revenue Service (IRS) in the Treasury Department issued guidance indicating that consumers that leased EVs weighing less than 14,000 pounds – normally falling under the Section 30D tax credits – could qualify under the Section 45W tax credits whether or not the leased vehicle was assembled in North America (IRS 2022). Leased vehicles assembled in Europe, South Korea, Japan or anywhere else were suddenly eligible for the tax credit.

Put differently, almost none of the constraints found in Section 30D – including the price and income caps – apply when US consumers lease vehicles to access the tax credit under Section 45W. Expensive European-assembled models from Porsche, BMW and Mercedes – and the high-income consumers who can afford them – suddenly became eligible for US tax credits. For European luxury brands, the benefit of the 29 December decision was thus potentially even greater than if the

United States had eliminated the North American assembly requirement in Section 30D by Congress amending the law.

The Section 45W leasing option will also dull the battery supply chain sourcing incentives, which are also found only in Section 30D. If consumers choose to take up the tax credit primarily via leasing under Section 45W, automakers will not face financial pressure to use battery components sourced from the United States, use recycled batteries or source critical minerals from the United States or free trade agreement partners. Section 45W thus reduces the incentive to create a separate redundant EV battery input supply chain outside of China.

In a second set of announcements in early 2023, the Biden Administration made additional decisions affecting implementation of the consumer tax credits. On 31 March, Treasury released its proposed rule regarding which countries would be considered 'free trade agreement' partners to satisfy the critical minerals sourcing criterion in Section 30D. It highlighted countries with which the United States *"has reliable and trusted economic relationships."* In addition to the 20 countries with which the United States had a Congressionally ratified FTA[109], the criterion for a critical minerals agreement would be one in which each side

> *"(A) reduces or eliminates trade barriers on a preferential basis, (B) commits the parties to refrain from imposing new trade barriers, (C) establishes high-standard disciplines in key areas affecting trade (such as core labor and environmental protections), and/ or (D) reduces or eliminates restrictions on exports or commits the parties to refrain from imposing such restrictions on exports"* (88 Federal Register 23370, 17 April 2023).

---

109 The 20 countries are Australia, Bahrain, Canada, Chile, Colombia, Costa Rica, the Dominican Republic, El Salvador, Guatemala, Honduras, Israel, Jordan, Korea, Mexico, Morocco, Nicaragua, Oman, Panama, Peru and Singapore.

The Biden Administration had foreshadowed these details on 28 March, when it announced and released the text of a critical minerals trade agreement with Japan[110]. On 10 March, European Commission President Ursula von der Leyen and President Biden announced that the EU and US would negotiate a similar agreement specifically "*to count toward requirements for clean vehicles in the Section 30D clean vehicle tax credit of the Inflation Reduction Act*"[111]. Countries including the United Kingdom, Indonesia and the Philippines immediately indicated they, too, would like to negotiate such an arrangement with the United States[112].

The purpose of such an agreement is obvious. If a country gets such a deal, it becomes a more attractive location for critical mineral supply chain investments, because of access to the $3,750 tax credit under Section 30D. What remains unclear is whether such an agreement would be simply a memorandum of understanding or if it would force a trading partner to adopt new laws or regulations. For the United States, these laws or regulations are currently being negotiated as executive agreements (Claussen, 2023), which do not require Congressional ratification. Negotiating them as such also means that a future administration could revoke them. This situation creates uncertainty for firms as they make decisions about where to locate substantial investments.

Some lawmakers were not pleased with the Biden Administration

110 See https://ustr.gov/sites/default/files/2023-03/US Japan Critical Minerals Agreement 2023 03 28.pdf.

111 White House, 'Joint Statement by President Biden and President von der Leyen', 10 March 2023, https://www.whitehouse.gov/briefing-room/statements-releases/2023/03/10/joint-statement-by-president-biden-and-president-von-der-leyen-2/.

112 See Graham Lanktree, 'Rishi Sunak Presses Joe Biden for a Trade Deal — Just Not the One the UK Wants Most', *Politico*, 11 April 2023, https://www.politico.eu/article/rishi-sunak-presses-joe-biden-for-trade-deal-uk-us-raw-materials-ira-supply-chains-china/; Stefanno Sulaiman, 'Indonesia to Propose Limited Free Trade Deal with US on Critical Minerals', *Reuters*, 10 April 2023, https://www.reuters.com/world/asia-pacific/indonesia-propose-limited-free-trade-deal-with-us-critical-minerals-2023-04-10/; and Brett Fortnam, 'The Philippines calls for FTA, critical minerals deal with the U.S.' *Inside US Trade*, 25 April 2023, https://insidetrade.com/daily-news/philippines-calls-fta-critical-minerals-deal-us.

implementing regulations of 29 December and 31 March, and its negotiations of such critical minerals agreements. In March, a bipartisan group called out the administration for not consulting with Congress, arguing that it was interfering with Congressional authority under the Constitution[113].

For its part, Congress also admitted to errors when drafting the original IRA text on the EV tax credits in haste in July 2022. Senator Manchin, who had negotiated the last-minute IRA details with Senate Majority Leader Schumer stated, "*I gotta be honest with you. I should have paused and said 'OK, I'm going to make sure our NATO allies are involved in this'*"[114]. In January 2023, Manchin also admitted that "*I did not realise the European Union is not a free trade agreement [economy]*"[115]. Such statements suggest that he may have welcomed Treasury's efforts at writing the implementing regulations that would make the EV tax credits more accessible to NATO allies and the EU. Writing in the *Wall Street Journal* on 29 March 2023, however, Manchin made clear his displeasure with the way in which Treasury was implementing the tax credit regulations to include partners like Japan and the European Union, by asking President Biden "*to instruct his administration to implement the Inflation Reduction Act as written and stop redefining its credits and other subsidies*"[116].

---

113 Margaret Spiegelman, 'Ways & Means Trade Chair: Guidance on EV Tax Credits "Unconstitutional"', *Inside US Trade*, 31 arch 2023, https://insidetrade.com/daily-news/ways-means-trade-chair-guidance-ev-tax-credits-unconstitutional.

114 Andrew Duehren, 'EU and Japan Strike Deal on Minerals Used in Batteries for Electric Cars', *Wall Street Journal*, 28 March 2023, https://www.wsj.com/articles/u-s-and-japan-strike-deal-on-minerals-used-in-batteries-for-electric-cars-bbf8b8ee.

115 Ari Natter, 'Manchin Says He Didn't Know US, EU Lacked Free Trade Agreement', *Bloomberg*, 19 January 2023, https://www.bloomberg.com/news/articles/2023-01-19/manchin-says-he-didn-t-know-us-eu-lacked-free-trade-agreement.

116 Joe Manchin, 'Biden's Inflation Reduction Act Betrayal. Instead of Implementing the Law as Intended, His Administration Subverts It for Ideological Ends', *Wall Street Journal*, 29 March 2023, https://www.wsj.com/articles/biden-inflation-reduction-act-betrayal-joe-manchin-debt-ceiling-budget-fossil-fuels-green-energy-dc37738e.

The full impact of these critical minerals agreements and the Treasury announcement of 31 March 2023 remains unknown. At one extreme, they could turn out to be meaningless. For example, if all consumers and automakers switch to transacting via lease instead of purchases, there would be no additional tax credit benefit from sourcing critical minerals from such a partner country. Or, if the executive agreement nature of the critical minerals deals does not create enough certainty about future access to the US tax credits, firms may not invest. At the other extreme, if consumers seek the tax credit under Section 30D instead, the ability to source inputs from such countries might create additional incentives to develop alternative supply chains outside of China.

Finally, on 12 April 2023, the Biden Administration proposed another policy to increase the take-up of EVs[117]. The Environmental Protection Agency announced new regulations that require two-thirds of new passenger cars to be all-electric by 2032. If implemented, the regulations would tend to increase consumption of all EVs, domestic or imported, relative to ICE vehicles.

6 Eligibility for US tax credits, US imports of electric vehicles, and leasing

It is too soon to look for the impact of these emerging regulations on the EV supply chain, but it is worth examining the US import market to provide context (Figure 6). The concern expressed by South Korean and European officials over the North American assembly provisions in the IRA is understandable. In the lead-up to the sudden announcement of its details (in July 2022), US imports of EVs from both the EU and South Korea had been growing. In the 12 months ending in July 2022, US imports were $3.3 billion from the EU and $1.8 billion from South Korea. Cutting off those exports would obviously hurt both economies.

---

117 See EPA press release of 12 April 2023, https://www.epa.gov/newsreleases/biden-harris-administration-proposes-strongest-ever-pollution-standards-cars-and.

Figure 6: US imports of electric vehicles from the EU and South Korea have continued growing despite the IRA

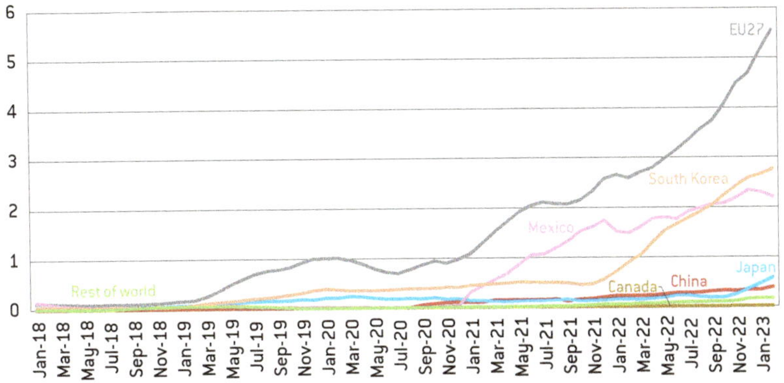

Source: US International Trade Commission Dataweb. Notes: The Harmonised Tariff Schedule code is 8703800000. The code was created in 2017 and did not exist prior to 2017.

There is no discernible impact of the IRA on the US electric vehicle import data at time of writing. The North American assembly provision went into effect on 16 August 2022 and has remained in place for purchased vehicles since. Adoption of the August provision was not followed by a reduction in US imports of EVs from either the EU or South Korea in the fourth quarter of 2022. The lack of decline suggests that US demand for EVs in this period was high, as US consumers continued to purchase imported EVs even though the Section 30D consumer tax credits discriminated against most foreign-assembled vehicles. It was only on 29 December that Treasury announced that leased vehicles were eligible for the consumer tax credit, even if assembled outside of North America. Thus, any positive impact from that announcement would only be expected to arise in the 2023 data.

However, at least three other interesting trends are apparent in the US import data. First, US imports of EVs from Mexico are increasing, thanks in part to sales of the Mustang Mach-E assembled at the Ford Cuautitlan Stamping and Assembly Plant (while US imports from Mexico were unaffected by the IRA's North American assembly requirement that went into effect in August 2022, they may be affected by the input sourcing requirements that went into effect in April 2023 discussed below). Second, like the EU, the US is importing relatively few battery EVs from Japan. Third, and unlike the EU, the US is not importing many EVs from China. These sales are probably limited by the 25 percent US trade war tariffs imposed in July 2018 on imports of cars from China, which remain in effect.

Stronger recent American take-up of all EVs, including imports, may reflect several additional factors. First, improvements to the EV charging infrastructure – including the roll-out of fast-charging stations – may have reduced 'range anxiety' concerns. Second, so few models may have been assembled in North America that consumers found it difficult not to buy imports. If more vehicle models are assembled in North America, that constraint would be relaxed over time.

Indeed, when the sourcing regulations announced on 31 March went into effect on 18 April, only 20 models from four automakers – Ford, GM, Tesla and Volkswagen – remained eligible for the full $7,500 tax credit under Section 30D. Another six models (one from Tesla, two from Rivian and three from Ford, including the Mustang Mach-E) were eligible for $3,750 of the credit. Apparently nine models from four automakers – Hyundai (Genesis), Nissan, Tesla and Volkswagen – were not able to adjust their input sourcing requirements in time to remain eligible for the tax credits on 18 April. For these and other non-eligible models, it remains to be seen whether automakers shift their input sources (and regain access under Section 30D), lease to consumers instead (and gain access under Section 45W), sell without the tax credit or discontinue the models entirely.

US imports of EVs may remain high, especially if consumers choose to lease instead of buy. In the short run, this may also be impacted by the fact that so few models satisfying the tax credits were available to buy.

Early indications suggest US leasing of electric vehicles increased considerably in the immediate aftermath of the Treasury announcement of 29 December 2022 (Figure 7). EV leasing rates increased from only 9.7 percent of new EVs entering the market in December 2022 to 34.3 percent by March 2023. The steady increase from January to March is consistent with dealers and consumers learning about and responding to the tax credit differential available under the leasing option. While the leasing rate of all US vehicles increased between December 2022 and March 2023, the uptick was much larger for EVs (in 2022, ICE vehicles still made up more than 90 percent of all new vehicles in the US market – see again Figure 1).

Figure 7: US electric vehicle leases have increased since the eligibility for IRA tax credits was expanded

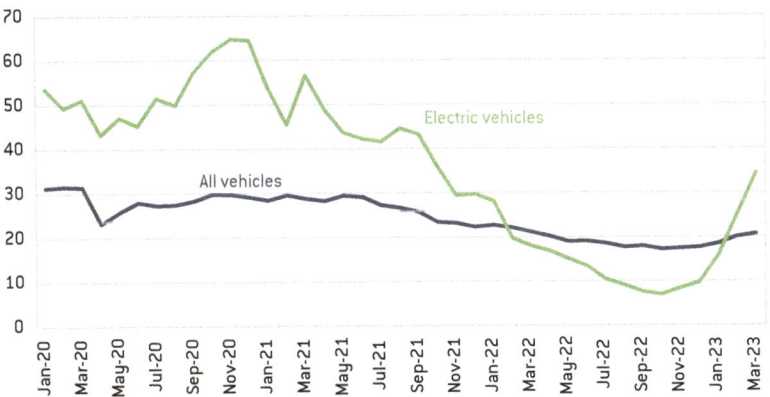

Source: Edmunds. Notes: On 29 December 2022, Treasury announced that EVs leased to consumers would be eligible for tax credits under Section 45W of the Inflation Reduction Act.

More generally, Figure 7 also illustrates how US lease rates, including for EVs, fell dramatically during the COVID-19 pandemic and remained extraordinarily low as of December 2022. Between 2010-19, on average, 25 percent of all new passenger cars put onto the market each year were leased, with slightly lower rates for light trucks[118]. Pandemic lockdowns and mobility restrictions resulted in a crash of US car production in early 2020. When mobility restrictions were lifted, there was a shortage of new cars – further exacerbated by supply chain disruptions, including semiconductor shortages – increasing demand for used cars, causing used-car prices to spike. As a result, many leased vehicles had higher market values at the end of their lease period than the option price set when the lease was first signed. That price differential led many consumers to purchase their previously leased cars outright, forgoing the need for another lease. This is one reason why leasing rates fell and have only recently begun to recover[119].

7 Conclusion

Section 30D of the IRA restricts eligibility for consumer tax credits on the purchase of EVs. For a consumer to receive the full subsidy, the vehicle must not only be assembled in North America, but the source of key inputs for its batteries must be sourced outside of China and from a restrictive set of locations. Furthermore, access requires that consumers satisfy legislatively mandated income caps and specific models meet price caps. On the other hand, the 29 December 2022 Treasury announcement meant that Section 45W of the IRA does not restrict eligibility for tax credits provided consumers lease the EV.

Thus, those Section 30D restrictions may be significantly dulled if consumers start leasing EVs and accessing tax credits under Section 45W instead. If consumers do not lease EVs, then the IRA's Section 30D constraints will bind and affect incentives in a number of ways. First, fewer models will be available and limited to those assembled in North America. Second, the binding nature of the EV supply chain constraints also found in Section 30D may further limit eligibility – eg only

---

118   Bureau of Transportation Statistics, 2023, https://www.bts.gov/content/new-and-used-passenger-car-sales-and-leases-thousands-vehicles.

119   Sean Tucker, 'Car Leases are Declining – Here's Why', *Kelley Blue Book*, 1 November 2022, https://www.kbb.com/car-news/car-leases-are-declining-heres-why/.

a few models were eligible for the full tax credit as of April 2023, when the input sourcing regulations first went into effect. More models may become eligible over time if automakers choose to assemble in North America and if their supply chains for inputs adjust. However, that outcome may also be influenced by the restrictiveness of other Treasury and Department of Energy Section 30D decisions that are still under consideration, as well as whether countries negotiate critical minerals agreements with the US Trade Representative.

However, even if consumers opt to buy instead of lease EVs, so that the battery input sourcing criterion binds, several questions remain. To address concerns over dependency on imports from an authoritarian regime with a history of restricting exports, how will the United States coordinate with trading partners to establish an additional EV battery input supply chain outside of China? In June 2022, the United States, the EU, Japan, South Korea, the United Kingdom and Australia established the Minerals Security Partnership[120]. How it will be used remains unclear. Where will the mining and the environmentally challenging refining take place? Incentivising industry to invest in an additional supply chain outside of China is resource intensive and requires policy coordination, including through potentially discriminatory policies. Those policies include subsidies (to favoured producers), tariffs (on Chinese production), or establishment of environmental, social and governance standards that China would be deemed unable to meet. Even adding Japan, the EU or the UK as 'free trade agreement' partners to provide them eligibility under Section 30D is unlikely to be sufficient on its own, as these economies currently mine or process few critical minerals.

From the EU's perspective, although the EV subsidies made the headlines, they were only one small part of its concerns with the IRA. And even they were only partially fixed. Whether EU EV exporters are

---

120 See US State Department press release of 14 June 2022, https://www.state.gov/minerals-security-partnership/.

affected will ultimately depend, in part, on whether consumers switch to leasing.

Another issue that could not be resolved is the IRA's producer tax credits for batteries and their inputs arising under Section 45X.

Furthermore, none of the tweaks arising from Treasury regulations tackled the larger and more fundamental European worry about the IRA: the divergence between the US and EU approaches to reducing carbon emissions and tackling climate change. Even ignoring the local content requirements and other discriminatory elements associated with all of the other tax credits for production of hydrogen, solar, wind and other forms of clean energy[121], Europe's primary concern is that the US approach is to subsidise energy while the EU has been planning to tax carbon. This policy divergence may make certain energy-intensive industries artificially competitive in the United States relative to their European counterparts. How great this impact will be is an empirical question.

To keep tabs on the issue, French and German economy ministers Bruno Le Maire and Robert Habeck requested additional US transparency[122]. Although transparency is obviously welcome, at least two challenges remain. First, take-up of the subsidies is difficult to project, because it depends on consumer responsiveness, producer responsiveness and many other factors. It will also be difficult to measure and report on publicly because much of the subsidisation arrives through credits and the tax code as opposed to direct government expenditures.

---

121 Many of the production tax credits in Section 45X may also distort trade by reducing purchases of imported inputs. As they are for domestic energy products that may be nontraded, the resulting outputs may not be trade distorting. However, the impact of reducing US energy prices (relative to the EU climate policy approach, which increases energy prices) will affect the relative competitiveness of other US and EU energy-intensive industries.

122 Christian Kraemer and David Lawder, 'France, Germany Protest US Green Subsidies on Washington Trip', *Reuters*, 8 February 2023, https://www.reuters.com/markets/europe/inflation-reduction-act-should-cover-most-possible-eu-companies-frances-le-maire-2023-02-07/.

Second, understanding the potential impacts of these other parts of the IRA on competitiveness will require more complex assessments than simply counting up the total amount of subsidies disbursed.

From the US perspective, the IRA also remains imperfect. As already described, the implementing regulations may impact economic outcomes in ways that diverge from the law's initial intentions.

Even putting that aside, additional domestic policy is needed to assist workers and communities adversely affected by the transition from ICE vehicles to EVs. Displaced workers need help reaching opportunities, both within the automobile and clean energy sectors and in other important and growing areas of the US economy (Hanson, 2023).

The IRA also raises longer-run fiscal concerns. Because its tax credits are uncapped, if consumer and producer take-up of incentives exceeds expectations, the federal government may need additional sources of tax revenue. One potential solution – included in the Build Back Better Act, which passed the House in 2021 but failed to pass the Senate, but was not included in the IRA – was a global minimum corporate tax that is consistent with that of the OECD (Clausing, 2022, 2023; the EU adopted a directive implementing the minimum tax at the end of 2022, Directive (EU) 2022/2523).

The US and EU may have resolved the most pressing bilateral frictions associated with their EV industries. But the European concerns associated with the IRA overall have not been fixed, and the considerable political-economic challenges associated with coordinating the US and EU green transitions are far from over.

References

ACEA (2022) *Overview—Electric Vehicles: Tax Benefits & Purchase Incentives in the European Union*, European Automobile Manufacturers' Association, 21 September, available at https://www.acea.auto/fact/overview-electric-vehicles-tax-benefits-purchase-incentives-in-the-european-union-2022/

Autor, D., D. Dorn and G. Hanson (2021) 'On the Persistence of the China Shock', *Brookings Papers on Economic Activity Fall*: 381–447, available at https://www.brookings.edu/bpea-articles/on-the-persistence-of-the-china-shock/

Bistline, J., N.R. Mehrotra and C. Wolfram (2023) 'Economic Implications of the Climate Provisions in the Inflation Reduction Act', *Brookings Papers on Economic Activity Conference Draft*, March

Bown, C.P. (2018) 'Why the United States Needs Allies in a Trade War Against China', *Harvard Business Review*, 11 December, available at https://piie.com/commentary/op-eds/why-us-needs-allies-trade-war-against-china

Bown, C.P. (2021) 'The US–China Trade War and Phase One Agreement', *Journal of Policy Modeling* 43(4) 805–43

Bown, C.P. (2022) 'Will New US Tax Credits Remake EV Supply Chains?' *Trade Talks*, episode 167, 3 October, available at https://tradetalkspodcast.com/podcast/167-will-new-us-tax-credits-remake-electric-vehicle-supply-chains/

Bown, C.P. and J.A. Hillman (2019) 'WTO'ing a Resolution to the China Subsidy Problem', *Journal of International Economic Law* 22(4): 557–78

Clausing, K. (2022) 'The Global Minimum Tax Lives on. America Has Abandoned It for Now but Will Likely Come around', *Foreign Affairs*, 17 August, available at https://www.foreignaffairs.com/united-states/global-minimum-tax-lives

Clausing, K. (2023) 'The international tax agreement of 2021: Why it's needed, what it does, and what comes next?' *Peterson Institute for International Economics Policy Briefs* 23-4, available at https://www.piie.com/publications/policy-briefs/international-tax-agreement-2021-why-its-needed-what-it-does-and-what

Clausing, K. and C. Wolfram (Forthcoming) 'Asymmetric Climate Policies and International Trade', *Journal of Economic Perspectives*

Claussen, K. (2023) 'What Is a Free Trade Agreement, Anyway?' *International Economic Law and Policy Blog*, 3 January, https://ielp.worldtradelaw.net/2023/01/what-is-a-free-trade-agreement-anyway.html

CBO (2022a) *Emissions of Carbon Dioxide in the Transportation Sector*, Congressional Budget Office, available at https://www.cbo.gov/system/files/2022-12/58566-co2-emissions-transportation.pdf

CBO (2022b) 'Summary Estimated Budgetary Effects of Public Law 117- 169, to Provide for Reconciliation Pursuant to Title II of S. Con. Res. 14', Congressional Budget Office and Joint Committee on Taxation, available at https://www.cbo.gov/publication/58455

EPA (2022) *EPA External Review Draft of Report on the Social Cost of Greenhouse Gases: Estimates Incorporating Recent Scientific Advances*, PA-HQ-OAR-2021-0317, Environmental Protection Agency, available at https://www.epa.gov/system/files/documents/2022-11/epa_scghg_report_draft_0.pdf

Goldman Sachs (2023) *Carbonomics: The Third American Energy Revolution*

Hanson, G.H. (2023) 'Local Labor Market Impacts of the Energy Transition: Prospects and Policies', *NBER Working Paper* 30871, National Bureau of Economic Research, available at https://www.nber.org/papers/w30871

IEA (2022) *Electric Vehicles, International Energy Agency*, available at https://www.iea.org/reports/electric-vehicles

IRS (2022) 'Frequently Asked Questions Related to New, Previously-Owned and Qualified Commercial Clean Vehicle Credits', RS Fact Sheet FS-2022-42, Internal Revenue Service, US Department of Treasury, available at https://www.irs.gov/pub/taxpros/fs-2022-42.pdf

Klier, T.H. and J.M. Rubenstein (2022) 'North America's Rapidly Growing EV Market: Implications for the Geography of Automotive Production', *Chicago Fed Economic Perspectives* 5, available at https://doi.org/10.21033/ep-2022-5

Kleimann, D., N. Poitiers, A. Sapir, S. Tagliapietra, N. Véron, R. Veugelers and J. Zettelmeyer (2023) 'How Europe should answer the US Inflation Reduction Act', Policy Contribution 04/2023, Bruegel, available at https://www.bruegel.org/policy-brief/how-europe-should-answer-us-inflation-reduction-act

Leruth, L., A. Mazarei, P. Régibeau and L. Renneboog (2022) 'Green Energy Depends On Critical Minerals. Who Controls the Supply Chains?' *PIIE Working Paper* 22-12, Peterson Institute for International Economics, available at https://www.piie.com/publications/working-papers/green-energy-depends-critical-minerals-who-controls-supply-chains

Noland, M. (2023) 'Electric Vehicle Uptake: Hawaii as a Natural Experiment', *PIIE Realtime Economics*, 4 April, Peterson Institute for International Economics, available at https://www.piie.com/blogs/realtime-economics/electric-vehicle-uptake-hawaii-natural-experiment

OECD (2022) *Pricing Greenhouse Gas Emissions: Key Findings for the United States*, Organisation for Economic Co-operation and Development, available at https://www.oecd.org/tax/tax-policy/carbon-pricing-united-states.pdf

OECD (2023) 'Raw Materials Critical for the Green Transition. Production, International Trade and Export', *OECD Trade Policy Paper* 269, Organisation for Economic Co-operation and Development, available at https://www.oecd.org/publications/raw-materials-critical-for-the-green-transition-c6bb598b-en.htm

Rapson, D.S. and E. Muehlegger (2022) 'The Economics of Electric Vehicles', *NBER Working Paper* 29093 (revised), National Bureau of Economic Research

Rennert, K., F. Errickson, B.C. Prest, L. Rennels, R.G. Newell, W. Pizer … D. Anthoff (2022) 'Comprehensive Evidence Implies a Higher Social Cost of CO2', *Nature* 610: 687–92, available at https://www.nature.com/articles/s41586-022-05224-9

Sheldon, T.L. (2022) 'Evaluating Electric Vehicle Policy Effectiveness and Equity', *Annual Review of Resource Economics* 14: 66988

Tesla (2020) 'Form 10-K. Annual Report Pursuant to Section 13 or 15(D) of the Securities Exchange Act of 1934', 29 January, available at https://www.sec.gov/Archives/edgar/data/1318605/000156459020004475/tsla-10k_20191231.htm

Tracy, B.S. (2022) *Critical Minerals in Electric Vehicle Batteries*, CRS Report R47227, Congressional Research Service, available at https://crsreports.congress.gov/product/pdf/R/R47227

US Treasury Department (2022) 'Anticipated Direction of Forthcoming Proposed Guidance on Critical Mineral and Battery Component Value Calculations for the New Clean Vehicle Credit', *30D White Paper*, 29 December, available at https://home.treasury.gov/system/files/136/30DWhite-Paper.pdf

12 A new pharma industrial policy for Europe? Lessons from COVID-19

Mathias Dewatripont

1 Introduction[123]

This chapter draws out lessons for industrial policy in the European Union from the COVID-19 vaccine experience. It reviews the process of development of safe and efficient vaccines and the issue of vaccine procurement.

The emergence of new efficient vaccines in record time has been a great success of public and private international cooperation. However, credit should go to the United States's 'Operation Warp Speed', from which Europe should learn important lessons.

This chapter also discusses how to improve the tradeoff between innovation and affordability, a challenge which is growing with the emergence of new, costly therapies thanks to the progress of science. In particular, opportunities should be taken in relation to the new role of the European Commission as representative of the 27 EU countries in price negotiations with pharmaceutical companies.

2 Vaccine development, authorisation and production[124]

The COVID-19 crisis and the question of vaccine development have been instructive in terms of what needs to improve in the EU. The

---

[123] The paper is based on Dewatripont (2022). I thank Sofia Amaral-Garcia, Philippe Aghion, Alain Fischer and Michel Goldman, with whom I collaborated on some of the work discussed here.

[124] This section is partly based on Aghion *et al* (2020).

crisis revealed the weaknesses of the US social system compared to Europe, and the mismanagement of the pandemic by the Trump Administration. Nonetheless, together with Congress, the Trump Administration pursued a determined and aggressive strategy to: (i) ensure US leadership in vaccine R&D, and (ii) secure supplies of future vaccines for US citizens.

Although the European Commission took the lead in negotiating advance purchase agreements with vaccine manufacturers on behalf of the 27 EU countries, and decided to provide loans to European biotechs engaged in vaccine development through the European Investment Bank, it fell short in terms of matching the US effort to incentivise vaccine innovation. This was because of a lower level of financial investment and insufficient coordination of research and innovation funding schemes (reflecting the more decentralised nature of R&D and health policies in Europe).

2.1 General considerations

Considering the race for a successful 'global product', a natural question concerns the optimal degree of competition and coordination. For COVID-19 vaccines, we observed an interesting mix of the two: although political authorities in China initially denied the upcoming disaster, Chinese scientists have been very open about their research results. In fact, the first vaccines to be authorised could be developed rapidly because Chinese scientists had published the genetic sequence of the virus as soon as it was deciphered, allowing universities and private firms, large and small, to compete aggressively to be the first in the race for a vaccine, with the help of private, and especially state, funding sources.

From the perspective of world welfare, the cooperation/open science part is obviously good. As for the competition on vaccine development, things are more subtle: on the one hand, more financial effort overall is good since it saves lives and accelerates exit from costly lockdowns. On the other hand, is there a risk of money being 'wasted' in funding more than 100 vaccine projects, including advance building of production facilities? As discussed by Bolton and Farrell (1990), in *"times of war"*, speed is essential, and more coordination is preferable to *"fine-tuning for the most efficient option,"* if such an optimal solution comes significantly later. We can, however, safely conclude that speed has not been hampered, given the rush we observed. If anything, the risk to be worried about concerned 'cutting corners' in excessively fast approval of vaccines that might not be safe or effective enough. But that risk appears to have been dealt with successfully, since more than 13 billion vaccine doses had been administered worldwide by February 2023, with few adverse side-effects. Authorisation bodies (Food and Drug Administration (FDA) in the US, European Medicines Agency (EMA) in the EU, etc) thus showed they were able to combine speed and safety.

2.2 The US versus the EU
As is well-known, the US is a clear leader in biotech innovation (see evidence summarised in Aghion *et al*, 2020). Moreover, it set up an articulated US-centric COVID-19 strategy – Operation Warp Speed (OWS) – which took advantage of the complementarity between developing vaccines and securing advanced supplies. It thereby brought together the two phases of negotiations with private entities, while relying on the combined expertise and financial weight of existing federal instruments, in particular the National Institutes of Health (NIH) and the Biomedical Advanced Research and Development Authority (BARDA). This gave the US a first-mover advantage.

Congress allocated almost $10 billion to OWS, of which more than $6.5 billion was allocated to BARDA and $3 billion for NIH research. By September 2020, BARDA had distributed more than $11 billion to more than 40 companies to fund the development of COVID-19 vaccines, diagnostic, therapeutics, rapidly deployable capabilities and others (see Aghion *et al*, 2020).

The EU, instead, pursued a less-coherent strategy overall, and with fewer financial resources invested directly in candidate vaccines. And while it looked more 'benevolent' than the US in terms of vaccine development, pushing for worldwide cooperation, through the Coronavirus Global Response, the Coalition for Epidemic Preparedness Innovations (CEPI) and the 'ACT-Accelerator' (see details in Aghion *et al*, 2020), it has been 'EU-centric' when trying to secure vaccine supplies for its member states and citizens. This strategy did not exploit sufficiently the complementarity involved in the process, which adds to the problematic complexity of funding sources (European budget, European Investment Bank (EIB), member states, etc).

By September 2020, there were more than 130 candidate vaccines in preclinical evaluation and 30 candidate vaccines in clinical evaluation. Among these 30 candidates, 13 received support from BARDA, CEPI and/or the EU/EIB (see Aghion *et al*, 2020). Among these, three received support from both BARDA and CEPI (University of Oxford, Moderna and Novavax), one received support from both CEPI and the EIB (CureVac), and one received support from BARDA and EIB (BioNTech). In all these cases, BARDA consistently provided higher funding amounts.

It is moreover striking that BARDA spent $8.69 billion out of its $10.8 billion on the five vaccines that were approved, as of December 2021, by the FDA and/or EMA (BioNTech-Pfizer, Moderna, AstraZeneca, Johnson and Johnson and Novavax). And obviously the funding did not go only to US companies, since AstraZeneca and BioNTech (which is the company that received BARDA funding, not Pfizer) are European. In fact the remaining $2.07 billion went to Sanofi, a French company, whose vaccine developed together with GSK received EMA approval in late 2022.

It is also interesting that a very significant chunk of the funding went to biotech companies Moderna and Novavax, and BioNTech. This confirms the importance of smaller firms in health innovation. That said, the success of the BioNTech-Pfizer alliance also shows the value of a close association with a big pharma company for scaling up the downward development and the production phases, even if Moderna's performance was quite impressive. And it is striking that, of the 'big four' pre-COVID-19 vaccine players – MSD, GSK, Sanofi and Pfizer – only the last emerged as a 'winner' of this race, and only thanks to its alliance with BioNTech.

Coming back to OWS, as stressed in 2020 by Moncef Slaoui[125], who was appointed OWS Chief Scientific Officer, there was a conscious decision to concentrate funding on three different technologies and two projects per technology (or 'dual sourcing'): BioNTech/Pfizer (Germany/US) and Moderna (US) for the mRNA technology, Johnson and Johnson (US) and Oxford/AstraZeneca (UK/Sweden) for the viral vector technology, and Novavax (US) and Sanofi/GSK (France/UK) for the protein subunit technology.

It is hard not to consider OWS as an overwhelming success of 'industrial policy', bringing together, as stressed by Slaoui: (i) significant public money, (ii) competences from the whole 'ecosystem': universities, BARDA, NIH, FDA, biotech companies, big pharma, and even the US Army, and (iii) a small unified decision-making structure to speed things up, at arm's length from politics. Of course, there was quite some luck: the most successful technology, mRNA, was readily available, thanks to years of research efforts (which, as argued by Veugelers (2021) had not benefited before COVID-19 from the support it deserved). And the vaccines turned out to be even more successful than what could have been expected. But still, this episode was a great success, which other jurisdictions should definitely try to learn from.

2.3 For an integrated EU treatment and vaccine development strategy

Europe (especially when adding the United Kingdom and Switzerland to the EU) is strong in health, with its universities, biotech companies, big pharma companies and public money, which is ample although

---

125 See Jean-François Munster, 'Moncef Slaoui au «Soir»: «Avec les vaccins, on va pouvoir contrôler cette pandémie»', *Le Soir*, 26 December 2020, https://www.lesoir.be/345671/article/2020-12-26/moncef-slaoui-au-soir-avec-les-vaccins-va-pouvoir-controler-cette-pandemie.

scattered (the EU being rightly seen as a regulatory giant but a budgetary dwarf). It is coordination that is suboptimal.

Therefore a renewed EU support strategy for the development and commercialisation of innovative technologies is desirable. This could be extended to other areas, for example, defence-related technologies, on the model of the Defense Advanced Research Projects Agency (DARPA) in the US, which, strikingly, has been instrumental also in a number of non-defence innovations. This should not be a renewed industrial policy amounting to 'picking one winner'. As in the case of COVID-19 vaccines, the BARDA-DARPA model mixes top-down and bottom-up approaches, in which government funds finance competing teams that work on making new technologies operational[126]. Once selected by the government, team leaders have full autonomy in deciding how to organise the research process and who to involve in that process. The various teams will typically compete not only within Europe, but also on a more global scale, with the US but also China. So, this is about competition-friendly industrial policy, as advocated by Aghion *et al* (2015).

Interestingly, by the end of 2020, the European Union had launched HERA, the Health Emergency Response and Preparedness Authority, with explicit reference to BARDA and the US innovation ecosystem. Let us see to what extent it can help in boosting European innovation in healthcare.

Let us end this section with three remarks. First, since speed is often crucial, flexibility has been key to the success of BARDA. This pleads for relaxing typical EU political constraints about *juste retour*, seven-year budgets and (near) unanimity voting rules. Second, BARDA has taken a global view, so funding should not be exclusively restricted to EU entities; in particular, despite Brexit, joining forces with the UK makes particular sense, given its academic and industrial expertise in the area (the same is true for defence). Third, the US success was not limited to BARDA. Pooling more resources at the EU level to create an EU

---

126 See Veugelers (2021) for a discussion of the various dimensions of this ecosystem.

equivalent of the NIH is worth considering. And the US has been able to use the leverage of the Defense Production Act to request private firm cooperation with OWS (not to mention the help of the US Army). The lessons of this US success are thus wide-ranging.

3 Securing supplies and setting up delivery systems

COVID-19 vaccines provided an opportunity for the European Commission to centralise discussions with vaccine producers in order to obtain sufficient vaccine supplies at an appropriate price.

The Commission was criticised in the first months of 2021 for insisting too much on low prices in their contractual negotiations with vaccine producers, and not enough on speed of delivery, in a world where the opportunity cost of delaying the recovery was huge. This criticism is not unfair, and countries including Israel, the UK and the US did get ahead of the EU in vaccination in the first half of 2021. This was particularly true in the first quarter of 2021. In this respect, while the UK and the US benefited from their close links with, respectively, AstraZeneca and Pfizer and Moderna to accelerate purchases, Israel showed that one does not have to be involved in R&D or production to be the first in terms of purchases: paying a high price is enough (Israel also allowed Pfizer/BioNTech to analyse in detail the impact of vaccination on the Israeli population, thereby contributing to global knowledge). Indeed, Israel seems to have paid between $47 and (more than) $100 – respectively around €38 and €81 at the time – for two doses of the Pfizer/BioNTech vaccine[127], much more than the €24 the EU paid for the same vaccine (the EU also paid less than €4 for two doses of the AstraZeneca vaccine and €36 for two doses of the Moderna vaccine in the original contracts signed by the Commission (these numbers are contractually meant to be secret but were disclosed in a tweet by the Belgian secretary of state for budget).

After the first quarter of 2021, EU vaccination took off and many

---

127 Stuart Winer, 'Israel has spent $788m on vaccines, could double sum — Health Ministry', *Times of Israel*, 16 March 2021, https://www.timesofisrael.com/israel-has-spent-788m-on-vaccines-could-double-that-in-future-health-ministry/.

western EU countries overtook the US, the UK and Israel in vaccination rates. And the Commission intervention favoured equal treatment between member states, while earlier a group of four countries (France, Italy, Germany and the Netherlands) had decided to join forces and bargain only for themselves. Thanks to the Commission, everyone agreed ultimately to go for centralised EU-wide bargaining.

As discussed by Dewatripont (2022), vaccination rates went up with little variance across most EU countries in the first months of 2021. Until May 2021, only Bulgaria was significantly slower than the other EU countries. During the course of May and June, some other eastern EU countries, including Romania, Slovakia, Poland and Czechia, also started to lag the rest of the pack. Other EU countries stayed close together until June, when divergence started to grow. But by this time, vaccine hesitancy had become the key constraint, not vaccine availability or logistical challenges. Joint European purchases therefore ensured equity between EU member states, a success which explains why HERA was subsequently tasked to buy monkeypox vaccines for most EU countries.

4 Insufficient public leverage on the innovation/affordability tradeoff of new drugs

The COVID-19 vaccine experience also offers lessons on this innovation/affordability tradeoff.

4.1 Excessive prices?

While the European Commission was criticised in the first half of 2021 for insisting excessively on low COVID-19 vaccine prices (instead of speed of delivery), containing prices of booster shots and improved COVID-19 vaccines could be a concern in the future. In this respect, the words of Frank D'Amelio, the Chief Financial Officer of Pfizer were not very reassuring: "In short, D'Amelio explained that Pfizer expects its COVID vaccine margins to improve. Under one pandemic supply deal, Pfizer is charging the US $19.50 per dose, D'Amelio said, which is 'not a normal price like we typically get for a vaccine—$150, $175 per dose. So, pandemic pricing'"[128].

This should remind authorities of the need to avoid rents above competitive rates of returns for vaccines and treatments. The question of high prices has become an even bigger issue at a time when accelerating scientific progress opens up new opportunities, for example with gene therapies (and mRNA could provide another boost to this trend), which is both very promising and challenging. For example, Fischer *et al* (2019, 2022) reported several cases of treatments approved by the FDA and/or EMA since 2018 costing between $373,000 and $2,100,000 per patient, for diseases affecting 1000 to more than 10,000 patients in Europe and the US. Since this increasing trend is going to persist, it is important to find ways to keep public health budgets under control, while ensuring that useful innovation can flourish.

In its official strategy documents, the European Commission (2021) has recognised this challenge, and has therefore stressed the need to ensure access to affordable medicines for patients, and to address unmet medical needs, in the areas of antimicrobial resistance and rare diseases in particular. In this respect, the Commission has stressed four strands of policy: (i) enhancing competition; (ii) working with national authorities to exchange information on sustainable health systems, pricing, cost-effectiveness, payment, procurement policies and affordability; (iii) enhancing transparency through guidelines on how to calculate the R&D costs of medicines; and (iv) using the annual European Semester cycle of economic policy coordination to assess national health systems and issue country-specific recommendations to ensure their accessibility, efficiency and sustainability.

While these are useful avenues, more could be done. Of course, while Pfizer, BioNTech and Moderna have been making good money,

---

128   Eric Sagonowsky, 'Pfizer eyes higher prices for COVID-19 vaccine after the pandemic wanes: exec, analyst', *Fierce Pharma*, 23 February 2021, https://www.fiercepharma.com/pharma/pfizer-eyes-higher-covid-19-vaccine-prices-after-pandemic-exec-analyst.

typical discussions about innovation in pharma in general pit critics of high prices and returns against industry advocates who stress the cost and risk of innovation. Obviously, economists would naturally assume that inducing private R&D to take place, especially in the *ex-ante* less 'attractive' areas of 'neglected' diseases (rare diseases, several infectious diseases, complex diseases like Alzheimer's, where industry is seen to be not active enough), requires the researcher/innovator to anticipate the (discounted) net benefit (B - C) of innovation to exceed (B - C)*, the net benefit of other potential uses of the innovator's resources. Policy can act in particular on the gross benefit B (which is the result of price negotiations with funders after authorisation) and also on the cost C[129].

On the other hand, there is no reason, for either (B - C) or (B - C)*, to be above competitive returns. However, evidence indicates that, while biotech firms earn on average a (B - C) that is higher than (risk-adjusted) market-consistent rates of return (having in fact a higher risk more than compensating their *ex-post* high return), big pharmaceutical companies have for decades earned annual risk-adjusted rates of return that are 3 percent in excess of the market (see Thakor, 2015).

This is partly linked to the lobbying power of big pharma companies, especially in the US, where prices have been high since George W. Bush convinced Congress to prevent Medicare from negotiating drug prices (see Danzon, 2018). This adds to the problem of generally weak competition today, which has led big firms to earn high returns,

---

[129] Note that neglected diseases have a number of specificities as far as this inequality is concerned: (i) B will typically be low when the potential market is small, either in terms of number of cases (eg rare diseases), or of low 'ability to pay' (diseases affecting poor countries); (ii) on the other hand, since low patient numbers reduce the threat to public budgets, higher prices per patient can at times be obtained, which raises B; (iii) as for C, it can be higher when the disease is complex (eg Alzheimer's); (iv) on the other hand, some neglected diseases can benefit from a fair amount of public funding, which lowers C, and finally (v) authorisation on the basis of lower sample sizes for randomised controlled trials, typical for rare diseases, lowers C again.

even leading to adverse macroeconomic consequences (see, for example, the discussion in Aghion *et al*, 2021). In this respect, one should reiterate that industrial policy should be competition-friendly, as stressed by Aghion *et al* (2015) and as successfully managed by OWS.

Moreover, not only is the equilibrium (B – C) 3 percent per year too high, but evidence points to an authorisation bias against 'truly creative' innovation through an excessive reward of 'marginal' innovation'. Fojo *et al* (2014) looked at US evidence on cancer therapies and stressed the unintended consequences of expensive marginal therapies that earn higher risk-adjusted returns than more innovative ones, and are unsurprisingly pursued by for-profit pharma companies. This indicates a flaw in the authorisation/pricing process for new therapies, since by making marginal innovation more lucrative, one raises the opportunity cost (B – C)* of engaging in truly innovative research. Industrial policy should try and address this problem.

4.2 Improving the innovation/affordability tradeoff

Unsurprisingly, the COVID-19 vaccine experience has generated debates about the distribution of the rewards of innovation between private companies and the public sector.

4.2.1 Improving bargaining positions

In fact, the emergence of the European Commission as a negotiator on behalf of the 27 EU countries echoes efforts by groups of EU countries to join forces in price negotiations with drug companies. Belgium, the Netherlands, Austria, Ireland and Luxembourg were the first such group[130]. Other initiatives are the Valletta group of southern European countries, the Nordic pharmaceuticals forum and the Visegrad group[131].

---

130   See https://beneluxa.org/.
131   Francesca Bruce, 'Europe's Biggest Multi-Country Access Alliance Picks Up The Pace', *Pink Sheet*, 28 July 2021, https://pink.pharmaintelligence.informa.com/PS144710/Europes-Biggest-Multi-Country-Access-Alliance-Picks-Up-The-Pace.

The goal of such initiatives is to put these countries in a better position to require more transparency about R&D, manufacturing and distribution costs of the drug.

Truly meaningful impact would however require further coordination. The COVID-19 vaccine episode should provide an opportunity to go more generally towards EU-wide coordination of negotiations with pharma companies, to limit their ability to put states in competition. Kyle (2007) showed in particular that new drugs are introduced earlier in jurisdictions that pay higher prices, which is in line with the priority given to Israel by Pfizer. One should therefore not draw the wrong lessons from the European COVID-19 negotiation: it should constitute a precedent worth building on in order to improve the bargaining power of European member states with pharma companies.

Rare diseases would be a natural area for EU-wide intervention. One objective reason for high prices is of course the limited market size of each country. A pan-EU purchase would offer the prospect of higher sales, thereby making lower prices more sustainable for industry. One could even envisage advance market commitments, like with vaccines (Levin *et al*, 2021), which should ideally be coupled with a percentage of profits to be refunded by the company in case these turn out to be higher than expected.

EU-wide coordination of the organisation of statistically significant clinical trials, which does represent a key challenge for rare diseases, would also make sense. And the same is true for the necessary coordination of national research and development funding beyond EU R&D funding, along the lines of NIH funding, in order to maximise synergies, especially for rare diseases.

Finally, COVID-19 vaccines are an extreme example of the asymmetric timing of the financial costs and benefits of health innovation. Early stages of the process are heavily subsidized – in this case not only R&D but even production – but price negotiations, and especially renegotiations, happen later on and risk insufficiently rewarding earlier subsidies through subsequent price discounts in the case of successful innovation. Public authorities should make their early support conditional on profit-sharing schemes in order to benefit from the upside of innovation.

4.2.2 Governance

Current healthcare innovation typically works as follows: its later stages are implemented by the private sector, often big pharmaceutical companies, which buy biotech firms, which are themselves built on publicly-funded research (universities, the NIH and BARDA in the US, etc). While this sequence is natural, achieving a fair distribution of the rewards of innovation is difficult in a system of large for-profit providers of new vaccines and therapies. The profit motive is a powerful driver with high rent-extraction costs, and economics has documented how information asymmetries and residual rights of control do allow producers to earn rents. One idea to limit these rents could be the introduction of common-good advocates on the boards of pharma companies. Another could be to transform (part of) them into 'benefit corporations', as advocated by Fischer *et al* (2019), so that shareholder value would stop being their overriding objective (an objective resulting from their legal charter and, since the 1980s, aggressively put into practice).

Change could be enacted by leveraging companies' corporate social responsibility. Concretely, payers could for example incentivise companies involved in expensive therapies to create *ad-hoc* subsidiaries for these activities and organise them according to the benefit corporation concept (Cummings, 2012) in order to subsequently obtain a B Corporation certification[132]. The benefit corporation declaration gives legal protection to companies to pursue social and environmental performance alongside value for shareholders. The boards of benefit corporations are required in their decision-making to consider other stakeholders in addition to shareholders. The application for B corporate certification further enhances accountability to social good, as the

---

132   See https://bcorporation.net/.

certification is done by an external third-party based on the company's verified performance on the B impact assessment, making the benefit corporation a certified B corporation.

By acquiring the status of certified B corporation, companies should be able to leverage the social impact of their pricing in their performance indicators, thus affording them the opportunity to bring their pricing down to a market-consistent level, in order to enhance their social performance.

Pushback is to be expected. But corporations themselves are increasingly recognising the need to generate long-term value for all stakeholders, instead of solely shareholders, and to shift their priorities from profit maximisation to optimising value creation, as demonstrated by the Business Roundtable 2019 Statement on the Purpose of a Corporation (Business Roundtable, 2019), to which several pharmaceutical companies are signatories. The next step would be for payers to consider making reimbursement of some therapies conditional on their commercialisation by certified B corporations. The greater objective should be a pricing policy that results from a credible alignment of the interests of industry, patients and payers.

5 Conclusion

This pandemic has been unique in its magnitude and should lead to a rethink of a number of features of the institutional system. In particular, the US OWS success should call for a strengthening of the EU biotech innovation system, not only through a BARDA-like HERA, but also through a better-coordinated EU health research budget similar to the NIH. More EU coordination on purchases is also desirable given the experience the European Commission has acquired in its contractual negotiations with vaccine producers. The objective should be to improve the terms of the innovation/affordability tradeoff. Given the magnitude of public funds poured into health innovation systems, society at large could obtain a larger share of successful innovation returns, without driving private players away from the market.

References

Aghion, P., S. Amaral-Garcia, M. Dewatripont and M. Goldman (2020) 'How to strengthen European industries' leadership in vaccine research and innovation', *VoxEU*, 1 September, available at https://cepr.org/voxeu/columns/how-strengthen-european-industries-leadership-vaccine-research-and-innovation

Aghion, P., C. Antonin and S. Bunel (2021) *The Power of Creative Destruction: Economic Upheaval and the Wealth of Nations*, Cambridge, MA: Harvard University Press

Aghion, P., J. Cai, M. Dewatripont, L. Du, A. Harrison and P. Legros (2015) 'Industrial Policy and Competition', *American Economic Journal: Macroeconomics* 7: 1-32

Bolton, P. and J. Farrell (1990) 'Decentralization, Duplication and Delay', *Journal of Political Economy* 98: 803-826

Business Roundtable (2019) 'Statement on the Purpose of a Corporation', available at https://system.businessroundtable.org/app/uploads/sites/5/2023/02/WSJ_BRT_POC_Ad.pdf

Cummings, B. (2012) 'Benefit Corporations: How to Enforce a Mandate to Promote the Public Interest', *Columbia Law Review* 112: 578-627

Danzon, P. (2018) 'Differential Pricing of Pharmaceuticals: Theory, Evidence and Emerging Issues', *Pharmacoeconomics* 36: 1395-1

Dewatripont, M. (2022) 'Which policies for vaccine innovation and delivery in Europe?' *International Journal of Industrial Organization* 84, 102858, available at https://doi.org/10.1016/j.ijindorg.2022.102858.

European Commission (2021) 'Making Medicines More Affordable', available at https://health.ec.europa.eu/medicinal-products/pharmaceutical-strategy-europe/making-medicines-more-affordable_en

Fischer, A., M. Dewatripont and M. Goldman (2019) 'Benefit Corporation: A Path to Affordable Gene Therapies?' *Nature Medicine* 25: 1813-1814

Fischer, A., M. Dewatripont and M. Goldman (2022) 'Improving the innovation/access tradeoff for rare diseases in the European Union after Covid-19', *VoxEU*, 29 September, available at https://cepr.org/voxeu/columns/improving-innovationaccess-trade-rare-diseases-eu-after-covid-19

Fojo, T., S. Mailankody and A. Lo (2014) 'Unintended Consequences of Expensive Cancer Therapeutics—The Pursuit of Marginal Indications and a Me-Too Mentality That Stifles Innovation and Creativity', *Journal of the American Medical Association Otolaryngology – Head Neck Surgery* 140: 1225-1236

Kyle, M. (2007) 'Pharmaceutical Price Controls and Entry Strategies', *Review of Economics and Statistics* 89: 88-99

Levin, J., M. Kremer and C. Snyder (2020) "Designing Advance Market Commitments for New Vaccines", *Working Paper* 28168, National Bureau of Economic Research

Thakor, R., N. Anaya, Y. Zhang, C. Vilanilam, K. Siah, C. Wong and A. Lo (2015) 'Just How Good an Investment is the Biopharmaceutical Sector?' *Nature Biotechnology* 35 :1149-1157

Veugelers, R. (2021) 'mRNA vaccines: a lucky shot?', *Working Paper* 13/2021, Bruegel

www.ingramcontent.com/pod-product-compliance
Ingram Content Group UK Ltd.
Pitfield, Milton Keynes, MK11 3LW, UK
UKHW022121230426
12048UKWH00011BA/645